LEARNING STRATEGIES CURRICULUM

Proficiency in the Sentence Writing Strategy

Instructor's Manual

Jean B. Schumaker, Ph.D. with Jan Sheldon, Ph.D.

The University of Kansas
Lawrence, Kansas
1999

Copy Editors: Jean B. Schumaker
Kirsten McBride

Cover Design: Michael Bingham

Text Design: John B. Naughtin

Figures: Trudy J. Rinne

Printed in the United States of America.
Revised 1991
Eleventh Printing 1994
Twelfth Printing 1996
Revised 1999
Fourteenth Printing 2000
Fifteenth Printing 2002
Sixteenth Printing 2004
Seventeenth Printing 2006
Eighteenth Printing 2010
Nineteenth Printing 2011

Registration of Instruction

**Proficiency in
the Sentence Writing Strategy**

**Strategic Instruction Model®
University of Kansas Center for
Research on Learning (KU-CRL)**

Name (Please Print) _____

Home Address _____

City, State _____ Zip _____

Phone (_____) _____

Home Email _____

Work Address _____

Work City, State _____ Zip _____

Work Phone (_____) _____

Work Email _____

Professional Developer's Name _____ Date of Session _____

Location of Session _____

District/Agency Sponsoring Professional Development _____

Completion of this registration form confirms participation in a strategy training session. All information must be completed. If your manual is lost, damaged, or left at a previous school, this registration will enable you to purchase a new manual. This original registration sheet, not a copy, must be completed each time you participate in a training session related to a new strategy.

_____Please place me on the KU-CRL email list to receive updates related to strategies instructor's manuals and other information about the Strategic Instruction Model. ☐Home Email   ☐Work Email

Additional information about this Learning Strategy and the Strategic Instruction Model (SIM®) can be found at: www.kucrl.org

University of Kansas
Center for Research on Learning
J. R. Pearson Hall
1122 W. Campus Road, Room 517
Lawrence, KS 66045-3101

CONTENTS

ACKNOWLEDGMENTS

The conceptualization, development, validation, and revision of the *Learning Strategies Curriculum* has benefited from the efforts of many individuals. We gratefully acknowledge the innumerable contributions of the following colleagues and professionals: Vickie Beals, Jean Brownlee, Fran Clark, Pegi Denton, Keren Hamburger, Keith Lenz, Ann Hoffman, Sue Nolan, John Schmidt, Conn Thomas, Mike Warner, and Ginger Williams. Additionally, the personnel of the Lawrence School District have been tremendous allies during the period of development and research on the *Learning Strategies Curriculum*. Specifically, we wish to credit and thank Carol Ann Buller, Steve Carlson, Ed Ellis, Don Herbel, Jerry Keimig, Karen Lyerla, Bruce Passman, Brad Tate, and Tony Van Reusen.

The *Sentence Writing Strategy* lesson materials were originally developed and field-tested in 1974 in a summer school program for junior-high students. We are grateful to our colleague, Dr. Jim Sherman, to the teachers, Burleigh Smith and Bob Sharkey, and to the students for their valuable help in this original development effort.

In the years since then, the students who participated in the original field test have graduated from high school (and some from college), and this *Instructor's Manual* has been developed and field tested. We would like to thank the Shawnee Mission School District in Kansas and Katie Alexander for allowing the original field test of this *Instructor's Manual* to take place in the Shawnee Mission South High School resource room. We deeply appreciate Katie's invention of the sentence formulas as well as the innumerable suggestions made by Jean Brownlee, Jan Bulgren, Pegi Denton, Kathleen Gabriel, Pat Jonason, Cathy Kea, and the teachers at Summit School in West Dundee, Illinois regarding improvements to be made throughout the manual. We also appreciate the critiques provided by countless teachers across the nation who have used this manual since the original field tests.

We wish to thank the staff of the Office of Research, Graduate Studies, and Public Service at the University of Kansas for their encouragement and financial support for Institute for Research in Learning Disabilities activities. This product also benefited from tremendous technical and moral support rendered by Institute Core Staff, research assistants, and support staff. Specifically, we would like to acknowledge the contributions of Muriel Hays, Trudy Rinne, Peggy Showalter, and Eleanor Womack.

Finally, we wish to acknowledge the major role of our colleagues, Drs. Gordon Alley and Don Deshler, in the overall conceptualization of learning strategy instruction as an instructional approach. Their thinking and knowledge have greatly influenced the development of this product. Additionally, Don Deshler's thoughtful suggestions throughout the revision process have helped polish this *Instructor's Manual* to its current condition. We are grateful for his help.

JBS, JS

"... writing is something you can never do as well as it can be done. It is a perpetual challenge and it is more difficult than anything else that I have ever done—so I do it. And it makes me happy when I do it well. "

Ernest Hemingway, 1935

This book is dedicated to all those students who will become happy writers under your guidance.

INTRODUCTION

WHAT ARE LEARNING STRATEGIES?

In almost every educational setting there are some students who are low achievers. Although the causes of low achievement are varied, in many instances students perform poorly because they have not learned "how to learn." Recent research has shown that students *can* be taught how to learn by teaching them learning strategies. A *learning strategy* is an individual's approach to a learning task. It includes how a person thinks and acts when planning, executing, and evaluating performance on the task and its outcomes. Learning strategy instruction focuses on both how to learn and how to effectively use what has been learned.

As students progress through the educational system, the curriculum places increasing demands on them to acquire and memorize large amounts of information and to demonstrate their knowledge and command of this information. The *Learning Strategies Curriculum* has been designed to enable students to cope effectively with such curricular demands and to teach them how to generalize their use of these skills to a variety of settings including mainstream classes and home and employment settings. The overriding goal associated with the *Learning Strategies Curriculum* is to enable students to learn skills and content and to perform tasks independently.

The *Learning Strategies Curriculum* (see Figure 1 on p. 2) consists of three instructional strands: the Acquisition Strand, the Storage Strand, and the Expression and Demonstration of Competence Strand. Each strand consists of several task-specific learning strategies that have been designed to improve a student's ability to cope with specific curriculum demands. The strategies in the Acquisition Strand enable students to gain information from written material (e.g., textbooks, novels, technical manuals). The Storage Strand strategies are designed to enable students to organize, store, and retrieve information. Finally, the Expression and Demonstration of Competence Strand consists of strategies that enable students to complete assignments, to effectively express themselves in writing, and to take tests.

The Expression and Demonstration of Competence Strand will now be described in more detail because the *Sentence Writing Strategy* is a member of that strand.

THE EXPRESSION AND DEMONSTRATION OF COMPETENCE STRAND

The Expression and Demonstration of Competence Strand is made up of several strategies. Briefly, the two *Sentence Writing Strategies* are designed to enable students to write four kinds of sentences: simple, compound, complex, and compound-complex. The *Paragraph Writing Strategy* enables students to write well-organized paragraphs. The *EDIT (Error Monitoring) Strategy* is used by students to systematically detect and correct mistakes in written products. The *Theme Writing Strategy* is designed to enable students to compose themes or essays of at least five paragraphs in length. The *Assignment Completion Strategy* helps students organize and manage their time so that they are able to complete homework assignments. The *Test-Taking Strategy* helps students apply effective test-taking procedures to classroom tests, and the *Essay Test-Taking Strategy* enables students to respond to essay questions.

Sequencing Instruction within the Expression and Demonstration of Competence Strand

Teachers often ask how to organize instruction in the Expression and Demonstration of Competence Strand. The most frequent of their questions are addressed in the following sections.

1. Which strategy should be taught first?

Initially, the strategy chosen for instruction should help the student meet a pressing curriculum demand. If students see the strategy as a tool that makes them successful in educational settings, getting their sustained commitment is easier. Thus, having a good understanding of the demands that lead to students' learning difficulties is important. This general rule is particularly true for the *Assignment Completion* and *Test-Taking* strategies. If a student is having difficulty completing homework assignments independently, the *Assignment Completion Strategy* should be taught first. On the other hand, if the student is having difficulty completing tests independently (e.g., does not answer all questions, does not know how to follow instructions on tests), the *Test-Taking Strategy* should be taught first.

In the case of the written expression strategies (*Fundamentals of Sentence Writing, Proficiency in Sentence Writing, Paragraph Writing, EDIT [Error Monitoring]*, and *Theme Writing*), they should be taught in the order in which they appear in Figure 1. That is, the *Sentence Writing Strategy* should be taught first unless the student has already mastered writing simple, compound, complex, and compound-complex sentences. This strategy is foundational to the other writing strategies. Thus, while the most pressing curriculum demand on a student may be paragraph writing, instruction in the *Paragraph Writing Strategy* is unlikely to be successful until the student has mastered at least simple and compound sentences.

If students demonstrate mastery of any of the writing strategies prior to instruction, instruction should begin in the next strategy. For example, if a student can write well-organized paragraphs using a variety of sentences, instruction should probably begin in the EDIT or *Theme Writing Strategy*. In general, *Assignment Completion* and *Test-Taking* are independent of any inststructional sequence and can be taught at any time.

2. Where should a student begin instruction in the *Sentence Writing Strategy*? Two options are currently available. If students need a thorough grounding in basic concepts and terms (e.g., subject, verb, infinitive, preposition), the instructional methods described in *Fundamentals in the Sentence Writing Strategy* (Schumaker & Sheldon, 1998) are most appropriate. This instruction can either be used as a developmental writing program or as a very fast "bring-them-up-to-speed" set of lessons. If students already have a basic understanding of these concepts, they might begin with the instruction described in this instructor's manual *(Proficiency in the Sentence Writing Strategy)*. Here, students learn more advanced sentence writing skills including writing compound, complex, and compound-complex sentences.

3. How many strategies in this strand need to be taught to improve student performance? The answer to this question depends on the student. For some, instruction in one or two strategies has been sufficient to impact school performance. For example, some students can receive their first learning strategy instruction in the *Test-Taking Strategy*, master the strategy immediately, and, as a result, improve their grades in content areas. For others, however, instruction in several strategies is required to bring about significant results. For example, some students need to learn some of the strategies in the Storage Strand (e.g., the *FIRST-Letter Mnemonic Strategy,* the *Vocabulary Learning Strategy,* and the *Paired Associates Strategy*) as well as the *Test-Taking Strategy* to improve their grades on tests to an acceptable level. This is also true for the written expression strategies because students in secondary settings are often required to write relatively error-free compositions. Students frequently see improvement in their grades on compositions only after they have learned at least three or four writing strategies.

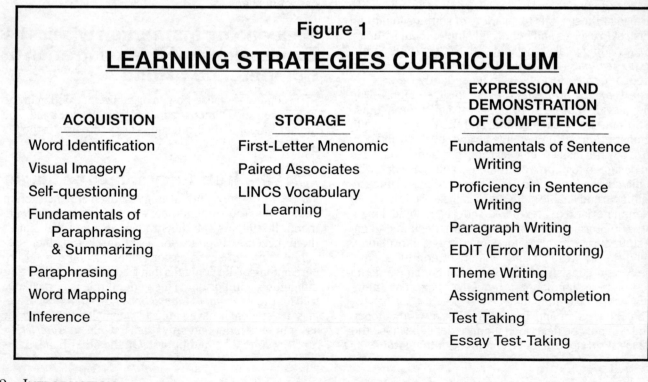

Figure 1
LEARNING STRATEGIES CURRICULUM

ACQUISTION	STORAGE	EXPRESSION AND DEMONSTRATION OF COMPETENCE
Word Identification	First-Letter Mnenomic	Fundamentals of Sentence Writing
Visual Imagery	Paired Associates	Proficiency in Sentence Writing
Self-questioning	LINCS Vocabulary Learning	Paragraph Writing
Fundamentals of Paraphrasing & Summarizing		EDIT (Error Monitoring)
Paraphrasing		Theme Writing
Word Mapping		Assignment Completion
Inference		Test Taking
		Essay Test-Taking

Since each of the strategies in this strand includes a specific set of skills required for efficient performance in advanced educational settings, teachers have systematically presented instruction in all of the strategies in this strand over a 3- to 6-year period. The *Sentence Writing Strategy,* for example, can be taught beginning in the elementary grades. Both the *Paragraph Writing Strategy* and the *EDIT* or *Error Monitoring Strategy* can be taught in late elementary or junior-high grades. The *Theme Writing Strategy* may be taught in the late junior-high and early high-school grades. Powerful cumulative effects have resulted from such systematic instruction since the combination of several mastered strategies can yield important changes in school performance for low-achieving students. Another advantage of sequencing instruction over several years is that it reduces the pressure on both students and teachers of having to fit all the instruction into a short period of time.

4. What kinds of results can I expect?
The *Learning Strategies Curriculum* has undergone a great deal of field testing to validate the efficacy of this instructional approach. Since 1979, the instructional procedures used for teaching the writing strategies have been tested in a host of different settings and with different kinds of students by staff members of the University of Kansas Center for Research on Learning (KU-CRL)* and associated school district personnel.

The results of these field tests have indicated that when the writing strategies are taught according to the procedures outlined in the *Instructor's Manuals,* significant gains are realized both in behaviors associated directly with the strategy (e.g., sentence writing) and in general competencies (e.g., writing achievement scores). Low achievers' use of learning strategies enables them to perform at levels that are competitive with those of their normally achieving peers. Thus, after learning the strategies, students who have previously been restricted to self-contained classrooms or special courses are able to succeed independently in mainstream classes. Further, students who previously were prime candidates for dropping out of school are earning well-deserved high school diplomas, and some have gone on to succeed in community college and university settings. Specific research has shown that students who receive instruction in the *Sentence Writing Strategy* consistently produce written products that contain 100% complete sentences and at least 40% complicated sentences (i.e., either compound, complex, or compound-complex sentences). In addition, their written products include more words, more sentences, and a greater variety of sentences than those of low achievers who have not received strategy training. These results were realized when the instructional steps outlined in the instructional

manuals were adhered to carefully. Finally, experience indicates that student performance will increase markedly when additional strategies are taught to supplement previously learned strategies.

The *Sentence Writing Strategy*

The *Sentence Writing Strategy* is used by students to write four types of sentences. As a result, they are able to respond more effectively to the complex writing demands in secondary and post-secondary settings. This instructional packet is designed to teach students a set of steps and key formulas that help them recognize and write different types of sentences. Instruction in this strategy is systematically sequenced so that students have ample opportunity to practice identifying and writing different types of sentences. Students who achieve mastery in each of the sentence types covered in this manual will also benefit from instruction in the other writing strategies. The instructional procedures and materials have been designed from a remedial perspective. Thus, the instruction does not cover every sentence variation or occurrence that might be covered in a developmental language course. Nevertheless, students who master all of the sentence types included in this manual will be able to write sentences that fit more than 14 different sentence structures.

HOW TO TEACH THE SENTENCE WRITING STRATEGY

In order for a learning strategy, like the *Sentence Writing Strategy,* to serve a student well, it must be learned to an automatic level. Just as we use repetition to teach beginning readers to master basic sound-symbol relationships, we teach older students to master task-specific learning strategies through much structured practice. The principles outlined in this section have been found to be critical for instructional success with the *Sentence Writing Strategy.* We strongly urge you to carefully read (and reread) this section. If your students are not making the anticipated progress, review this section and evaluate your instructional practices in light of the principles expressed here.

The Instructional Sequence

The *Sentence Writing Strategy* is taught in four parts (see Figure 2); however, before any instruction begins, a pretest is given to obtain a measure of each student's sentence-writing skills. In Part I of the instruction, the skills involved in writing simple sentences are taught. In Part II, the skills involved in writing compound sentences are taught and integrated with the skills of writing simple sentences. In Part III, students learn to write

---

*Research reports and monographs are available from the KU-CRL on the validation research conducted on the *Learning Strategies Curriculum.* Write to 1122 W. Campus Rd., University of Kansas, Lawrence, KS 66045, for information on the available literature.

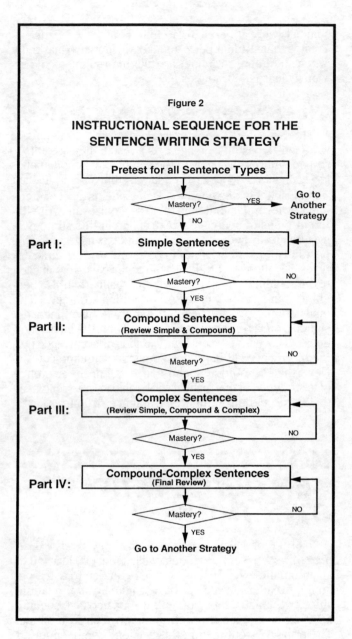

Figure 2

**INSTRUCTIONAL SEQUENCE FOR THE
SENTENCE WRITING STRATEGY**

Pretest for all Sentence Types

Mastery? — YES → Go to Another Strategy

NO

Part I: **Simple Sentences**

Mastery? — NO

YES

Part II: **Compound Sentences**
(Review Simple & Compound)

Mastery? — NO

YES

Part III: **Complex Sentences**
(Review Simple, Compound & Complex)

Mastery? — NO

YES

Part IV: **Compound-Complex Sentences**
(Final Review)

Mastery? — NO

YES

Go to Another Strategy

complex sentences and integrate them with the skills of writing simple and compound sentences. Finally, in Part IV, students learn to write compound-complex sentences and integrate the skills of writing all four types of sentences. Students must reach mastery in one part of the instruction before moving to the next. Thus, the instruction is a building process whereby students are required to integrate new skills with previously learned skills.

This four-part instruction can be adapted to a variety of needs. For example, a student can receive instruction in all four parts in a large block of time (e.g., 30 minutes per day for 9-10 weeks). Alternatively, instruction in a single part can be provided, whereupon instruction can shift to other strategies if necessary. At some later time the student may return to instruction in the *Sentence Writing Strategy* to learn additional sentence types. For example, some junior-high teachers prefer to teach Parts I

and II in the seventh grade, Part III in the eighth grade, and Part IV in the ninth grade. This sequence is acceptable as long as the specified maintenance activities are implemented when writing instruction is not being provided.

One final caution: since the instruction builds on previous activities, teaching the parts in a different sequence than the one shown in Figure 2 or teaching Parts II, III, or IV without Part I is not advisable. That is, even though a student can write simple sentences, he must go through the simple sentence instruction because it provides him with vocabulary and a knowledge base upon which subsequent parts build. Thus, the foundation provided in the simple sentence instruction is critical for success in the other parts, and each subsequent part logically builds on previous instruction.

Critical Instructional Procedures

Research has shown that 98% of all the low-achieving students who have been taught learning strategies have mastered them if the 8-stage instructional procedure to be described is followed carefully. As you will note, the *Instructor's Manual* is organized around the same eight stages.

Figure 3 (on p. 5) summarizes the eight instructional stages and the sequence in which they are to be followed. After receiving a pretest (Stage 1), the student proceeds through instructional stages 2-8 for each part of the instruction (i.e., for each type of sentence that is targeted). Once instruction for one type of sentence is well under way in "Stage 8: Generalization," the student can begin instruction at "Stage 2: Describe" for the next type of sentence to be learned. The sequence of instructional stages 2-8 is recycled for each type of sentence to be learned until all four sentence types have been mastered.

Stage 1: Pretest and Make Commitments. In this stage, students are tested to determine their current habits with regard to writing four types of sentences: simple, compound, complex, and compound-complex. To establish how well students can write sentences, you will ask them to perform an assignment comparable in difficulty to one they might receive in their regular educational setting. After this assessment, you will inform students of their strengths or weaknesses relative to the skills assessed. This will help them understand, in part, why they may be ineffective writers and will serve as the basis for gaining their commitment to learn an alternative strategy that will help them become better writers. Our experience has told us that motivation throughout the instructional process will be higher if students make a verbal commitment to improve their skills before instruction begins.

Stage 2: Describe. The Describe Stage in the teaching process is designed to paint a picture that details the nature of a given strategy and the advantages of using it. After you generally define the *Sentence Writing Strategy* for the students, you will provide them with rationales

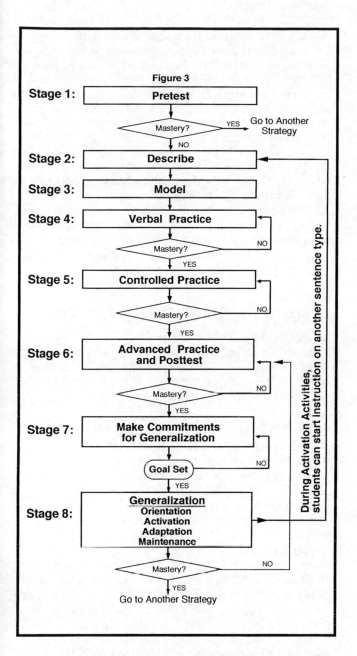

Figure 3

Stage 1: Pretest

Mastery? — YES → Go to Another Strategy

NO

Stage 2: Describe

Stage 3: Model

Stage 4: Verbal Practice

Mastery? — NO

YES

Stage 5: Controlled Practice

Mastery? — NO

YES

Stage 6: Advanced Practice and Posttest

Mastery? — NO

YES

Stage 7: Make Commitments for Generalization

Goal Set — NO

YES

Stage 8: Generalization
Orientation
Activation
Adaptation
Maintenance

Mastery? — NO

YES

Go to Another Strategy

During Activation Activities, students can start instruction on another sentence type.

showing them how they can benefit from mastering each part of the strategy. Your exploration of this topic will include examples of situations where students can use the *Sentence Writing Strategy* and the advantages of applying it compared to their old writing habits. Additionally, you will give students an idea of the kinds of results they can expect after learning the strategy. In many respects, your students are like critical consumers shopping for new cars. Before making a purchase, consumers often ask some essential questions about the costs and benefits of the new car, including price, finance charges, warranty, gas mileage, and required maintenance. If the benefits outweigh the costs, consumers are willing to give up some of their resources (money) for new cars. Similarly, when low-achieving students are offered a solution to their learning problems, they become critical consumers try-

ing to decide whether to give up some of their resources (in this case, time and effort) to acquire a new strategy. To help them make a sound choice, you will show them some associated costs (e.g., the amount of time it will probably take them to reach mastery) and the benefits they can expect (e.g., how much their written expression will improve).

Once the students have bought the idea of learning the *Sentence Writing Strategy,* you will help them set some goals with regard to how fast they want to learn it. Finally, you will provide them with a thorough description of the steps and formulas involved in using the *Sentence Writing Strategy* to write a particular type of sentence (i.e., simple, compound, complex, or compound-complex).

Stage 3: Model.
Most of us learn a skill better if we can see it performed rather than just hearing a description of what to do. That is, we learn skills best through imitation. In the Model Stage, you will demonstrate all the *Sentence Writing Strategy* steps while writing particular kinds of sentences and while thinking aloud, so the students can witness the necessary cognitive processes as well as the overt behaviors involved in performing the strategy. Each aspect of the strategy must be presented clearly and explicitly. Students should be encouraged to ask questions to ensure they understand your demonstration. In the final part of the demonstration, you will involve the students as much as possible to check their understanding of the strategy steps.

Stage 4: Verbal Practice.
Before students are asked to use the strategy, they must learn to define certain concepts and name the strategy steps at an automatic level. During this instructional stage, therefore, you will ask students to verbally rehearse the definitions of important terms and the strategy steps. This process is designed to facilitate self-instruction and independence when students perform the strategy in the future. The Verbal Practice Stage can be very effectively and quickly carried out with a group of students through "rapid-fire" practice. Using this method, you will point to each student in succession and require the contribution of the next definition or the next step of the strategy. Later in this stage, you will individually quiz students to determine their mastery of the concepts.

Stage 5: Controlled Practice and Feedback.
As soon as students demonstrate both understanding and verbal mastery of the definitions, steps, and procedures involved in the strategy, they should begin using the strategy to write a particular kind of sentence. Specific lessons are provided in the accompanying *Student Lessons* volume (Schumaker & Sheldon, 1985) for this purpose. The major goal of this stage is to give students ample opportunity to practice using the new strategy to write new kinds of sentences in situations that are largely devoid of many of the demands in their regular courses. By practicing the strategy under controlled con-

ditions, students can build their confidence and fluency in performing the strategy steps. Some students feel that the time spent working with controlled materials is a waste because they are not dealing directly with assignments from their required courses. In these cases, be sure to explain the reasons for such practice.

Provide students individual feedback each time they practice the strategy. Individual feedback is perhaps the most important instructional element of the entire teaching process. Research has shown that students make the greatest gains when they receive specific and well-timed feedback. Without such feedback, low-achieving students often continue to practice incorrect responses which delays their mastery of the targeted strategy.

Stage 6: Advanced Practice/ Posttest and Feedback.
The real test of students' mastery of a strategy is their ability to apply it to grade-appropriate assignments: the assignments with which they were unable to cope originally. Thus, the purpose of this instructional stage is to give students ample opportunity to practice the strategy in the types of assignments used in the criterion environment (i.e., the regular educational setting). The last practice attempt at this level will serve as the student's posttest for the type of sentence being learned.

This stage embodies an important aspect of promoting acquisition durability. Specifically, you should use it to fade the instructional prompts and cues given liberally in earlier stages. In this manner, the student becomes more responsible for taking the initiative and getting more actively involved in using the strategy. The role of individual feedback during this stage is as critical as during Stage 5; however, rather than you assuming total responsibility for the feedback process, you will involve students by asking them questions about their responses, thus enabling them to analyze the appropriateness of their performance.

Stage 7: Make Commitments for Generalization.
This stage involves encouraging an analysis of student progress and obtaining student commitment to use the new strategy in a variety of settings. The generalization activities that follow will not be successful if students do not make a personal commitment to generalize the strategy they have just mastered. This stage also involves making a commitment to the student to help her generalize the strategy.

Stage 8: Generalization.
A frequently overlooked instructional stage in teaching skills to low achievers is *generalization*. We tend to be satisfied if students demonstrate competency within a remedial setting or controlled materials; however, the real measure of the effect of instruction is the degree to which students can generalize the acquired strategy to a variety of settings and maintain use of the strategy over time. Research has shown that generalization instruction must be specifically scheduled. Four distinct phases are addressed in generalization instruction. First, an Orientation Phase is designed to make students aware of situations and circumstances in which they can use their newly learned strategy and the way in which they may need to adjust the strategy to meet unique situations. Second, an Activation Phase allows students to practice using the strategy in a broad array of settings and situations. Here, students are given specific assignments requiring application of the strategy. Third, in the Adaptation Phase, students learn how to adapt the cognitive processes in the strategy to other types of tasks. Finally, the Maintenance Phase is designed to periodically check if students are continuing to use the strategy appropriately. The old adage, "If you don't use it, you'll lose it," is particularly applicable to strategy usage.

Other Instructional Issues

During field testing of the *Learning Strategies Curriculum,* a number of questions have arisen related to the most effective way of delivering the special kinds of instruction required. Some of the more frequently asked questions are presented below.

How important is following the instructions in this manual?
In compiling this *Instructor's Manual,* the procedures to be used in teaching the *Sentence Writing Strategy* have been covered as completely as possible. This has been done to provide you specific guidelines for putting each of the instructional stages into practice. Teachers who have tested our materials have indicated that following the instructions as they are presented to secure student learning is critical. They have stated that picking and choosing the information to be presented without frequently referring to the instructions have resulted in confusion and poor student performance. Students rarely master a strategy under such conditions.

Each of the instructions provided here is based on sound learning theory and empirical research. Low achievers need the special instructional sequences and conditions outlined in this manual if they are to be expected to learn. Thus, we strongly recommend that you teach the *Sentence Writing Strategy* as specified.

In what settings are the learning strategies best taught?
The learning strategy instruction described this *Instructor's Manual* was designed primarily for small groups of students (approximately 4-7). We have found that students benefit from observing other students' responses while learning the strategies. Small-group instruction also allows the instructor ample opportunity to provide individual feedback to students on a regular basis. This does not mean that learning strategies cannot be taught to individuals (in

a one-to-one format) or to larger groups. For the most part, the instructions in this manual can be followed for either teaching arrangement. Some teachers have taught the *Sentence Writing Strategy* successfully to as many as 30 students at one time by having some students practice independently or in cooperative groups, while the teacher provided feedback and additional instruction to other students. With groups of this size, you may need the assistance of an aide for grading student work. Also, you will need to take care to schedule sufficient opportunities to give specific feedback to each student regarding written assignments. You may choose to use a feedback form through which written feedback can be provided to each student daily. Require students to review the feedback form and, if necessary, obtain help from you or a peer before starting a new lesson.

Usually, the learning strategies can most effectively be taught in a remedial setting such as a resource room, a learning center, or a remedial class. However, to apply a mastered strategy, students must be placed in an actual curricular setting.

How much should I try to involve the student in the instructional process? A great deal! Remember, an overriding

instructional goal of learning strategy instruction is to make students active and independent learners and performers. This goal is best accomplished by deliberately involving students at critical points in the instructional process. Thus, throughout the instructions in this manual you will find that students are required to perform tasks that you normally do for them and to think for themselves. For example, after the student has completed the pretest in Stage 1, discuss the results with him and obtain his commitment to learn the strategy. In Stage 2, students should be asked to set specific goals relative to mastering the strategy. In Stages 5, 6, and 8, students should be responsible for acquiring their own materials and completing their assignments. In Stage 7, they should write a specific goal for generalizing their use of the strategy. Throughout the instructional process, adhere to the following Three-Statement Rule: **"The teacher will make no more than three statements without having a student make a response."** The student response can be either oral (i.e., answering a question) or written (i.e., taking notes). In short, student involvement is essential throughout the instructional process to secure the students' vested interest as well as to accomplish the overall instructional goal of making students active participants in the learning process. Emphasis has been placed on active academic responding because it has been found to correlate with academic achievement. That is, if they are academically active, students will make more achievement gains than if they are passive. Thus, our emphasis is on making students academically active (i.e., by having them speak, read, or write) the entire time they spend in a learning strategy class.

In addition to ensuring that students remain academ-

ically active during the learning process, make sure that the majority of your instructional activities are consistent with the overall goal of helping them become independent learners. For example, if a student asks how to respond to an item on one of the lessons, ask the student a probing question that causes her to arrive at a solution somewhat independently rather than simply giving her the correct answer. In this manner, you can make the student a more active and independent participant in the learning process, consistent with the overall instructional goal. By simply providing the student with the correct answer, on the other hand, you can make her more dependent upon you. Also, structure your learning setting so that students can access materials and begin work independently. In addition, think of ways in which, through actions and words, you can communicate to the students that they are capable of being independent learners.

The *Instructor's Manual* seems to provide everything needed to teach the student. What does the teacher provide? The teacher is often de-

scribed as the mediator between instructional materials and students. This portrayal fits instruction in learning strategies. For example, this *Instructor's Manual* and associated *Student Lessons* might be thought of as the technology for teaching this learning strategy. Your success in teaching the *Sentence Writing Strategy* will, in large measure, be a function of two factors. First, it depends on how carefully and skillfully you follow the outlined procedures (e.g., giving appropriate feedback, ensuring that students reach mastery). Your skills as a teacher who can pinpoint a student's problems in each instructional stage and who can get a student to change his behavior will play a major role in each student's learning process. Second, the success of the learning process also relies on how much excitement and commitment you bring to the teaching process! In short, your mind set and enthusiasm for how much students can improve their learning by acquiring learning strategies can greatly enhance the instructional process.

What factors make for good feedback? The following four characteristics are critical

in providing adequate feedback. First, feedback should be positive. That is, you need to point out at least three appropriate aspects of the student's performance. This will be reinforcing to the students and make them aware of behaviors that should be continued. Second, feedback should be *corrective*. That is, students should be made aware of the specific aspects of their performance that are incorrect and how they can improve. The more specific your corrective feedback is, the more quickly a student's performance will improve. To help a student learn quickly, (a) categorize the types of errors she is making, (b) specify those categories of errors to the student, (c) help the student create ministrategies for avoiding those errors in the future, (d) demonstrte how to perform those ministrategies, (e) have the student show you how she performs the ministrategy on at least one example, (f) provide feedback until she performs the ministrategy correctly, and (g) prompt the student to write goals for future practice attempts.

Third, feedback should be given *individually*. Experience has shown that feedback given to groups of students has relatively little impact on changing a given student's performance. Fourth, feedback should be given immediately *after* one performance of a strategy and *before* the next. The timing of feedback is important; it should fall as close to a student's response as possible. Most instructors are aware of the importance of giving feedback immediately after a student completes work, but often forget how important it is to do so right before a student makes the next response. This is particularly important for low-achieving students because they should not continue to practice their incorrect habits. Thus, a simple reminder before students begin their work can be helpful by making them aware of responses to be avoided. Again, to promote independence, ask the students to specify how *they* are going to try to improve immediately before each practice attempt.

How important is "mastery" performance?
Students will be unable to generalize a given learning strategy (our major instructional goal) until they can proficiently perform the strategy at the specified mastery levels. Specifically, two dimensions constitute mastery performance: *correct performance* of a given strategy and *fluent use* of the strategy. Typically, the earlier phases of instruction focus on students acquiring and performing the correct strategy steps. After they have learned the steps in the correct order, the instructional emphasis must shift to increasing the speed with which students use the strategy. Older students are often required to express large amounts of information quickly. If a learning strategy is to serve a student well, mastery performance must be thought of both in terms of correctness and fluency.

What do I do if a student bogs down when learning a strategy?
This question is difficult to answer because many factors may account for a student's poor progress in learning a given strategy. The following are key checkpoints and possible solutions. First, a student may have begun to learn a strategy that is too difficult. That is, the student may lack some critical prerequisite skills for acquiring the strategy. For example, if the student is having difficulty applying the *Sentence Writing Strategy* to writing simple sentences, he may need supplemental instruction on some key prerequisite skills, such as subject and verb identification. Thus, teaching these skills and providing supplementary practice in this area may be necessary before resuming instruction in the *Sentence Writing Strategy*.

Second, students sometimes bog down because they lose sight of the benefits of mastering a given strategy. Take time to sit next to the student while she is completing a lesson. Ask the student to think aloud so you can hear her thought processes while she works. Provide elaborated feedback on those elements of the strategy that the student is omitting or performing incorrectly. Third, sometimes students lose sight of the benefits of mastering a given strategy. Thus, you may have to restate some rationales about how the use of the strategy can help students and specify performance levels they can expect to achieve after mastering the strategy. Your enthusiasm and credibility will also help re-excite students. Fourth, a creative choice of stimulus materials and topics will contribute to maintaining student interest and allow students to reach their goals more quickly.

How do I keep all students together in the group, or should I even try?
Students can be taught as a group during the Describe and Model Stages of the teaching procedures. During the Verbal Practice, Controlled Practice and Feedback, and Advanced Practice/Posttest and Feedback Stages, however, students learn at different rates. Consequently, some will require additional practice to reach mastery. Since instruction in each part of the *Sentence Writing Strategy* after the Verbal Practice Stage is individually based, there is no reason to try to keep the students together after this stage. Students who are learning quickly should be allowed to continue to learn quickly and meet their goals. Once they reach mastery in Stage 8, they can work on other kinds of skills if you want them to wait for the other group members to catch up before beginning a new sentence type or a new strategy. If you prefer, advanced students can be taught to be effective peer tutors. Such an arrangement not only provides the necessary practice for the tutee, it also allows the tutor to review the strategy. Alternatively, many teachers allow their students to progress through the four parts of the strategy at their own pace. They do not require the students to wait for each other, or ask them to wait for only one or two students so that the Describe and Model Stages can be presented to a small group of two or three students.

MANAGING INSTRUCTION

Effective learning strategy instruction is contingent upon a well-organized instructional setting and a clear plan for managing the instructional process. Some helpful ideas are presented below.

Decide Who Needs Learning Strategy Instruction

Every student in your classroom should not automatically receive learning strategy instruction. Consequently, each student's needs should be carefully considered before a decision is made to initiate learning strategy instruction. The *Learning Strategies Curriculum* has been designed and found most appropriate for students in the middle grades (5-6) through post-secondary education. Students who have responded most favorably to the curriculum are those typically classified as low achievers, underachievers, culturally different, or learning disabled.

Specifically, we have found that, with few exceptions, most students can benefit from instruction in at least part of the *Sentence Writing Strategy*. Students who have severe spelling disabilities may benefit from prerequisite or simultaneous instruction in morphographic spelling skills.* Similarly, students who have difficulty discriminating subjects and verbs may need instruction in these prerequisite skills prior to beginning the instruction described in this manual. Use the *Fundamentals in the Sentence Writing Strategy* program (Schumaker & Sheldon, 1998) to provide such prerequisite instruction.

Set Your Own Goals

Instructors should set goals regarding how much to accomplish with each student within a specified period of time. Without clearly defined goals, many teachers tend to fall a little behind schedule each week, resulting in significant slippage by the end of a semester. Use your limited instructional time well so that you can address the large number of deficiencies many low-achieving students exhibit. Well-defined and ambitious goals will increase the intensity of your instruction as well as the overall progress of your students.

Throughout this manual we have included time estimates for the instructional stages. These are averages for instructors who are proficient in teaching the strategy, and are based on the assumption that a student will receive instruction in the *Sentence Writing Strategy* for approximately one-half hour per day. (If the student receives learning strategy instruction for one hour each day, instruction in two strategies can be provided per day.) On the student's goal chart, one day is equal to one 25- or 30-minute instructional period.

A note of caution: Our experience has repeatedly shown that instructors usually take *twice* as long to help their students reach mastery the first time they teach a strategy compared to the second time. As you become familiar with the stages, the instructional materials, and the best ways to provide effective feedback, your teaching efficiency will increase markedly. Therefore, the first time you teach the *Sentence Writing Strategy* do not become discouraged if your students are not learning as quickly as the estimates in this *Instructor's Manual* indicate they should be.

---

* See Dixon, R. & Englemann, S. (1979). Corrective spelling through morphographs. (Science Research Associates, 155 N. Wacker Dr., Chicago, IL 60606. 800-621-0476)

Getting Organized!

The investment of a couple of hours before you begin instruction in the *Sentence Writing Strategy* to set up student folders and make copies of needed materials will facilitate delivery of the instructional content. We recommend that you set up a manilla folder (or three-ring notebook) for each student, labeled with the name of the student and the name of the strategy. An envelope should be affixed to the inside front cover of the folder for holding the student's Formula Card and *Sentence Checklists*. The folder should contain a major section for each of the sentence types to be learned. Some teachers use colored paper, others use tabbed dividers to designate where one section begins and another ends. A separate *Progress Chart* (pp. 175-178), *Generalization Progress Chart* (p. 179) and Assignment Sheet (see p. 47 for a description) will be needed for each sentence type (simple, compound, complex, compound-complex), and should be placed at the beginning of the section designated for that sentence type in the students' folders.

Some teachers have provided organizational dividers for students to use in their folders. This helps the students learn how to store their products in an orderly fashion and helps you find their products and other stored materials quickly. If you choose to provide organizational dividers for each major section, the following tabs are appropriate: Cue Cards, Verbal Practice, Controlled Practice, Advanced Practice, and Generalization. A separate set of tabs should be used for each sentence type to be taught. Alternatively, separate folders with appropriate dividers can be used for each sentence type to be taught.

In addition, to get started, you will need an ample supply of *Sentence Score Sheets* (p. 174) and at least one *Management Chart* (p. 180). The *Score Sheets* should be stored in a separate folder labeled "Sentence Score Sheets." The students' names should be written on the *Management Chart(s)*, and the *Chart(s)* should be posted in a place accessible to the students.

Also, copy needed lessons from the *Student Lessons* volume (Sheldon & Schumaker, 1985). Make a folder for each lesson labeled with the lesson name and number (e.g., Simple Sentence Lesson 1A), and insert a large number of copies of the lesson in the folder. For Advanced Practice Lessons, insert stimuli (e.g., pictures, magazine or newspaper articles) in the folder as well (see p. 54 for a description of appropriate stimuli). Put all the lesson folders in a cardboard box or a file drawer in the correct sequence (as sequenced in the *Student Lessons* volume).

Once you have prepared and gathered the materials as indicated in the remainder of this manual, structure the learning setting so that students have independent access to them. That is, put the student folders in a place the students can access as they enter the learning setting. They should be able to quickly look at their assignments for the day, gather the necessary supplies, and get started within the first 2-3 minutes they are present in the learning setting. This kind of arrangement fosters student independence and eliminates time usually wasted while students wait for attendance to be taken and instructions to be given. Such time is better spent in active academic responding. Decide how you can best capitalize on the time students spend with you, and organize your learning setting accordingly.

WHAT THIS MANUAL INCLUDES

If you have thumbed through the remainder of this manual, you may feel overwhelmed! There is no need to be because everything has been organized for your convenience. The purpose of this section is to introduce you to the contents of the manual. You will note that it is divided into four major sections: Instructional Methods, Evaluation Guidelines (Appendix A), Instructional Materials (Appendix B), and Enrichment Activities (Appendix C).

Instructional Methods

This section is organized according to the eight instructional stages (e.g., Pretest and Make Commitments, Describe) mentioned earlier. To assist you in teaching each stage most effectively, its contents have been organized as follows:

What your goal is. This part tells you what you are to accomplish during a given stage.

What you need. This section lists everything you will need to teach a given stage. Do not be intimidated by the long lists! We expressly overincluded to ensure that you would not be caught short during instruction.

How to prepare. This section lists the steps you should follow to become prepared for the upcoming lesson. You must be well prepared so that you can focus on the students and not on the words in your manual while you are teaching. Since a lively instructional pace and student involvement are critical, advanced preparations are definitely required.

How much time to allow. This section will help you plan how much you can accomplish during the available instructional time. Most activities will fit into half of a 50-minute or one-hour class period. These time designations are merely estimates, however.

What to do. This section contains detailed instructions for each stage. Most teachers like to have the *Instructor's Manual* open to this section and in front of them as they provide the instruction. The bold-faced headings should serve as cues. After becoming familiar with a given strategy, you will merely need to glance at the bold-faced cues to know what to do or say. If necessary, you can look at the text occasionally and cue yourself about what questions to ask or what to do next. The things you need to do are presented in brackets. The things you need to say are shown in quotes and bold-faced type. Some teachers like to go through the manual and highlight in yellow what

to say or what questions to ask. When you are talking to students, you do not have to use the precise wording in the manual. Use your own words so that your natural teaching style is not altered; however, do not alter the *intent* of instructional steps or substeps and the content provided. Adhere to the Three-Statement Rule (see p. 7)—student involvement is *essential*.

What to require. This section specifies the mastery level you should expect of your students. Without mastery at each stage, students are unlikely to ever use a given strategy. The investment of your time and energy in providing strategy instruction to students is most likely to have a significant impact on their lives if you require them to reach the mastery levels as indicated.

Where to go from here. This part tells you what to do next, depending on how a student has performed.

How to trouble-shoot. This section includes suggestions for working with students who are not progressing. You may have additional ideas of your own. Research has shown that learning strategy instruction as specified in this *Instructor's Manual* is successful for most students. If students experience difficulty even after you have tried the ideas in the troubleshooting section, it may be due to a problem like absenteeism.

Appendix A: Evaluation Guidelines

Appendix A contains the information you will need in order to learn how to score sentences written by students and how to record their progress. Included are: the *Sentence Scoring Instructions* (pp. 137-143)—a set of guidelines for use when evaluating students' sentences; the *Calculation Procedures* (pp. 143-144)—a step-by-step guide to be used in determining a student's performance levels; the *Progress Chart Explanation* (p. 144)—a guide for graphing the students' percentage scores on the *Progress Chart;* the *Example Progress Chart* (p. 145)—an illustration of how to fill out the *Progress Chart;* a *Pretest Sample* and a *Practice Sample* (p. 146)—illustrations of the types of products you may receive when assessing student proficiency in writing sentences; the *Example Sentence Score Sheets* (p. 147)—illustrations of how to fill out the *Sentence Score Sheet* based on the *Pretest Sample* and *Practice Sample;* the *Scoring Explanation* (pp. 148-149)—a description of the reasons behind each scoring decision for the *Example Sentence Score Sheets;* and a *Percentage Table* (p. 149)—a chart that can be used to convert the number of points earned on Controlled Practice Lessons into the percentage of points earned. You will need to refer to these materials frequently the first time you teach the *Sentence Writing Strategy.* Thereafter, you should review them periodically to refresh your memory about the performance level to require of your students.

Appendix B: Instructional Materials

Appendix B includes most of the materials you need to teach the *Sentence Writing Strategy*. The *Topic List* (p. 152) is to be used to stimulate writing for the Pretest. You may make an overhead transparency of the *List* or you can write it on the board. The *Cue Cards* (pp. 153-167) have been designed to highlight the essential information required to perform the *Sentence Writing Strategy* steps. Use these as masters for overheads or as models for posters, or use them as references while writing the information on the chalkboard as you discuss each step or point. The *Example Sheets* (pp. 168-169) can be used as masters for making a copy for each student receiving instruction. The appropriate *Verbal Practice Checklist* (pp. 170-173) is to be used in Stage 4 to keep track of a student's attempts to reach criterion on defining concepts and naming the different steps involved in the *Sentence Writing Strategy*. The *Sentence Score Sheet* (p. 174) is for scoring a student's written performance on the Pretest, on practice attempts during Advanced Practice, on Generalization attempts, and on Maintenance Probes. The *Progress Charts* (pp. 175-178) are contracting and self-recording devices to be used by students to set their goals and record their progress. Use of the *Progress Charts* will prove motivational for most students. The *Management Chart* (p. 180) enables you to review at a glance all students' progress in learning the *Sentence Writing Strategy*. It should also be used by the students as a self-recording device. Finally, the *Sentence Checklists* (p. 181) are to be used by the students to check their work on Advanced Practice Lessons and during Generalization activities. You can use the *Checklists* to evaluate the mix of sentences a student has written.

Permission is granted to the owner of this *Instructor's Manual* to copy the materials in Appendix B for personal use in providing *Sentence Writing Strategy* instruction. You may make one copy of the *Cue Cards* on paper or overhead transparencies to present information to students learning the *Sentence Writing Strategy*. You may make copies of the *Examples Sheets, Verbal Practice Checklists,* the *Score Sheet,* the *Progress Charts,* and the *Management Chart* as needed for student instruction in your own instructional setting. Copying these materials for other instructors or any other purpose is in violation of copyright law. Research has shown that individuals who do not receive appropriate instruction in the use of these materials do not use them effectively. Thus, if someone is interested in obtaining these materials, encourage her to get authorized instruction in their use. If you want to copy the materials in Appendix B for any purpose other than instruction with students, permission to do so must be obtained from the copyright holder. No other materials or excerpts of this manual may be copied or used without the copyright holder's permission.

Appendix C: Enrichment Activities

The *Enrichment Activities* (pp. 183-190) are to be used with advanced students after they master particular parts of this strategy. They should be used with students who learn quickly or who express an interest in learning more about a particular sentence type. For most students, stressing the basic information in this manual and foregoing the enrichment activities will be appropriate. The enrichment activities have been included in response to a demand by teachers who teach at the post-secondary level.

WHAT ELSE YOU NEED

This manual includes all the materials you need to teach the *Sentence Writing Strategy* except the lessons through which the students will practice using the strategy. These can be found in the *Student Lessons* volume of *Proficiency in the Sentence Writing Strategy* (Sheldon & Schumaker, 1985). Permission is granted to the owner of this *Instructor's Manual* to copy lessons from the *Student Lessons* volume for personal use in providing instruction to students learning the *Sentence Writing Strategy*. The lessons are to be used only in conjunction with the instruction provided in this *Instructor's Manual*. They are not designed to be used independent of that instruction. Copying of these lesson materials for other instructors or any other purpose in any form is in violation of copyright law.

In teaching this strategy, some teachers have used English textbooks as a source of additional example sentences for their presentations as well as references for clarifying any questions that may arise regarding sentence structure during instruction of the strategy. In addition, teachers have developed a picture library and a topics library that can be used as sources of stimuli for different writing assignments to fit individual students' interests.

REFERENCES

Schumaker, J.B., and Deshler, D.D. (1992). Validation of learning strategy interventions for students with learning disabilities: Results of a programmatic research effort. In B.Y.L. Wong (Ed.), *Contemporary intervention research in learning disabilities: An international perspective.* (pp. 22-46). New York: Springer-Verlag.

Schumaker, J.B., and Sheldon, J.B. (1998). *Fundamentals in the Sentence Writing Strategy.* Lawrence, KS: The University of Kansas Center for Research on Learning.

Sheldon, J., and Schumaker, J.B. (1985). *Proficiency in the Sentence Writing Strategy: Student Lessons.* Lawrence, KS: Edge Enterprises, Inc.

INSTRUCTIONAL METHODS

STAGE 1: PRETEST AND MAKE COMMITMENTS

What your goals are:

- To obtain a measure of students' ability to use a variety of sentence structures in their writing.
- To obtain student commitment to learn to write different kinds of sentences.
- To make a commitment to guide student learning.

What you need:

- Chalkboard or other large writing surface (e.g., easel pad, blank overhead transparency)
- Writing implement appropriate for the chosen writing surface (e.g., chalk, colored pen)
- Ruled paper
- Pencils
- *Topic List* (p. 152)
- *Sentence Scoring Instructions* (pp. 137-143)
- *Example Sentence Score Sheets* (p. 147)
- *Sentence Score Sheet* (one per student) (p. 174)
- *Example Sentence Progress Chart* (p. 145)
- *Simple Sentence Progress Chart* (p. 175) (one per student)
- Student folders (see p. 9 for description) (one per student)
- *Management Chart for Instruction in Simple Sentences* (p. 180)

How to prepare:

1. **Decide who will take the pretest.** Read the section on p. 8 entitled, *"Decide who needs learning strategy instruction."* Determine which students fit the characteristics, and schedule these students for the Pretest.

2. **Check your supplies of *Simple Sentence Progress Charts*, *Sentence Score Sheets,* and student folders.** Make sure you have at least one *Simple Sentence Progress Chart* and one *Sentence Score Sheet* for each student. Prepare student folders if you do not have at least one per student (see p. 9).

3. **Gather the other listed materials.** Make one copy of the *Management Chart* and put the word "Simple" in the blank of the title on the chart.

4. **Read the instructions below.** Familiarize yourself with the order of events to take place in the instructional setting and the instructions you will be giving the students.

5. **Familiarize yourself with the scoring procedures.** Read the Evaluation Guidelines (pp. 137-144) to become familiar with the scoring procedures for sentences as well as the calculation and charting procedures.

6. **Prepare the *Topic List*.** Make a transparency of the *Topic List* or list the topics from the *Topic List* in a location that is visible to the students. Add topics you think will interest particular students.

7. **List the types of sentences on the board.** Under the heading "Types of Sentences," list the following: simple sentence, compound sentence, complex sentence, compound-complex sentence.

How much time to allow:

Allow approximately 15-20 minutes for students to write six sentences. Students may take more time if necessary, but no more than 60 minutes should be scheduled for the test. Allow approximately 10 minutes to explain the test results to each student individually.

What to do:

1. **Give students an advance organizer.** "We need to determine the quality and kinds of sentences you can write before we begin your writing instruction. Therefore, you are going to write a group of sentences about one of the topics on the board."

2. **Distribute paper and pencils if necessary.**

3. **Give specific instructions.** "Choose one of the topics from the list on the board, and write at least six sentences about it. Write the topic at the top of your paper along with your name and today's date. Try to make your sentences as different in structure from each other as possible."

[Point to the list of sentence types on the board.]

"Try to include as many as possible of the following kinds of sentences in your paragraph: simple, compound, complex, and compound-complex."

4. **Solicit and answer questions.** [Solicit questions from the students and answer them. If they ask about a particular sentence type, give them a short definition. For example: "A compound sentence consists of two or more independent clauses." Do not give examples of any of the sentence types.]

5. **Monitor students' work.** [As the students write, circulate among them to ensure that they are following your instructions. Encourage students to choose a topic and get started quickly. If students ask you to help them spell words, provide assistance. *Do not* provide assistance in structuring sentences.]

6. **Collect the test materials.** [When a student indicates that she has completed the task, check that she has written at least six sentences (as indicated by the use of periods, capital letters, or both). If at least six sentences have been writ-

ten, collect the paper for scoring. If the student has not written six sentences, encourage her to write the necessary number of additional sentences.]

7. **Evaluate each student's sentences.** [Using the *Sentence Scoring Instructions* and a *Sentence Score Sheet,* evaluate each of the student's products. (Refer to the *Pretest Sample* on p. 146 and the corresponding *Example Score Sheet I* on p. 147, if necessary.) Calculate the percentage scores. (Refer to the Calculation Procedures on pp. 143-144 for instructions.) Record the results on the student's *Simple Sentence Progress Chart.* (See the *Example Progress Chart* on p. 145 for a model and the *Progress Chart Explanation* on p. 144 for instructions.)]

8. **Communicate test results to the student.** [Using the student's product and the completed *Sentence Score Sheet,* describe to each student privately how he is currently performing. In a matter-of-fact way, describe the kinds of sentences he does and does not write well. Explain how the scores were calculated and how they were plotted on the *Progress Chart.* Define the mastery levels and describe how the student functions in relation to them. If the student did not reach the required mastery levels, explain how such a performance will hinder his success in school, leisure-time, and work settings, and relate the problem to the student's personal goals in such settings. Solicit and provide specific examples to illustrate how the student's inability to write complete and interesting sentences will hinder him in reaching his goals.]

9. **Make your commitment to the student.** "You and I need to create a partnership to create success for you in the area of writing. I need to work hard at teaching, and you need to work hard at learning how to write. I am willing to commit to you that I will do my very best to teach you the *Sentence Writing Strategy.*"

[Write a statement of commitment on a piece of paper such as, "I will do my very best to teach (student's name) to write a variety of complete sentences." Write your signature below the statement.]

10. **Obtain the student's commitment to learn.** [Ask the student, given her pretest performance, to write a goal indicating her commitment to learn a strategy for writing complete and interesting sentences. Have her write and sign a long-term goal to that effect (e.g., "I want to learn the *Sentence Writing Strategy*"). Place the signed goal statement in the student's IEP file.

If the student indicates that he does not wish to write a goal about learning the strategy or seems uncertain, spend additional time explaining, in a matter-of-fact way, how the strategy might help in required courses, job training, writing a letter of application for a job, writing a complaint to a landlord, and other situations related to the student's long-term goals. If he still does not wish to write the goal to learn the strategy, invite him to attend the discussion for the Describe Stage. Often, when a student sees other students willing to learn a strategy and realizes that the strategy appears simple, he will want to learn the strategy. This approach is preferable, since students need to perceive themselves as being in control and responsible for choosing what they learn.]

11. **Fill out the *Management Chart.*** [Fill in the title and enter the names of students who have chosen to learn the *Sentence Writing Strategy* on the *Man-*

agement Chart. Post the chart in an easy-to-see location. Place the current date under "Pretest" for each student to indicate who has completed this step.]

What to require for mastery:

Percentage of complete sentences. One hundred percent (100%) of the sentences in a student's product must be complete.

Percentage of complicated sentences. At least fifty percent (50%) of the sentences in a student's product must be complicated.

Percentage of correctly punctuated complicated sentences. At least sixty-six percent (66%) of the complicated sentences must be correctly punctuated.

Sentence mix. A minimum of three different sentence types must be used.

Where to go from here:

If the student does not reach the required mastery levels but appears to have mastered some basic skills related to sentence writing, go to STAGE 2: DESCRIBE. If, on the other hand, the majority of the student's sentences are incomplete or run-on sentences, begin instruction for that student in the *Fundamentals in the Sentence Writing Strategy* program (Schumaker & Sheldon, 1998).*

If the student reaches the mastery levels, proceed to another strategy (e.g., the *Paragraph Strategy* or the *Error Monitoring Strategy*).

How to trouble-shoot:

Occasionally, you will encounter students who cannot spell well enough to write a single sentence. Teach these students morphographic spelling skills** before giving the pretest for the *Sentence Writing Strategy.* After students learn some spelling skills, morphographic spelling skills and the *Sentence Writing Strategy* can be taught simultaneously.

You may also encounter students who write one long run-on sentence that covers the majority of the page. Asking such students to write five more sentences will be fruitless, for they have no idea of what a sentence is. Therefore, accept the run-on sentence as the Pretest.

Another problem you might encounter is a kind of writer's block. A student may have no confidence in her writing skills or may, for other reasons, appear stuck and unable to write a single sentence. In such a case, help the student choose a topic, and ask her to write it down. Next, in the left-hand margin of a sheet of paper, place the numbers 1, 2, 3, 4, 5, and 6 spread out over the length of the paper. Ask the student to write a sentence that relates to the topic next to each number. If the student still appears stuck, you might suggest the content for one or two sentences. *Do not* dictate sentences for the student to write. For example, you might say, "Your topic is 'Summer Activities.' What's one summer activity? (The student answers, "Swimming.") Good. Write the first sentence about swimming." Accept as many sentences as the student can write, and note how much help you provided.

---

* See Schumaker, J.B., & Sheldon, J.B. (1998). *Fundamentals in the Sentence Writing Strategy.* Lawrence: University of Kansas Center for Research on Learning.
** See Dixon, R., & Englemann, S. (1979). *Corrective spelling through morphographs.* Palo Alto, CA: Science Research Associates. (SRA/McGraw-Hill, 220 E. Danieldale Road, DeSoto, TX 75115. 1-888-772-4543)

PART I: SIMPLE SENTENCES
STAGE 2: DESCRIBE

What your goals are:

To provide students with a description of:
- Rationales for learning the *Sentence Writing Strategy*.
- General characteristics of situations where students will be able to apply the *Sentence Writing Strategy*.
- Example situations where they can use the *Sentence Writing Strategy*.
- The results they can expect after learning the *Sentence Writing Strategy*.
- Requirements for simple sentences.
- Formulas to be used in writing simple sentences.
- Steps of the *Sentence Writing Strategy*.

What you need:

- Chalkboard or other writing surface (e.g., poster board, easel pad, blank overhead transparencies, paper)
- Writing implement appropriate for chosen writing surface (e.g., chalk, colored pens)
- Overhead projector and screen (if using overhead transparencies)
- *Sentence Writing Cue Cards #1-6* (pp. 153-167)
- *Example Sheets* (pp. 168-169) (one per student)
- *Pretest Sample* and *Practice Sample* (p. 146)* (one per student)
- 4" × 6" cards (one per student)
- Your own 4" × 6" Formula Card
- Student folders
- Paper for student notes
- Pencils
- Large calendar
- *Management Chart for Instruction in Simple Sentences* (p. 180)

How to prepare:

1. **Make copies of the *Cue Cards*, the *Example Sheets*, the *Pretest Sample*, and the *Practice Sample*.** If you are using overhead copies of the *Cue Cards,* the *Example Sheets,* and the *Pretest Sample* and *Practice Sample,* make them prior to the instructional session. If you are not using overhead projection, make one paper copy of each of the *Cue Cards,* which can easily be used for reference as you present the information to the students, and copies of the *Pretest Sample* and *Practice Sample* that the students can share. Regardless of the presentation method you are using, make one paper copy of the *Example Sheets* for each student.

---

* Alternatively, you may use pretest and practice samples written by your own students. Erase the student's name from each product before copying it.

2. Gather the other listed materials. Make a model 4" × 6" Formula Card if necessary (see instructions on p. 34). Gather the other materials needed.

3. Familiarize yourself with the instructions below.

How much time to allow:

Allow 2-3 hours to present the information. If you present the information on two or three different days, start the second and third day's lesson with a quick review of information presented on the previous day.

What to do:
Preliminary Activities

1. Give the students an advance organizer. "Today we are beginning a unit on the *Sentence Writing Strategy* with a lesson on the first kind of sentence you will learn, the *simple sentence*. Most of you will learn how to write four kinds of simple sentences within the next 2-3 weeks. By the end of 9 or 10 weeks, most of you will be writing at least 14 different kinds of sentences. You will know how to write complete sentences and how to vary your sentences to make them interesting."

2. Discuss rationales for learning the *Sentence Writing Strategy.* "Before we begin learning about simple sentences, let's discuss why it's important to know how to write complete and interesting sentences."

a. Discuss benefits in school. "How do you suppose improved sentence-writing skills might help you in school?"

[Solicit responses such as: grades will improve, teachers will think the students are trying hard and will give them the benefit of the doubt in choice situations, and they will be able to pass the minimal competency test on sentence writing.]

b. Discuss benefits in employment. "How can writing complete and interesting sentences help you make a good impression on people outside school, such as a future employer?"

[Elicit responses such as they will be able to make a good impression when they write letters of application or fill out job applications, and when they write a letter asking for help, a favor, or support.]

"If you write incomplete or run-on sentences in your job application, what kind of an impression would you make? Would you be likely to be called in for an interview?"

[Elicit negative responses.]

c. Discuss general benefits. "That's right, and the *Sentence Writing Strategy* can help you in another way: it can help you say what you really mean. Can you think of times when it's *very* important that people clearly express their ideas in writing?"

[Elicit responses such as writing a statement for the police on what happened to cause an accident, writing a letter to your girlfriend explaining why you were seen with another girl, etc.]

d. Summarize. "As you can see, learning the *Sentence Writing Strategy* can help you get better grades in school, make a good impression on the people who read your writing, and express yourself better in important situations."

3. Discuss general characteristics of situations where the *Sentence Writing Strategy* can be used, and cite example situations. "You can use the *Sentence Writing Strategy* any time you have to write one or more sentences. Let's think of as many situations as we can where writing one or more sentences is necessary."

[Elicit responses, and list them on the board. Prompt students to think of situations at school (e.g., writing a book report, answering an essay question on a test, writing an answer to a question that appears at the end of a history chapter), in the community (e.g., completing a job application, writing a thank-you note, writing a letter), and at work (e.g., writing a note to a co-worker or employer, writing a letter to a customer).]

"These are all excellent examples of situations where you can use the *Sentence Writing Strategy.* You've seen that this strategy can help you in a variety of situations—at school, at home, and on your job."

4. Provide information on the results students can expect. "Other students who have learned the *Sentence Writing Strategy* have been very pleased with the way the strategy helps them. Let's look at some examples."

[Distribute copies of the *Pretest Sample* and *Practice Sample,* or display them on the overhead projector.]

"These are two products written by the same student. The *Pretest Sample* was written before the student learned the *Sentence Writing Strategy.* The *Practice Sample* was written after he learned the *Sentence Writing Strategy.*"

"How are these pretest and practice products different?"

[Solicit responses such as:

The Pretest Sample	The Practice Sample
Is short.	Is much longer with more words and sentences.
Consists of incomplete sentences.	Consists of complete sentences.
Contains only one sentence type.	Contains a variety of sentence types.
Has unclear ideas.	Expresses ideas that are clear and easy to understand.
Makes a bad impression.	Makes a good impression.
Is uninteresting.	Is very interesting to read.]

"That's right, and these are exactly the kinds of improvements you can expect in your writing. You'll find that writing becomes easy for you, so you'll write more. Your sentences will be well written, and your ideas will be easy to understand. Best of all, your writing will be interesting to read."

5. **Set goals.** [Distribute the students' folders and ask them to turn to the *Simple Sentence Progress Chart.* Explain that they need to set their goals for how fast they want to learn to write simple sentences.

Using the calendar for reference, have the students write on their *Progress Charts,* in the section labeled "Goals Section," a target date under each heading next to the words "Target Dates." Explain that they can change the goal dates at any time depending on their progress.

Starting with the current day's date, have the students write a target date for completion of each stage. The following timeline may be suggested:

STAGE 2:	DESCRIBE	3 or 4 days
		(depending on your plan)
STAGE 3:	MODEL	1 day
STAGE 4:	VERBAL PRACTICE	1-2 days*
STAGE 5:	CONTROLLED PRACTICE AND FEEDBACK	3-12 days*
STAGE 6:	ADVANCED PRACTICE/POSTTEST AND FEEDBACK	1-4 days*
STAGE 7:	MAKE COMMITMENTS FOR GENERALIZATION	1 day
STAGE 8:	GENERALIZATION	10-15 days*

Help the students match the number of days they choose to dates on the calendar.

Discuss with the students why they should master simple sentences quickly (i.e., so they can learn other important skills and strategies within the school year).]

6. **Prompt the students to make Cue Cards.** "As I said, today we're beginning a unit on simple sentences. While we talk about simple sentences, you need to take notes so you can make your own Cue Cards."

[Ask the students to take out paper and pencils, or distribute paper and pencils.]

"You can keep the Cue Cards in your folder, so you will be able to refer to them whenever you need to. For each Cue Card that I show you, use a separate piece of paper."

Basic Definitions

7. **Give the definition for a simple sentence.** A *simple sentence* is a sentence that is made up of one independent clause."

[Write the definition for a simple sentence on the board, or uncover the definition on the transparency of *Cue Card #1.* Remind the students to begin making their

---

* Within this range, students choose the number of days that fits their individual learning rates on the previous activities.

first Cue Card. From this point on, prompt the students to take notes and get out new sheets of paper when necessary.]

8. Give the definition for an independent clause. "**Does anyone know what an independent clause is?**"

[Elicit a response like, "It's a clause that can stand alone."]

"**Good. An _independent clause_ is a group of words that makes a complete statement and can stand alone. That means that the group of words makes sense by itself.**"

[Write this part of the definition for an independent clause on the board, or uncover the definition on the transparency of *Cue Card #1.*]

"**An example simple sentence or independent clause is, 'Susan ran.' **"

[Write the sentence on the board.]

"**This is a group of words that can stand by itself. It can stand by itself because it has two important things.**"

"**Does anyone know what those two important things are?**"

[Elicit the response, "A subject and a verb."]

"**That's right. It has a subject (Susan) and a verb* (ran).**"

[Draw a vertical line between "Susan" and "ran." Write "subject" over "Susan" and "verb" over "ran."]

"**Every independent clause and, therefore, every simple sentence contains two things: a subject and a verb.**"

[Write the two parts of an independent clause on the board, or uncover that part of the definition on the transparency of *Cue Card #1.*]

9. Give the definition for the subject of a sentence. "**Who knows what the definition for the subject of the sentence is?**"

[Elicit a response like, "It's a person, place, or thing."]

"**That's right. The _subject_ is what the sentence is about. To be more precise, the subject of the sentence is the person, place, thing, quality, or idea the sentence is about.**"

[Write the definition on the board, or uncover the definition on the transparency of *Cue Card #2.*]

---

* If you wish to use the word "predicate" instead of "verb," please adjust the remaining instruction accordingly. "Verb" has been used here to simplify the vocabulary load for language-deficient students.

"The kind of words we use for the subject of a sentence are naming words known as <u>nouns</u>. Nouns name the person, place, thing, quality, or idea the sentence is about."

10. **Discuss examples of subjects.** "Let's look at some examples of each of these kinds of nouns. For example, in the sentence, 'John went for a walk,'. . ."

[Write the sentence on the board, or uncover the sentence on the transparency of *Cue Card #2.*]

". . . the subject is a person."

"What word serves as the subject of this sentence?"

[Elicit the answer, "John." Discuss the remaining examples on *Cue Card #2* in the same manner, asking the students to identify the subject for each. Explain that qualities can be characteristics or feelings and that ideas are abstract thoughts or concepts.]

"Let's think of other examples of nouns that can be used as subjects for sentences."

[Write five columns entitled "Persons," "Places," "Things," "Qualities," and "Ideas" on the board. Ask the students to provide examples of each type of subject. Give them feedback, as necessary, and write each correct response in the appropriate column on the board.

Prompt students to suggest pronouns like "he," "she," "it," and "we" to be entered in the columns. Continue discussing the types of subjects until the students can make the distinction.]

"To review, what's the definition of a subject?"

[Elicit the definition.]

11. **Give the definition for verb.** "So far, we've been talking about the subject of the simple sentence."

"What's the other part of a simple sentence called?"

[Elicit the answer, "Verb."]

"That's right. The <u>verb</u> is a word that shows the subject's state of being or action. That is, it tells what the subject is or does."

[Write the definition for "verb" on the board, or uncover the definition on *Cue Card #3.*]

12. **Discuss examples of verbs.** "If the verb shows some sort of action, it is usually easy to pick out. That means it shows physical or mental activity. An activity is something that is done in the mind or through physical motion. It is something you can *do*."

[Put the example sentences on the board, or use the transparency of **Cue Card** **#3** to display the examples.]

"In the sentence, 'Sally sneezed,' the verb denotes physical activity, an activity the subject does with her body. What is the activity?"

[Elicit the answer, "Sneezed."]

"Correct. In the sentence, 'John thinks,' the verb shows a mental activity (an activity the subject does with his mind). What is the mental activity?"

[Elicit the answer, "Thinks."]

"Sometimes the verb shows the subject's state of being or condition. Words like 'is,' 'are,' and 'were' are verbs that show the subject's state of being. For example, in the sentence, 'Jesse is happy,' 'is' is the word that shows the state of being. It links or connects the subject 'Jesse' with what Jesse is. For this reason, words used to show state of being are called _linking_ _verbs_."

"Let's think of examples of three types of verbs: physical action verbs, mental action verbs, and linking verbs."

[Write three columns on the board entitled, "Physical Action Verbs," "Mental Action Verbs," and "State-of-Being or Linking Verbs." Ask the students to provide examples of each type of verb and to make their own lists of the examples. Give them feedback as necessary and write each correct response in the appropriate column on the board. Prompt them to name the nine linking verbs, "am," "are," "be," "been," "become," "is," "seem," "was," and "were," by writing two sentences on the board containing words that can be linked (e.g., "The clouds _____ beautiful." or "Sam _____ crazy.") and asking students to suggest linking words that fit in the blanks. Continue discussing the different kinds of verbs until the students understand the distinctions. Discuss with the students ways to remember the linking verbs.]

"To review, what's a verb?"

[Elicit the definition.]

Verb-Subject Identification

13. Explain the Verb-Subject Identification Procedure. "**You must know how to find the verbs and subjects in the sentences you write because this will help you know whether you have a complete sentence. A complete simple sentence contains a subject and a verb. An incomplete sentence has a subject but no verb or has a verb but no subject. You should avoid leaving out a vital part of the sentences you write.**"

"To identify the verb and subject of a sentence, you will need to go through a two-step procedure."

  a. Describe Step 1. [Uncover the first step on the transparency of **Cue Card** **#4,** or write the step on the board.]

"First, look for the word that shows mental or physical action or a state of being. That is, you need to look for an action verb or a linking verb and write a "V" above it. For example, in the sentence, 'Kevin reported the theft', . . ."

[Write the sentence on the board, or uncover the sentence on the transparency of *Cue Card #4.*]

". . . first look for the word that shows action or state of being."

"What is the word that shows action or something you can do in this sentence?"

[Elicit the answer, "Reported," and write a "V" above "reported."]

b. **Describe Step 2.** "Once you've found the verb, you need to complete the second step."

[Uncover the second step on the transparency of *Cue Card #4,* or write the step on the board.]

"In the second step, you ask yourself, 'Who or what?,' and add the verb you've found. For our example, where the verb is 'reported,' you should ask yourself, 'Who or what reported?,' to find the subject."

"What is the subject in this sentence if you ask the question, 'Who or what reported?' "

[Elicit the answer, "Kevin," and write an "S" above "Kevin."]

"That's right. 'Kevin' is the subject. I've written an 'S' above 'Kevin' to show this is the subject."

c. **Provide another example.** "Let's look at another example. In the sentence, 'Paula is an astronaut', . . ."

[Write the sentence on the board, or uncover it on the transparency of *Cue Card #4.*]

". . . is there an action verb (something you can do)?"

[Elicit the answer, "No."]

"That means there must be a linking verb. What is it?"

[Elicit the answer, "is." Write a "V" above "is."]

"After we find the verb, what's the next step in our Verb-Subject Identification Procedure?"

[Elicit the answer, "Ask the 'Who/What Question' to find the subject."]

"Right. What's the answer if we ask, 'Who or what is?' "

[Elicit the answer, "Paula." Write an "S" above "Paula."]

"That's right, 'Paula' is the subject."

"Always look for the action or linking verb first, and then ask yourself the 'Who/What Question' to find the subject."

14. **Practice finding subjects and verbs.** [Distribute the *Example Sheets* and direct the students to look at Example Set I. If possible, use an overhead transparency of the *Example Sheet* showing Example Set I. Call on the students to perform parts of the Verb-Subject Identification Procedure on each sentence. Call on one student to read the sentence, on another student to find the verb, and on yet another student to find the subject. Write a "V" above the verb and an "S" above the subject. Ask the students to do the same on their copies of the *Example Sheets*. Keep the pace lively, and call on students randomly. Discourage the students from working ahead of the group, and encourage them to attend to the discussion. Provide feedback, and instruct everyone to write a "V" above the verb and an "S" above the subject. Use as many of the sentences as necessary to ensure that the students understand the procedure for identifying the subject and the verb. Emphasize the idea that the verb should always be identified first.]

Example Set I

     S   V
1. Jane went to the pool.

     S V
2. Paul is a very nice guy.

      S   V
3. Cakes lined the store window.

     S V
4. I love chocolate ice cream.

      S   V
5. Bikes are very expensive

     S V
6. Dad is strict.

      S   V
7. Bananas taste good.

      S   V
8. Kathy has a son named Jimmy.

      S   V
9. Raccoons raid our garbage cans every night.

       S   V
10. Flowers are in bloom everywhere.

15. **Introduce noun phrases.** **"So far, the sentences we have talked about were sentences in which the complete subject consists of one word—a noun. However, sometimes two or more words are used for the subject. When several words are used together like that, they are called a *noun phrase*. The noun phrase is the complete subject. For example, when we apply the Verb-Subject Identification Procedure to the first sentence in Example Set II, 'The old gray mare limped down the lane,' what is the verb?"**

[Elicit "limped," and write a "V" above it. Instruct the students to do likewise.]

"Right. When we ask the 'Who/What Question,' what group of words gives us the answer?"

[Elicit the answer, "The old gray mare."]

"That's right, 'The old gray mare' is the _complete subject_. It is the group of words or the noun phrase that tells what the sentence is about. The word 'mare' is the _main subject_. It is the most important word in the complete subject. It is the one word without which you would not know what the sentence was about. In this class, whenever you are asked to identify the subject of a sentence, remember to identify the one word that tells what the sentence is about. You do not need to identify the complete subject. Write an "S" above the main subject."

[Write an "S" above "mare."]

"Let's look at some other examples in Example Set II. First, I will demonstrate how to identify verbs, complete subjects, and main subjects. Then I'll ask you to do it."

[Model using the Verb-Subject Identification Procedure on the second sentence in Example Set II. Mark the verb "soared" with a "V." After asking yourself, "Who or what soared?," answer, "The silver-winged plane." Then think aloud to show how you figure out which word is the main subject. Demonstrate leaving each of the words in the noun phrase out of the sentence. Explain that leaving out the word "plane" destroys the meaning of the sentence. Therefore, it is the main subject. Mark the main subject "plane" with an "S." Ask each student to analyze part of one sentence. Have one student read the sentence, one student identify the verb, and one student identify the main subject of the sentence. Keep the pace lively. Provide help and feedback as necessary. Prompt the students to begin with the first step of the identification procedure each time. As the students respond, instruct them to mark the verb with a "V" and the main subject with an "S" on their _Example Sheets._]

Example Set II

                       S   V
1. The old gray mare limped down the lane.

                       S   V
2. The silver-winged plane soared.

                      S   V
3. Johnny's baby sister cried for hours.

                   S   V
4. The first three girls giggled.

                   S   V
5. Fourteen good pilots died in the war.

              S   V
6. The chairman of the meeting left early.

                     S   V
7. The chrome-plated motorcycles glistened in the sun.

$$\overset{\text{S}}{} \qquad \overset{\text{V}}{}$$

8. The pioneers in our family fled from England.

$$\overset{\text{S}}{} \quad \overset{\text{V}}{}$$

9. The dog's buried bones rotted in the ground.

$$\overset{\text{S}}{} \quad \overset{\text{V}}{}$$

10. Carol's best china plate broke into a hundred pieces.

16. **Introduce verb phrases.** "Just like several words can form the subject of a sentence, the verb can consist of two or more words. This is called a _verb phrase_. For example, in the first sentence in Example Set III, 'The bus must have gone by now,' the words 'must have gone' are the verb phrase."

[Draw an arch above the three words and mark them with a "V" like this:

$$\overset{\text{V}}{\overparen{\text{must have gone}}}$$

Instruct the students to do likewise on their _Example Sheets_.]

"These three words form the _complete verb_. The word 'gone' is the main verb."

[Point to "gone."]

"It shows the action. Without it, the action of the bus would be unknown."

a. **Introduce helping verbs.** "Verb phrases are formed by putting one or more _helping verbs_ in front of a main verb. Here is a list of helping verbs."

[Display the transparency of _Cue Card #5,_ or write the list on the board.]

"You will notice that the linking verbs are circled on this list of helping verbs. They can be used in front of another verb. For example, the linking verb 'am' can be used as a helping verb in a sentence like, 'I am swimming.' 'Swimming' is the main verb."

[As the students copy the list to make their own Cue Cards, ask them to suggest sentences in which each helping verb is used by itself with a main verb. Provide feedback as necessary.]

"Two or more of these helping verbs can be used in combination in front of the main verb. Usually one helping verb is used in combination with one of the helping verbs that starts with the letter 'h.' For example, you could combine the helping verbs 'could' and 'have' to say, 'I could have eaten.' You can also use a helping verb in combination with 'be,' 'been,' or 'being' in front of the main verb. These three words have been placed in a box on the Cue Card because they are not used by themselves in front of a main verb. They can only be used in combination with other helping verbs. For example, you could say, 'I have been swimming all afternoon.' What are some other combinations of the helping words on this list?"

[Elicit combinations such as "Might have," "May have been," "Should have," "Would have," and "Would have been."]

b. Practice identifying complete verbs and main subjects.

"Any time you are asked to identify the verb of a sentence in this class, you should identify the helping verb or verbs *and* the main verb in any sentence that has a verb phrase. After you find an action verb, always check to see if there are one or more helping verbs to the left of the action verb. Make an arch above the helping verbs and the main verb, and write a 'V' above the arch."

"Let's look at some sentences and identify the complete verb and the main subject."

[Direct the students to look at Example Set III on their *Example Sheets*. Show how you would use the Verb-Subject Identification Procedure on the second sentence. State that you are looking for more than one word for the verb. Say that you will first look for something a person can do. Explain that since a person can work, "work" is the main verb. Then state that you will look for a helping verb to the left of the main verb "work." It can be right in front of the verb or a few words away. Identify the helping verb, "could," by checking your list of helping verbs. Draw an arch above "could" and "work," and write a "V" above the arch. Put an arrow at each end of the arch to indicate that those two words represent the verb and not the word "not." State that the word "not" is <u>not</u> a verb or a helping verb. Explain that "not" should never be marked as a verb, but that it can be used in the "Who/What Question." Ask yourself, "Who or what could not work?," and answer, "My best friend." Figure out the main subject, and mark "friend" with an "S." Have the students take turns on parts of the procedure for the remaining sentences. One student should read the sentence, one should find the action verb, one should find the helping verb(s), and one should find the main subject. Provide feedback as necessary. Mark the main subject with a "S" and the complete verb with an arch and a "V."]

Example Set III

1. The bus must have gone by now.
2. My best friend could not work tonight.
3. The light green grapes have been eaten.
4. The committee of environmentalists is working to solve the smog problem.
5. Steven's aunt is not following her new diet.
6. The old rickety wagon should not have been filled to the top.
7. The merry pied piper would have played a happy tune.

         S   V

8. A stray sunbeam could have pierced through the clouds.

        S   V

9. The paint on the old gray house was peeling.

        S   V

10. The peace treaty might have been signed today.

17. Introduce simple sentences in which the verb comes first.

"In some simple sentences, the verb comes before the subject of the sentence. For example, in the sentence, 'Down the street moved the bulls', . . . "

[Write the sentence on the board.]

". . . what is the action word?"

[Elicit "Moved." Write a "V" above it.]

"Right! Is there a helping verb?"

[Elicit the answer, "No."]

"Good. Who or what moved?"

[Elicit "Bulls," and write an "S" above it.]

"As you can see, the verb in this sentence appears in front of the subject. Sometimes the subject appears between the helping verb and the verb. This happens most often in a sentence that is written in the form of a question. In the sentence, 'Will you go to the movie tonight?' . . ."

[Write the sentence on the board.]

". . . what is the action word?"

[Elicit "Go."]

"Is there a helping verb?"

[Elicit "Will," and make an arch with arrows pointing to "will" and "go." Write a "V" above the arch.]

"Who or what will go?"

[Elicit "You," and write an "S" above it.]

"As you can see, the helping verb comes before the subject and the main verb appears after the subject in this question. Thus, the subject of a simple sentence does not always have to come first. Be sure to take this into account as you look for subjects and verbs."

18. Introduce infinitives. "Sometimes words in sentences show action without being the main verb of the sentence. Let's look at an example."

[Write, "Chad hoped to go sledding." on the board.]

"In this sentence, several words represent things you can do. What are they?"

[Elicit "Hoped," "Go," and "Sledding."]

"Which one is the main verb of the sentence (shows the subject's action or state of being)?"

[Elicit the answer, "Hoped," and write a "V" above it.]

"That's right. Any verb that has the word 'to' in front of it is an _infinitive_; it is not the main verb of the sentence. When you have a sentence with several action words in it, check for the word 'to.' Never identify as the main verb a word that has 'to' in front of it."

Types of Simple Sentences

19. Introduce simple sentences with compound subjects. "So far, we've been talking about simple sentences with one subject and one verb. They represent one kind of simple sentence. A second kind of simple sentence contains two or more subjects. We call two or more subjects in a simple sentence a _compound subject_. When we use the Verb-Subject Identification Procedure on the first sentence in Example Set IV, 'Bill and Sue want to go to the movies,' we will find that it contains two subjects."

"Who wants to try the Verb-Subject Identification Procedure on this sentence?"

[Choose a student to demonstrate the identification procedure. If the student chooses "go" as the verb, emphasize the rule about never choosing a word with "to" in front of it as the verb. When he finds the verb, "want," direct the students to mark it with a "V." When he asks himself, "Who or what want?," he should answer, "Bill wants" and "Sue wants." Direct the students to mark "Bill" and "Sue" with an "S."]

"You will notice that the word 'and' separates the two subjects. When you see the word 'and,' it's a cue that there might be two or more subjects in the sentence."

[Direct the students to look at the remaining sentences in Example Set IV. Have different students perform the various Verb-Subject Identification Steps on each sentence. Have one student identify the complete verb and one student identify the compound subject. Emphasize looking for an action verb first. If an action verb is found, encourage a search for a helping verb. Make sure the students' helping verb lists are handy. If an action verb is not found, emphasize looking for a linking verb. Emphasize finding the main subjects for each sentence. Instruct the students to mark each main subject with an "S" and to create an arch for the complete verb on their own _Example Sheets._]

Example Set IV

        S   S   V
1. Bill and Sue want to go to the movies.
      S   S   V
2. Jason and his friends work together.
             V
            S   S
3. Are the car and truck parked outside?
        S   S   V
4. The park and sidewalks were covered with snow.
        S   S   V
5. Hiding and seeking are fun activities.
        S   S   V
6. The old man and his black cat have lived long lives.
        S   S   V
7. The station and its surrounding parking lot become dangerous after 9:00 p.m..
        S   S   S   V
8. Arnie, Karen, and Ty went to buy a new van.
        S   S   V
9. Peace and war are direct opposites.
             V
            S   S
10. Did Marty and Kathy travel 500 miles just to speak at the conference?

20. **Introduce simple sentences with compound verbs.** "Just like simple sentences can have a compound subject, they can also have a *compound verb*. In the first sentence in Example Set V, 'Sally swam and played all afternoon,' two words represent the action. What are they?"

[Elicit the answers, "Swam" and "Played," and direct the students to mark each word with a "V."]

"Right. These two words form the compound verb. Again, notice that they are separated by the word 'and.' The word 'and' immediately following one verb is a cue to look for another verb."

[Direct the students to look at the remaining sentences in Example Set V. Have different students identify the verbs and the subject in each sentence. Follow the same instructions as presented for Example Set IV with regard to emphasizing particular concepts and procedures. Direct the students to mark the subject with an "S" and the complete verbs with a "V" on their own *Example Sheets.*]

Example Set V

        S   V   V
1. Sally swam and played all afternoon.
        S   V   V
2. The dogs had barked all night and slept all day.
        S   V   V
3. Michelle came home yesterday and did not work all day today.
             S   V   V
4. The basketball team rode on a bus and flew in a plane to attend the game.

         S   V   V

5. The park is dark and spooky at night and can be delightful on sunny days.

                 V   V
               S

6. Did Jane call her father and tell him the news?

     S V   V

7. I miss my sister and want to see her again soon.

          S   V   V

8. Children should not be allowed to watch T.V. and should be encouraged to play.

               V   V
               S

9. Will you sit by the sea and paint the ships?

           S   V   V

10. The books were stacked on the floor and were ruined by the flood.

21. Introduce sentences with compound subjects and compound verbs. "Some simple sentences have both a compound subject and a compound verb. In the first sentence in Example Set VI, 'The ponies and calves scampered and played in the field,' there are two verbs and two subjects."

"Who wants to try the Verb-Subject Identification Procedure on this sentence?"

[Have a volunteer identify the verbs first, ask herself the "Who/What Question" including both verbs, and answer it. Direct the students to mark the verbs ("scampered" and "played") with a "V" and the subjects ("ponies" and "calves") with an "S" on their *Example Sheets*.

Ask different students to complete the various steps of the Verb-Subject Identification Procedure on the remaining sentences. Direct the students to mark each complete verb with a "V" and each main subject with an "S."]

Example Set VI

          S   S   V   V

1. The ponies and calves scampered and played in the field.

        S   S   V   V

2. Kathy and her father do not like to play tennis and hate to jog.

        S   S   V   V

3. The Army and the Navy had a football game and filled the stadium.

          S   S   V   V

4. The two boys and their fathers were sick and did not attend the Father-Son banquet.

        S   S   V   V

5. Parties and dances are usually fun and can be thrilling.

        S   S   V   V

6. Cards and dice were used at the party and had been scattered everywhere.

        S   S   V   V

7. Radio towers and tall buildings must have lights and must be visible at night.

        S   S   V   V

8. Candles and flowers can brighten the table and can make guests feel special.

        S   S   V   V

9. Tape and string are needed to secure packages and can be used for other things.

        S   S   V   V

10. The graduates and their parents posed for pictures and celebrated with a party.

22. Introduce the simple sentences formulas. "To summarize, we've talked about four different kinds of simple sentences. We can represent these by four formulas for writing simple sentences."

[Write the four formulas on the board as follows.]
    Simple Sentences

        S   V
      SS   V
        S   VV
      SS   VV

"In all the formulas, what do you think the 'S' represents?"

[Elicit the answer, "A subject."]

"What do you think the 'V' represents?"

[Elicit the answer, "A verb."]

"Good. The 'S' can be a single noun or a noun phrase. The 'V' can be a single verb or a verb phrase."

"The first formula represents a simple sentence with what in it?"

[Elicit the answer, "A subject and a verb."]

"That's right, that's all that's required: one subject and one verb. The subject can come first in the sentence, or the verb may come first."

"In the remaining formulas, what do you think the 'SS' and 'VV' stand for?"

[Elicit the answers, "Compound subject" and "Compound verb."]

"That's correct. What kind of a sentence do you think this second formula stands for?"

[Elicit the answer, "A simple sentence with a compound subject and one verb."]

"Right. What's included in this third kind of simple sentence?"

[Point to the third formula. Elicit the answer, "One subject and a compound verb."]

"Exactly. What does the fourth formula stand for?"

[Elicit the answer, "A simple sentence with a compound subject and a compound verb." Ask the students to look at their *Example Sheets* and to put the correct formula at the top of each Example Set. Discuss which formula is appropriate for each set.]

23. **Make the Formula Cards.** [Distribute the 4" × 6" cards. Show the students your 4" × 6" card with only the simple sentences formulas on it. Instruct the students to write their names at the top of the card and divide it into four quadrants like yours. At the top of the upper-left quadrant they should write the title, "Simple Sentences"; directly under the title they should write the four formulas.]

"We will call these cards your 'Sentence Formula Cards.' You will use the card to help you remember the different kinds of sentences. Keep the card in the envelope at the front of your folder and take it out for reference each time you write sentences. Whenever we learn a new type of sentence, we will add new formulas to the card."

"Why do you think the formulas that you have written on your cards might be helpful?"

[Elicit the answers that the formulas make remembering the different types of simple sentences easy and that the formulas will help them to remember to use a variety of sentences in their papers.]

24. **Describe the steps of the *Sentence Writing Strategy*. "You must follow four simple steps when you want to write a simple sentence. As we talk about the steps, make your own Cue Card."**

    a. **Step 1: Pick a formula.** "The first step in writing a sentence is 'Pick a formula.' "

    [Display "Pick a formula" from *Cue Card #6.*]

    "This means that you choose one of the formulas on your card to guide you when you write your sentence."

    b. **Step 2: Explore words to fit the formula.** "Once you've chosen a formula, explore words to fit the formula."

    [Display "Explore words to fit the formula" from the second step on *Cue Card #6.*]

    "This entails thinking of the words that best express the idea you have in mind as well as words that fit the formula. Remember, you may use noun phrases and verb phrases consisting of several words to replace each 'S' or 'V' in the formula."

    c. **Step 3: Note the words.** "Once you've thought of the words, write them down. Step 3 is 'Note the words.' "

    [Display "Note the words" from *Cue Card #6.*]

"When you write the words, capitalize the first letter of the first word in the sentence, and put a period at the end of the sentence. Your sentence will not be a sentence if you fail to capitalize the first letter of the first word or fail to put a period at the end."

d. **Step 4: Search and check.** **"After you've written the sentence, do the Search and Check Step."**

[Display "Search and Check" from *Cue Card #6*.]

"This fourth step helps ensure that your sentence is complete and fits the formula you chose in Step 1."

"The 'Search' part of 'Search and Check' means that you search for and find the verbs and subjects. What should you do first to search for the verbs and subjects?"

[Elicit statements about finding the action or state-of-being words first.]

"That's right. You'll need to first identify the complete verb or verbs."

[Display "Look for the action or state-of-being word(s)" on *Cue Card #6*.]

"Be sure to look for helping verbs as well as main verbs."

"What might cue you to look for a helping verb?"

[Elicit an answer like, "Any time you see an action verb, you should look for a helping verb."]

"What might cue you to look for more than one verb (a compound verb)?"

[Elicit the answer, "When the word 'and' appears immediately after a verb."]

"What action words are not to be identified as the verb?"

[Elicit the answer, "Those that have the word 'to' in front of them."]

"Good. After you have found the verb or verbs in a sentence, what do you do?"

[Elicit a response about asking oneself the "Who/What Question" to find the subject.]

"Correct. You'll need to ask the 'Who/What Question' to help you find the subject or subjects."

[Display "Ask the 'Who/What Question' " from *Cue Card #6*.]

"What might cue you that there are two subjects in the sentence?"

[Elicit the response, "When the word 'and' appears immediately after a subject."]

"After you have identified the verbs and subjects, you'll need to do the 'Check' part of the Search and Check Step. You'll need to read the whole sentence one last time to see if it makes sense and to make sure you haven't left out any words. If you leave out any words, the sentence is not acceptable because it will not be understandable. Also check that you have started the sentence with a capital letter and ended it with a period."

[Display the items to be "checked" from *Cue Card #6.*]

25. **Describe the mnemonic device "PENS."** **"Do you notice anything unusual about these four steps that will help you remember them?"**

[Elicit the mnemonic device "PENS," and underline the letters "P," "E," "N," "S" on the board or transparency.]

"Why is 'PENS' a good word for helping us remember the *Sentence Writing Strategy* steps?"

[Elicit the response that pens can be used to write sentences.]

"That's true. Any time you need to remember the four steps for writing a sentence, think of the word 'PENS,' and you'll be able to quickly recall them."

26. **Compare the *Sentence Writing Strategy* to the students' previous writing habits.** [Ask the students to compare the *Sentence Writing Strategy* steps to the way they used to write sentences. Elicit responses such as: they didn't have a set of steps to follow so they didn't know how to proceed; or they didn't have formulas to follow to make writing easy. Ensure that the students understand the advantages of the *Sentence Writing Strategy* compared to their previously used approaches.]

27. **Emphasize speed.** [Explain to the students that, at first, writing each sentence will take a few minutes. This is to be expected since they need to practice a new skill many times before they become fluent users of it. Point out that after a while they will become such fluent writers that they will not have to check the Formula Cards because they will know the formulas and will be able to write a sentence completely and correctly without actively thinking of all the steps. Emphasize the expectancy that most of them will be able to write a sentence in less than a minute after a few weeks of practice.]

28. **Give the post-organizer.** **"Today we've begun to learn about the *Sentence Writing Strategy.* It consists of four steps and two substeps that we can remember by using the mnemonic device "PENS":** *Pick* **a formula,** *Explore* **words to fit the formula,** *Note* **the words, and** *Search* **and** *Check.* **That's all there is to it."**

29. Solicit questions. [Ask the students if they have any questions. Answer any questions.]

30. Record the completion date for Stage 2. [Ask the students to turn to the *Progress Charts* in their folders and record the day's date for completing Stage 2. Instruct the students to place their Cue Cards and Formula Cards in their folders. Have one student record the day's date under the Describe Stage heading on the *Management Chart* for each of the students in the group.]

Where to go from here:

After the students write the completion date on their *Progress Charts* and on the *Management Chart,* go to STAGE 3: MODEL.

How to trouble-shoot:

If a student has difficulty identifying subjects and verbs correctly during the exercises, begin instruction for that student in the *Fundamentals in the Sentence Writing Strategy* program (Schumaker & Sheldon, 1998),* or use selected lessons from that program to remediate particular skill deficits. For example, if a student identifies an infinitive as the verb of the sentence, utilize the lesson on infinitives. If the student identifies the object of the preposition as the subject of the sentence, utilize the lesson on prepositions. If the student does not identify helping verbs correctly, utilize the lesson on helping verbs.

---

* Schumaker, J.B., & Sheldon, J.B. (1998). *Fundamentals in the Sentence Writing Strategy: Instructor's Manual.* Lawrence: University of Kansas Center for Research on Learning.

PART I: SIMPLE SENTENCES
STAGE 3: MODEL

What your goals are:
- To demonstrate writing simple sentences using the *Sentence Writing Strategy* while thinking aloud, so students can witness all the processes involved.
- To involve students in the demonstration to check their understanding of the cognitive processes involved.

What you need:
- Chalkboard or other writing surface
- Writing implement for chosen surface
- Your own Formula Card
- *Cue Cards #1-6* (pp. 153-158)
- Student folders
- *Management Chart for Instruction in Simple Sentences*

How to prepare:
1. **Gather the needed materials.**

2. **Read the instructions below.** Become familiar with the kind of demonstration you should give and the order of events specified.

3. **Practice using the strategy.** Run through the demonstration by yourself a few times to become a fluent user of the steps of the *Sentence Writing Strategy.* For each type of simple sentence, be sure to have a topic firmly in mind. When you give the demonstration, you should be able to focus on the students as much as possible. Therefore, you must be well prepared; however, do *not* make notes for use during the demonstration. It should appear spontaneous and should be a good model of exactly how you want the students to perform as they use the strategy.

How much time to allow:
Allow approximately 15-20 minutes for the demonstration.

What to do:
1. **Review the *Sentence Writing Strategy.*** * [At the beginning of the lesson, ensure that the student folders have been distributed, and review the *Sentence Writing Strategy* with the students. Ask the students to define: a simple sen-

---

* This review is not necessary if the instruction takes place on the same day as the instruction for STAGE 2: DESCRIBE.

tence, an independent clause, a subject, a verb, a compound subject, and a compound verb. Ask the students to name the strategy steps and the four kinds of simple sentences, to specify where they can use the strategy, and to explain how the strategy can help them. Have them refer to their Cue Cards and Formula Cards if necessary.]

2. **Give an advance organizer.** "Now I will demonstrate how to use the *Sentence Writing Strategy* when writing simple sentences. I'm going to tell you everything I'm thinking while I use the strategy, so you can understand how I expect you to talk to yourself as you use this strategy. Watch and listen carefully because I will expect you to do everything I do, except that you will not have to think out loud as you use the strategy. Instead, you will speak to yourself silently."

   "Do you have any questions before I begin?"

   [Answer any questions.]

3. **Demonstrate writing a simple sentence with the *Sentence Writing Strategy*.** "Let's see, to begin I say, 'Sentence Writing: PENS' to remind myself of the four strategy steps."

   a. **Step 1: Pick a formula.** " 'P' stands for 'Pick a formula,' so the first thing I'll do is look at my Formula Card."

      [Look at your Formula Card.]

      "Hmm . . . I want to write the first kind of simple sentence, one with a single subject and a single verb."

      [Point to the formula, "S V."]

   b. **Step 2: Explore words to fit the formula.** "Now that I've chosen my formula, I must do the 'E' step. I need to explore words to fit the formula. Hmm . . . I have to write a sentence about the jobs of a cowboy, so 'cowboy' can be my subject and 'finds the stray cattle' can be the action sequence that tells about one aspect of his job. Let's see, my sentence will be 'A cowboy finds the stray cattle.' "

   c. **Step 3: Note the words.** "Now that I've thought of the words for my sentence, I need to do the 'N' step and note the words on paper. I'll write them on the board, so you can see them."

      [Write, "A cowboy finds stray cattle." on the board.]

      "As I write, I have to capitalize the first letter of the first word and put a period at the end of the sentence."

   d. **Step 4: Search and check.** "Now I have to do the 'S' step to make sure that I have a complete sentence. First, I need to search for the verbs and subjects. I need to identify one verb, because for this formula . . ."

[Point to the formula on the card.]

"... I need one verb. First, I'll look for an action verb. The first action word that I see in this sentence is 'finds.' "

[Point to "finds."]

"Are there any helping verbs? No. Is the word 'to' in front of 'finds'? No. Are there any other action or state-of-being words in this sentence? No. That's good. That means I've found the complete verb and the only verb in the sentence. I only need one verb for the sentence formula I chose.' "

"Next, I look for the subject by asking, 'Who or what finds?' The cowboy finds."

[Point to "cowboy."]

"Is there any other subject who finds? No. That means that 'Cowboy' is the only subject in this sentence, and I only needed one subject for my formula. Thus, my sentence checks out against the formula. Finally, I need to check my sentence over one last time to make sure that it makes sense and I didn't leave anything out. 'A cowboy finds the stray cattle.' That makes sense. The sentence starts with a capital letter and ends with a period, so I'm finished with this sentence."

4. **Involve the students in the demonstration.** [For the three remaining types of simple sentences, ask the students to tell you what should be done next and to suggest responses for each strategy step. Provide a general topic for each sentence, but ask the students to come up with the subject(s) and verb(s), and the final wording of the sentence. Have a student write the sentence on the board; ask other students to check it. Provide corrective feedback as needed.]

5. **Give the post-organizer.** "We have learned about simple sentences and the *Sentence Writing Strategy*, and you have seen how to use the strategy to write the four kinds of simple sentences. Next, you will learn how to instruct yourself to use the *Sentence Writing Strategy*."

6. **Solicit and answer questions.**

7. **Record the completion date for STAGE 3.** [Ask the students to turn to the *Progress Charts* in their folders and record the day's date for completing Stage 3 in the appropriate box under the Stage 3 label and next to the words "Date Completed." Have one student record the day's date on the *Management Chart* for each student in the group under the heading for the Model Stage.]

Where to go from here:

After all questions have been answered and completion dates have been recorded, go to STAGE 4: VERBAL PRACTICE.

PART I: SIMPLE SENTENCES
STAGE 4: VERBAL PRACTICE

What your goals are:

- To ensure that each student understands the requirements for simple sentences and the concepts involved in writing them.
- To ensure that each student memorizes the *Sentence Writing Strategy* steps to a criterion of 100% correct performance.

What you need:

- Chalkboard or other writing surface
- Writing implement appropriate for the chosen writing surface
- Student folders
- *Simple Sentence Verbal Practice Checklist* (p. 170 or p. 182) (one per student)
- *Simple Sentence Quiz* (in the *Student Lessons* volume) (one per student)
- *Cue Cards #1-6* (pp. 153-158)
- *Management Chart for Instruction in Simple Sentences*

How to prepare:

1. **Check your supply of *Simple Sentence Verbal Practice Checklists* and *Simple Sentence Quizzes*.** If necessary, make copies of the *Verbal Practice Checklist* and *Simple Sentence Quizzes*. Put them in separate folders that are labeled appropriately.

2. **Gather the other materials listed.**

3. **Read the instructions below.** Familiarize yourself with the order of events that should take place, the rapid-fire verbal rehearsal technique, the instructions to be given to the students, and the mastery requirements.

How much time to allow:

Most students will reach mastery on naming the strategy steps, providing definitions, and naming the kinds of simple sentences within 25 minutes. Others, however, may need to work on reaching mastery during an additional 25-minute instructional period. The written quiz takes approximately 10-15 minutes for a student to complete, and most students reach mastery on the first attempt.

What to do:

1. **Review important definitions, the formulas, and the strategy steps.** [Distribute the student folders. Ask the students to define a simple sentence, an independent clause, a subject, a verb, a compound subject, and

a compound verb. Ask them to name the formulas and the steps for writing a simple sentence. Ask them to name the two steps for identifying verbs and subjects. Write their responses on the board. If necessary, refer the students to their Cue Cards and Formula Cards.]

2. **Give an advance organizer.** "Today you are going to learn to name the steps of the *Sentence Writing Strategy.* You will also learn the definitions for a simple sentence, independent clause, subject, verb, compound subject and compound verb, and the four types of simple sentences. If you know these steps and definitions well, you will be able to tell yourself what to do when you use the strategy while writing."

3. **Introduce rapid-fire verbal rehearsal.** * "To help you learn the strategy steps, we are going to do an exercise called 'rapid-fire verbal rehearsal.' I'll be pointing at each of you in succession. When I point to you, I want you to name the next step of the strategy. This is called 'rapid-fire' because you are supposed to fire back the name of a step as rapidly as you can. When I point to you, name the step as quickly as you can, and try not to look at the board. If you need to look at the board, you may; however, don't rely on the board too much because I'm going to erase it after a few rounds of rapid-fire rehearsal. Instead, rely on the mnemonic device 'PENS.' "

4. **Explain what to say.** "This is what to say when naming the steps: the first person I point to says, 'Pick a formula'; the second person, 'Explore words'; the following, 'Note the words'; and the next, 'Search and check.' "

5. **Conduct the exercise with cues on the board.** "Let's see how fast we can go and how quickly we can memorize these steps."

"Are there any questions?"

[Answer any questions.]

"O.K., let's begin."

[Point to a student. If she hesitates, instruct her to name the first step of the *Sentence Writing Strategy.* When she names the step say, "Good" or "Right"; point immediately to the next student to signal that he is to name the second step.

Each time a student correctly names a step, make a brief positive comment before pointing to another student. If the student cannot remember a given step, prompt him by providing the letter cue and, if necessary, by pointing to the step on the board. Each time you begin a new round with the first step of the strategy, point

---

* If you are teaching only one student at a time, you can vary this procedure by participating in the rapid-fire verbal rehearsal of the steps and taking turns saying the steps with the student (i.e., you say a step, then the student says a step, you say a step, then she says a step, etc.). If you are teaching a large group (more than 15 students), demonstrate the rapid-fire exercise to the whole class by leading one small group. Then divide the class into small groups and select a leader for each group. Circulate among the groups as they practice to ensure the students learn the steps.

to a different person than the one who started the previous round. This allows everyone to say each step.]

6. Conduct the exercise without cues. [After several rounds in which the students quickly name the steps, erase the steps from the blackboard.]

"Now that I've erased the board, you have to rely totally on your own memory. Remember to use the letters in the word 'PENS' to help you think of the steps. Let's begin."

[Conduct several more rounds, each starting with a different person. If a student cannot remember a given step, point quickly to the next person. Continue this verbal practice until you are certain the majority of the students know the steps.]

7. Conduct a rapid-fire question-and-answer exercise to memorize the definitions. **"Now let's use the rapid-fire technique to memorize important definitions and the types of simple sentences. I will ask you a question, and, if I point to you, give me the answer to the question as quickly as you can. Here are the questions I'll ask and their answers."** *

1. **What's a simple sentence?**
   A sentence with one independent clause.
2. **What's an independent clause?**
   A group of words that can stand alone and that have a subject and a verb.
3. **What's a subject?**
   The part of the sentence that names what the sentence is about.
4. **What's a verb?**
   A word that shows the action or state of being of the subject.
5. **What's a compound subject?**
   Two subjects in an independent clause.
6. **What's a compound verb?**
   Two verbs in an independent clause.
7. **What's one kind of simple sentence?** * *
   S   V
   SS   V
   S   VV
   SS   VV

"Are there any questions?"

[Answer any questions.]

"O.K., let's begin."

[Conduct the rapid-fire verbal exercise for the definitions and kinds of simple sen-

---

* These definitions should fit what you have written on the board.
** Ask this question four times in succession. Each time, require a student to say a different formula than those previously contributed by others.

tences as instructed above for the strategy steps. Complete several rounds with the definitions on the board. Erase the board. Start each new round with a different person. Continue the verbal practice until you are certain the majority of the students can say the definitions and name the kinds of simple sentences. This procedure should be conducted at a lively pace and with great enthusiasm on the part of the instructor. It is a quick way of ensuring that most of the students know the steps and definitions for the strategy cold. Occasionally, you will encounter students who cannot name the appropriate step or definition when asked to participate. Such students will need individual help later. Do not continue the rapid-fire verbal rehearsal if only one student is faltering.]

8. **Allow time for individual review.** [After the verbal practice exercises, explain to the students that they must be able to: (a) name all four strategy steps; (b) define a simple sentence, an independent clause, a subject, a verb, a compound subject, and a compound verb; (c) name four kinds of simple sentences in an oral quiz; and (d) get 90% of their answers correct on a written quiz. Explain that as each student is ready, she can come to you for the oral and written quizzes. Give the students time to rehearse and study by themselves or with a partner. Allow them to refer to their notes and other materials in their folders if necessary.]

9. **Conduct the oral quizzes.*** [When a student indicates he is ready, have him meet with you privately. Ask him to orally list the steps of the *Sentence Writing Strategy,* to define the items listed on the *Simple Sentence Verbal Practice Checklist,* and to name the four kinds of simple sentences without referring to the Cue Cards, Formula Cards, or notes and without receiving other assistance. Use the *Simple Sentence Verbal Practice Checklist* to keep a record of a student's attempts at passing the oral quiz. Place a checkmark next to each step or item the student names or accurately defines. (If a step is named out of order, the student does not receive credit for it.) Determine the percentage of step definitions and kinds of simple sentences correctly named.]

10. **Conduct the written quiz.** [When a student passes the oral quiz (see the mastery criterion below), give her a copy of the *Simple Sentence Quiz* to complete independently at her seat. Ask the student to return the completed quiz to you as soon as she is finished. Determine the percentage of questions answered correctly using the table on p. 149.]

11. **Provide feedback.** [Show the student the completed checklist, and describe which steps and definitions he named correctly. Point out the steps the student omitted or named out of sequence. If the student missed a step or steps, have him tell you the mnemonic letters to be used to remember it. Then ask him to name the words that go with each letter. If the student missed a definition or a formula, help the student figure out a way to remember it. Finally, ask the student to recite the steps or definitions or formulas to himself or another student five times.

---

* If you are instructing a large class (i.e., more than 15 students) and cannot give oral quizzes to all the students individually due to time constraints, construct a written quiz that requires the students (a) to name the strategy steps, (b) to match the six terms to their definitions, and (c) to write the four formulas. Administer the quiz to the class as a whole. Require a score of 100% correct. Readminister the quiz to individuals who do not meet the criterion after they have had a chance to review and rehearse.

If the student has answered a question on the written quiz incorrectly, discuss the concept covered by the item. If appropriate, have the student suggest a way to remember how to handle similar items in the future. Orally present the student with a similar item to determine if she has understood your feedback. If not, explain the item again, and recheck for understanding. Have the student plot the percentage of questions answered correctly on the *Simple Sentence Quiz* on her *Progress Chart* on the vertical line above the "Q."]

What to require for mastery:

To reach mastery on the oral quiz, the student must correctly list each of the *Sentence Writing Strategy* steps in order and correctly answer all of your oral questions without referring to a Cue Card and without receiving other assistance.

To reach mastery on the written quiz, the student must correctly answer at least 90% of the items on the *Simple Sentence Quiz.*

Where to go from here:

If the student achieves mastery on both quizzes, congratulate him, and instruct him to record the day's date on his *Progress Chart* in the box under "Stage 4," next to the words "Date Completed." On the *Management Chart,* have him record the date under the "Verbal Practice" heading. Have him place the *Simple Sentence Verbal Practice Checklist* and written quiz in his folder and proceed to STAGE 5: CONTROLLED PRACTICE AND FEEDBACK.

If the student does not reach mastery on the oral quiz, provide feedback, and have her rehearse the pertinent information individually or with a partner. Give the student additional oral quizzes until she reaches the mastery criterion.

If the student does not reach mastery on the written quiz, provide feedback, and ask him to complete another copy of the written quiz once you are sure he understands the concepts.

How to trouble-shoot:

If a student fails to name all the strategy steps after three oral quizzes, try one or more of the following procedures:

1. Have someone (yourself, another student, a paraprofessional) give the student the first word of each step as a cue (i.e., "Pick," "Explore," "Note," and "Search"). After receiving the cue, the student must name the entire step or rule. When the student can do this well, only the first letter should be provided as a cue (i.e., "P," "E," "N," or "S"). The student should then be required to cue himself using the letters.

2. Use a chaining technique whereby somebody provides some of the steps with the student suggesting others. For example, give the first three steps of the strategy, and require the student to provide the last step several times. Give the first two steps, and ask the student to provide the last two steps several times. Then provide the first step, and require the student to name the last three steps. Finally, require the student to name all the steps independently.

If a student fails to give the correct definitions for the terms after three oral quizzes, try one or more of the following procedures.

1. Have the student write the definitions that were missed on 3″ × 5″ cards. The question should be written on one side of the card with the answer on the other side. The student should continue to test herself using the cards until she has answered all the questions correctly three times. Then another oral quiz should be administered.

2. Write the definitions and the terms on a sheet of paper and ask the student to match each term with the correct definition. Repeat this procedure several times, and then readminister the oral quiz.

3. Make up a game that requires the student to compete with someone to learn the definitions she has missed. Give the student time to review, and have her play the game with you or a peer. Award points for correct definitions. After the game, readminister the oral quiz.

PART I: SIMPLE SENTENCES
STAGE 5: CONTROLLED PRACTICE AND FEEDBACK

What your goals are:
- To ensure that students master the skills involved in writing four types of simple sentences.

What you need:
- *Simple Sentence Lessons 1A, 1B, 1C, 1D* (the *#1 Series*), *2A, 2B, 2C, 2D* (the *#2 Series*), and *3A, 3B, 3C, 3D* (the *#3 Series*) (in the *Student Lessons* volume)
- *Evaluation Guidelines* and *Answer Keys* for the lessons listed above (in the *Student Lessons* volume)
- Twelve lesson folders for *Simple Sentence Lessons 1A-3D*
- Student folders
- Pencils
- *Cue Cards #1-6* (pp. 153-158)
- Chalkboard or other writing surface and appropriate writing implement
- *Management Chart for Instruction in Simple Sentences*

How to prepare:
1. **Check lesson folders.** If necessary, make additional copies of the lessons (see p. 9 for a description of lesson folders).

2. **Gather the other materials listed.**

3. **Read the instructions below.** Become familiar with the order of events to take place and the instructions you will be giving the students.

4. **Plan assignments.** After the first day of this practice activity, the students will progress at individual rates. Thus, they will be working on different lessons. Before class, review the students' progress and determine what lesson each student needs for the day. Record the date of the assignment and the lesson number on a sheet labeled "Assignment Sheet" that has been placed in the student's folder. Thus, the student need only read his updated Assignment Sheet each day to know what to do, provided he has received feedback on the previous day's lesson.*

---

* If you have a large class, you may want to insert the appropriate lesson in each student's folder to preserve order in your class at the beginning of the lesson. Also, if you have a large class, design a method of giving students feedback on areas in which they need improvement (e.g., in the form of a feedback sheet that specifies categories of errors that have been made). If you use this feedback method, spend the first few minutes of class circulating among the students to ensure that they understand the feedback sheets and to review pertinent concepts with students who need a lot of help.

How much time to allow:

Simple Sentence Lessons 1A, 1B, 1C, and 1D take approximately 10 to 15 minutes to complete. *Simple Sentence Lessons 2A, 2B, 2C, 2D, 3A, 3B, 3C,* and *3D* take approximately 20 to 25 minutes to complete. Some students will finish the sequence in as few as three days; others will require 12 days or more.

What to do:

1. **Review the *Sentence Writing Strategy.*** * [Using the rapid-fire format, ask the students to define a simple sentence, an independent clause, a subject, a verb, a compound subject, and a compound verb. Have them name the steps of the *Sentence Writing Strategy,* the steps for identifying verbs and subjects, and the four kinds of simple sentences. Ask them to describe when and why they should use the *Sentence Writing Strategy.*]

2. **Give an advance organizer.** [Give one of the following advance organizers, as appropriate, when a student begins a new type of lesson. Make sure the student has the lesson before you give the advance organizer for it.]

   a. **Give an advance organizer for the first practice day.** "Today and for several more days, we will practice using what we've learned about simple sentences. You will be completing a series of lessons that will help you learn to write the four kinds of simple sentences. To reach mastery on a lesson, you must earn 90% of the points possible. When you reach mastery on one type of lesson, you will progress to a different one. You must reach mastery on three types of lessons to be allowed to go on to Advanced Practice. All of you will begin with *Simple Sentence Lesson 1A.*"

   [Distribute the *Simple Sentence Lesson 1A.* Explain how to use the Assignment Sheets in the students' folders and how to find the appropriate lessons in the future.]

   "*Simple Sentence Lesson 1A* requires you to apply the Verb-Subject Identification Procedure on 10 sentences. First you must find the verb or verbs in the sentence. Then look to the left of each verb for a helping verb. If there's one or more helping verbs, make an arch over the helping verbs and the verb and write a 'V' above the arch. Thus, for each complete verb, you may have two or more words under the arch. Be sure to look for a second verb if you see the word 'and.' "

   [Ask the students to define a verb phrase, helping verb, main verb, and compound verb. Review the concepts if necessary.]

   "Once you mark the complete verb, you must ask yourself the 'Who/What Question' to identify the subjects of the sentence. Write an 'S' above it. If a subject is represented by one noun, write an 'S' above it; if it is represented by a noun phrase, write an 'S' above the main subject only.

---

* This review should be conducted at the beginning of *each* practice day.

Be sure to look for a second subject if you see the word 'and.' Write an 'S' above it as well."

[Ask the students what a noun phrase is and what the main subject is. Review the concepts if necessary.]

"You also need to write the formula for the sentence on the line to the left of the sentence. For each sentence, you will earn 1 point for the correct formula, 1 point for correctly identifying the main subjects, and 1 point for correctly identifying the verbs. Thus, there are 30 points possible for the lesson. You must earn 27 points for mastery."

"Here's an example of what you need to do."

[Write, "The old lady and Janet walked down the street and saw a parade." on the board without "S"s and "V"s. Model using the Verb-Subject Identification Procedure. Have the students help you complete each step. Ask them which formula the sentence fits, and write the formula "SS VV" to the left of the sentence. Solicit questions and answer them. Explain that you expect the students to finish the lesson in 15 minutes. Conduct guided practice if needed.

Proceed to instructional step 3 on p. 50.]

b. Give the advance organizer for *Simple Sentence Lesson 2A.* "This lesson requires you to complete a sentence to match a certain formula. That is, the formula has been picked for you, and one subject has been chosen for the sentence. You must determine what is missing in the sentence to match the formula and finish the sentence. You need to do the last three steps of the strategy: explore words to fit the formula, note the words, and search for the verbs and subjects and check your work. Mark each verb with a 'V' and each subject with an 'S.' Here's an example of what you need to do."

[Write, "SS VV" and "Jan . . .", on the board. Show how you would analyze what is missing in the sentence compared to the formula. Then ask the student(s) for suggestions on how to finish the sentence. Write the sentence on the board. It should look something like this: "Jan and Jim screamed for help and struggled to climb on board the life raft." Use the Search and Check Step to find the verbs and subjects and check the sentence for completeness. Conduct more guided practice if needed.]

"For each sentence, you can earn 1 point if your sentence matches the formula and 1 point if it is complete (i.e., if your sentence has no words missing and contains a period at the end). You can also earn 1 point if you've marked the verbs and the subjects in your sentence correctly. You must earn 27 points for mastery. You should complete this lesson in 20-30 minutes."

[Solicit questions and answer them. Proceed to instructional step 3 on p. 50.]

c. Give the advance organizer for *Simple Sentence Lesson 3A.* "This lesson requires you to write 10 sentences: two for each of the four kinds of simple sentences and two of your own choice. For each of the first eight sentences, you will need to do the last three steps of the *Sentence Writing Strategy.* On each sentence you must: explore words to fit the formula, note the words, and search for the verbs and subjects and check your work. You do not have to mark the verbs and the subjects. Just be sure to check your work. For the last two sentences, you will need to do all four 'PENS' Steps including picking the formula. Write the formula you have chosen on the blank in front of the sentence. Your sentences can be about any topic, and they should have different subjects and verbs. You will not receive credit for your sentences if they are similar. You'll get 2 points if your sentence matches the formula and 1 point if it is complete and correct. Remember, to write a complete and correct sentence, you must capitalize the first letter of the first word of the sentence and put a period at the end of the sentence. The sentence has to make sense and have no words missing. You must earn 27 points for mastery. You should complete this lesson in 20-30 minutes."

[Elicit and answer questions. Conduct guided practice if needed.]

3. **Direct the students to begin practicing.** [Remind the students to tell themselves the appropriate steps of the *Sentence Writing Strategy* as they work on each sentence. If the students have practiced before, ask them individually to specify the areas in which they will try to improve. Have them write specific goals for improvement, if necessary. Allow them to refer to their Formula Cards and *Example Sheets* when needed.]

4. **Supervise individual practice.** [Circulate among the students. Look at their initial work on the lesson. Give immediate corrective feedback (see below). If a student is not following the instructions for the lesson, provide additional instruction. Instruct students to correct any incorrect work.]

5. **Collect the materials.** [Have the students put their completed lessons in their folders in order of completion so that they are easy to find.]

6. **Evaluate student responses.** [Use the appropriate Answer Key or Evaluation Guidelines (in the *Student Lessons* volume) to award points for correct responses. Translate the number of points earned into a percentage score using the *Percentage Table* on p. 149.]

7. **Provide individual feedback to students.** [Show the student his scored lesson sheet. Have the student plot the score for the percentage of points earned on his *Simple Sentence Progress Chart.* Ask him to compare the newly plotted point to previous ones in the same lesson series. Provide feedback as follows.]

a. **Provide positive feedback.** [Enthusiastically point out at least three things the student did correctly or well. For example, for *Lesson 1A* tell the student what formulas she wrote correctly, what subjects she correctly identified, and what verbs she correctly identified.]

b. **Provide corrective feedback.**

(1.) Specify a category of errors. [Make a Category of Errors Statement about one kind of error the student has made. For example, state that the student is not identifying the second verb in sentences with compound verbs, or that the student is not putting a period at the end of sentences, or that he is not matching the sentences to the specified formulas.]

(2.) Review the pertinent concept. [Ask the student to define the concept or review the step associated with the error. For example, ask the student to define a compound verb and state how compound verbs are separated (i.e., with the word "and").]

(3.) Specify what to do. [Explain to the student what she should do to avoid the type of error in the future. If necessary, invent a mini-strategy that the student can use to avoid the error in the future. For example, describe a mini-strategy for checking for a capital letter and a period.]

(4.) Provide a model. [Next, show the student what he should do to avoid the type of error in the future, thinking aloud so the student can witness all the processes involved.]

(5.) Have the student practice. [Require the student to show you how to proceed in the future using a different example than the one you used for the model. Provide feedback as needed, and continue having the student practice until you are certain the student knows what to do.]

(6.) Have the student paraphrase the feedback. [Ask the student to tell you in her own words what she needs to do to avoid the error in the future. Provide corrective feedback as needed.]

(7.) Have the student correct his work. [Ask the student to correct incorrect items that fit the category of errors you have discussed. The student may make oral or written corrections depending on the situation. For example, a student who has left off the second verb in a sentence requiring a compound verb should erase the period at the end of the sentence and add the second verb.]

(8.) Have the student write a goal related to the error category. [Have the student write a goal specifying in a positive way what she will do on future practice attempts.]

(9.) Repeat Corrective Feedback steps 1-7 for each category of error made.

8. Readjust goal dates. [Ask the student to evaluate his progress with respect to the goal date he set for Stage 5. If the student is ahead or considerably behind schedule according to recorded goal dates, ask him whether, in light of his progress to date, he wants to change the target dates on his *Progress Chart*. Discuss possible changes. Have the student make necessary adjustments.]

9. Have the student file completed products chronologically in the student's folder.

What to require for mastery:

The student must earn at least 90% (27 points) of the 30 points possible on one lesson in the *#1 Series,* on one lesson in the *#2 Series,* and on one lesson in the *#3 Series. Do not* require additional practice. It will destroy student motivation. This program was designed with lots of review activities built into it along the way.

Where to go from here:

If the student earns 90% or more of the points on a given lesson, she should receive the first lesson in the *next* numbered series. For example, if the student scores 90% on *Lesson 1A,* she should next receive *Lesson 2A.* Repeat instructional steps 1-9 above, providing the appropriate advance organizer for the new lesson.

If the student earns less than 90% of the points on a lesson, she should receive the next lesson in the *same* numbered series. For example, if the student earns 70% of the points possible on *Lesson 1A,* she should complete *Lesson 1B* next. Repeat instructional steps 1 and 3-9 above with the new lesson.

Continue having the student progress through the lessons alphabetically (A→ B→ C→ D→ A, etc.) if he earns less than 90% of the points, and to the next numerical series (1→ 2→ 3) when the student earns 90% or more of the points.

Do not require a student to complete additional lessons in the same numbered series after he reaches mastery in a series. This wastes valuable student time and destroys motivation.

When the student completes a lesson in the *#3 Series* at or above the mastery level, congratulate her, and ask her to record the day's date on her *Progress Chart* in the box under "Stage 5" and next to the words "Date Completed." Also ask her to record the day's date on the *Management Chart* under "Controlled Practice and Feedback." Proceed to STAGE 6: ADVANCED PRACTICE/POSTTEST AND FEEDBACK with that student.

How to trouble-shoot:

If a student does not show progress in identifying verbs and subjects in the *#1 Series* after four lessons, he needs remedial work on this skill. Use supplementary materials to teach the student to identify subjects and verbs.

If a student completes the fourth lesson in the *#2* or *#3 Series* (e.g., *Lesson 2D*) without reaching mastery, give her the first lesson again (*Lesson 2A*). Alternatively, design additional lessons, but ensure that the requirements in the new lessons are the same as the those in the lessons provided.

If a student continues to make the same error on more than one lesson, have him write a goal *before* he starts each lesson reflecting his intention to correct the error (e.g., "I will earn all the points for identifying helping verbs today."). Also have him write a one-sentence plan for reaching the goal (e.g., "I will check in front of each action verb to see if it has one or more helping verbs.").

Some students have difficulty identifying the subject in sentences like this one:
Twelve of my friends came to the party.

The subject in this sentence is "Twelve." Some students will identify the word "friends" as the subject. Explain that "friends" is the object of the preposition. The object of a preposition can never be the subject of the sentence. If the student is not familiar with prepositions, spend some time on this concept and ensure that the student can recognize some common prepositions. Teach the lesson in the *Fundamentals in the Sentence Writing Strategy** program on prepositions if necessary.

Likewise, if students confuse infinitives with the main verb of a sentence, teach the lesson on infinitives in the *Fundamentals* program. If they have trouble with helping verbs, teach the lesson on helping verbs.

Some students have trouble identifying the verb in a sentence like this one:
  The players were exhausted.

They will identify "were exhausted" as the complete verb. The verb should be "were." When the students are unsure about a word that follows a linking verb, they should ask themselves this question, "Is it something the subject can do or something the subject can *be*?" Only if the word is an action word (something the subject can *do*) should it be identified as part of the complete verb. Teach the lesson in the *Fundamentals* program on linking verbs if additional instruction is needed.

If a student makes grammatical or spelling errors, give her corrective feedback on those errors and have her correct them; however, do not penalize the student for such errors at this point. The goal here is to have the students write sentences and focus on sentence structure.

Provide a special dictionary or a computerized spelling checker for students who have difficulty spelling words. Some dictionaries list the correct spelling of words by their misspelled forms. Others have simple formats.** Students experiencing difficulty with spelling may benefit from learning morphographic spelling skills.***

If a student has difficulty thinking of content for sentences required in the *#3 Series,* suggest some ideas or give the student a couple of pictures as stimuli for content.

Some students find the task of writing 10 sentences as required in the*#3 Series* to be difficult. If this is the case, assign 5 sentences one day and 5 sentences the next. Gradually require the student to write more sentences each day until he can write 10 sentences in the allotted time without difficulty.

---

* See Schumaker, J.B., & Sheldon, J.B. (1998). *Fundamentals in the sentence writing strategy.* Lawrence: University of Kansas Center for Research on Learning.
** See, for example:
  Krevinsky, J., & Linfield, J.L. (1983). *The bad speller's dictionary.* New York: Random House.
  Miller, S.M. (1971). *Webster's new world speller/divider.* New York: Simon & Schuster.
  Moore, G.N., Talbot, R.A., & Woodruff, G.W. (1975). *Spellex word finder.* Billerica, MA: Curriculum Associates, Inc.
  Moore, G.N., Talbot, R.A., & Woodruff, G.W. (1984). *Funk & Wagnall's speller.* New York: Harper & Row Publishers.
  Moore, G.N., Talbot, R.A., & Woodruff, G.W. (1983). *Webster's new world misspeller's dictionary.* New York: Simon & Schuster.
*** See Dixon, R., & Englemann, S. (1979). *Corrective spelling through morphographs.* Palo Alto, CA: Science Research Associates. (See p. 9 for the address and phone number for ordering this material.)

PART I: SIMPLE SENTENCES
STAGE 6: ADVANCED PRACTICE/POSTTEST AND FEEDBACK

What your goals are:

- To ensure that students can write simple sentences in response to a grade appropriate assignment.

What you need:

- *Simple Sentence Lessons 4A, 4B, 4C, 4D* (the *#4 Series*) (in the *Student Lessons* volume)
- Four lesson folders for *Simple Sentence Lessons 4A-4D*
- Pictures and other stimuli to elicit written responses for the lessons
- Student folders
- *Cue Cards #1-6* (pp. 153-158)
- Pencils
- *Simple Sentence Checklist* (p. 181) (two per student per lesson)
- *Sentence Score Sheet* (p. 174) (one per lesson per student)
- *Sentence Scoring Instructions* (pp. 137-143)
- *Management Chart for Instruction in Simple Sentences*
- Stapler or paper clips

How to prepare:

1. **Check the lesson folders.** Make sure that each of the four lesson folders contains sufficient copies of the lessons and at least two stimulus items.* Stimulus items may be interesting pictures cut from magazines, a stimulating newspaper article, a short magazine article, or two small objects (e.g., two different shells, two different coins, two miniature animals). The items should accommodate fulfillment of the lesson requirements (i.e., students must write sentences using two subjects and two verbs). Keep these initial assignments simple since many students will have difficulty writing six sentences on the same topic. Make sure the appropriate lesson number is circled on each lesson sheet.

2. **Gather the other materials listed.** Copy additional *Simple Sentence Checklists* and *Sentence Score Sheets* if necessary.

3. **Read the instructions below.**

---

* If you have a large group of students, you will need to figure out ways to make stimulus items available to several students at the same time. For example, you can show a slide picture on an overhead screen or you can make 20 copies of a newspaper article.

4. Plan assignments. Specify on each student's Assignment Sheet what lesson she is to complete, the stimulus item to be used or the topic to be addressed for the lesson. If possible, integrate use of previously learned strategies into the assignments to ensure maintenance of these strategies. For example, if a student has mastered the *Paraphrasing Strategy,* you might ask her to read a magazine article using the *Paraphrasing Strategy* and to complete the writing lesson using the information she learned from the article.

How much time to allow:

Students usually require 20-30 minutes to complete one lesson in the *#4 Series.* If you are asking students to read something before completing the lesson, allow additional time.

What to do:

1. Review the *Sentence Writing Strategy.* [Ensure the student folders are distributed. Using the rapid-fire format, ask the students to define a simple sentence, an independent clause, a subject, a verb, a compound subject, and a compound verb. Ask them to name the steps of the *Sentence Writing Strategy,* the steps of the Verb-Subject Identification Procedure, and the kinds of simple sentences. Then distribute *Lesson 4A.*]

2. Give an advance organizer. "You have mastered the skill of writing simple sentences in isolation. Now you must practice writing them in groups of sentences about the same topic, so you will know how to use simple sentences when you receive an assignment in your classes or when you have to write an answer to an essay question. For the next lesson you must write at least six sentences about the same topic. The topic is listed on your Assignment Sheet. Within the six sentences you must include all four types of simple sentences you've learned to write. You can write these four sentence types in any order. For two of the six sentences, you can use whatever formula you want."

"Use all four 'PENS' Steps for each sentence. Before you write a sentence, pick a formula from your Formula Card, explore words to fit it, write the sentence, search for the verbs and subjects, and check to make sure it is complete. While you're writing all six sentences, use this checklist to make sure you've written each kind of sentence required."

[Distribute the *Simple Sentence Checklists.*]

"Read each sentence you've written and put a tally mark on the *Checklist* next to the kind of sentence it is. Staple (or paper clip) your *Checklist* to the lesson when you're finished."

"In order for you to reach mastery, all your sentences must address the topic, be complete and correct, and four of them must fit the four required formulas. The other two must be simple sentences of your choosing. Remember, to be complete and correct, your sentences must make sense, have no words left out, and have beginning capitalization and end punctuation. It should take you 20 to 30 minutes to complete this lesson."

3. Direct the students to begin practicing.-9. File completed products. [Follow the instructions provided for steps 3-9 under Stage 5: Controlled Practice and Feedback (pp. 50-51). Encourage the students to refer to their Formula Cards as they work. Use the *Sentence Scoring Instructions* (pp. 137-143), a *Sentence Scoring Sheet,* and a *Simple Sentence Checklist* to evaluate each student's product. Provide individual feedback after each lesson.]

What to require for mastery:

Percentage of complete sentences. One hundred percent (100%) of the sentences must be complete; they must all be about the topic and make sense. All sentences must be designated as such with beginning capitalization and end punctuation.

Sentence mix. The four kinds of simple sentences must be represented.

Where to go from here:

If the student meets the mastery requirements on a given lesson, congratulate him and ask him to record the day's date on his *Progress Chart* in the box under "Stage 6" and next to the words "Date Completed." Also ask him to record the day's date on the *Management Chart* under "Advanced Practice/Posttest and Feedback." Proceed to STAGE 7: MAKE COMMITMENTS FOR GENERALIZATION (p. 117).

If the student meets the mastery requirements, wants to learn more about simple sentences, and has the instructional time available, proceed to APPENDIX C: ENRICHMENT ACTIVITIES (p. 183) and then to STAGE 7: MAKE COMMITMENTS FOR GENERALIZATION (p. 117).

If the student does not meet mastery, assign the next lesson in the series after providing feedback. For example, if the student does not reach mastery on *Lesson 4A,* assign *Lesson 4B.* Make sure a new topic is provided for each lesson. Repeat instructional steps 1-9 above with each new lesson.

How to trouble-shoot:

Occasionally, you will encounter a student who cannot get started on the writing assignment. For such a student, write the numbers 1 through 6 along the left-hand margin of the paper. Have the student write a formula to the left of the number and a sentence on the topic to the right of the number. As the student becomes more comfortable with this task, fade out the use of numbers and written formulas, and require that each *sentence* be followed by another on the same line.

Often students will write a hodgepodge of sentences about a topic without any organization and without a topic sentence. This is acceptable at this point. The students will learn more advanced organizational skills in the *Paragraph Writing Strategy.*

Again, if students make spelling or grammatical errors, provide corrective feedback, but do not penalize them.

PART II: COMPOUND SENTENCES
STAGE 2: DESCRIBE

What your goals are:
To provide students with a description of:
- Rationales for varying sentence structures.
- Requirements for compound sentences.
- Formulas to be used in writing compound sentences.
- Application of the *Sentence Writing Strategy* to the writing of compound sentences.

What you need:
- Chalkboard or other writing surface and appropriate writing implement
- Overhead projector and screen (if using overhead transparencies)
- *Sentence Writing Cue Cards #7-10* (pp. 159-162)
- Student folders (containing Formula Cards, *Example Sheets,* etc.)
- Paper for student notes
- Pencils
- Large calendar
- *Compound Sentence Progress Chart* (p. 176) (one per student)
- *Management Chart for Instruction in Compound Sentences* (p. 180)
- Your own Formula Card

How to prepare:
1. Make a copy of the *Cue Cards.* If you are using overhead transparencies of the Cue Cards, make these prior to the instructional session. Otherwise, make one paper copy of each of the Cue Cards for reference during your presentation.

2. Gather the other listed materials. Make additional copies of the *Compound Sentence Progress Charts* (p. 176) if necessary. Expand your own Formula Card to include the compound sentence formulas. Fill in the title and the students' names on the *Management Chart for Instruction in Compound Sentences.*

3. Familiarize yourself with the instructions below.

How much time to allow:
Allow approximately 20-30 minutes for the presentation of the information, depending on whether you are presenting to an individual or a group of students.

What to do:
1. Review. [Using the rapid-fire format, ask the students to name the steps of the *Sentence Writing Strategy,* to give reasons why they should use the strategy, and to specify situations in which they can use the strategy.]

2. Give an advance organizer. "For the last couple of weeks you've been working on simple sentences. Today we begin a unit on the second major kind of sentence you will learn, the _compound sentence._"

[Write "Compound Sentence" on the board, or show only the title of the transparency of *Cue Card #7.*]

"We will be discussing why varying your sentences is important, you'll set some goals, we'll go over the requirements and formulas for compound sentences, and we'll talk about using the 'PENS' Steps to write compound sentences."

3. Discuss rationales for using a variety of sentences. "Compound sentences are different from simple sentences. Thus, if you use both compound and simple sentences, your writing will become more interesting."

"Why might you want to make your writing interesting?"

[Elicit and prompt responses such as teachers might give students better grades, they might qualify for school activities like writing for the newspaper or yearbook, their letters will be more interesting so people will be more likely to write back, job applications will be more correct and appealing so employers will be more likely to invite them for an interview, etc.]

4. Set goals. "The process we will follow in learning to write compound sentences is similar to the process we used to learn to write simple sentences. Today we will do the Describe and Model Stages. Tomorrow we'll work on Verbal Practice, and then you'll begin work on some practice lessons. Let's take some time now to set goals for how fast you want to learn to write compound sentences. Most of you should be able to complete this unit through Stage 7 in 2-3 weeks."

[Distribute student folders, *Compound Sentence Progress Charts,* and pencils. Using a calendar for reference, have the students write on their new *Progress Charts* a target date under each stage heading and next to the words "Goal Date." Suggest that they start with the current day's date and allow the following number of days for each stage:

STAGE 2:	DESCRIBE	1 day
STAGE 3:	MODEL	1 day
STAGE 4:	VERBAL PRACTICE	1-2 days*
STAGE 5:	CONTROLLED PRACTICE AND FEEDBACK	5-20 days*
STAGE 6:	ADVANCED PRACTICE/POSTTEST AND FEEDBACK	1-4 days*
STAGE 7:	MAKE COMMITMENTS FOR GENERALIZATION	1 day
STAGE 8:	GENERALIZATION	10-15 days*

* Within this range, students choose the number of days that fits their individual learning rates on the previous activities.

Help the students choose the number of days that matches their individual learning styles and translate the number of days chosen into dates on the calendar. Discuss why they should learn compound sentences quickly.]

5. **Review the definitions for a simple sentence and an independent clause.** "Let's review what we learned about simple sentences for a minute. What does every simple sentence contain?"

[Elicit, "A subject and a verb."]

"Right. That's the minimum. When we have a subject and a verb that make sense, we call that a simple sentence. What else do we call it?"

[Elicit, "An independent clause." Display *Cue Card #7.*]

"Yes. Each simple sentence is made up of *one* independent clause."

6. **Define a compound sentence.** "In contrast, a <u>compound</u> <u>sentence</u> contains two or more independent clauses. Most often, a compound sentence has two independent clauses."

[Write the definition on the board or uncover the definition on the transparency of *Cue Card #7.* Prompt the students to make their own Cue Cards from this point on.]

"What is included in an independent clause?"

[Solicit the answer, "A subject and a verb."]

"What are four ways to make independent clauses?"

[Elicit the four formulas for simple sentences, and write them on the board.]

"That's right. You can use those four kinds of independent clauses to build compound sentences. Most often you will use two of the first kind of independent clause ('S V') to build compound sentences."

7. **Provide an example of a compound sentence.** "Writing a compound sentence is like putting two simple sentences together into one. The following sentence is a compound sentence."

[Write the first example from *Cue Card #7* on the board, or uncover it on the transparency.]

"What is the first independent clause in this compound sentence?"

[Elicit the answer, "The students finished class," and underline this clause.]

"Right. What is the second independent clause?"

[Elicit the answer, "they went to lunch," and underline this clause.]

"Correct. Each of these independent clauses can stand by itself as a sim-

ple sentence. Let's use the Verb-Subject Identification Procedure on each independent clause in this sentence."

[Solicit a volunteer to apply the Verb-Subject Identification Procedure to the first independent clause and another volunteer for the second independent clause. Mark the verbs with "V"s and the subjects with "S"s. Ask the students which simple sentence formula was used for each independent clause.

Present each of the remaining examples on **Cue Card #7.** Ask the students to identify the independent clauses, the verbs and subjects, and the simple sentence formula used for each independent clause.]

8. **Contrast compound sentences to simple sentences with compound subjects and compound verbs.** "How many subjects and how many verbs does each of these compound sentences have?"

[Elicit the response, "Two subjects and two verbs."]

"That's true, but even though compound sentences have two subjects and two verbs, they are different from simple sentences with compound subjects and compound verbs. What formula do we use to write a simple sentence with a compound subject and a compound verb?"

[Elicit the answer, "SS VV," and write the formula on the board next to the words "Simple Sentence."]

"In contrast, if you were to write a formula for our three example compound sentences on the board using the 'S' and 'V' symbols, what would it be?"

[Elicit the answer, "S V S V," and write this formula on the board next to the words "Compound Sentence."]

"How are these two formulas different?"

[Elicit a response like, "In the simple sentence, the subjects are together and the verbs are together. In the compound sentence, the subjects are separated by a verb and the verbs are separated by a subject."]

"That's right. Let's look at some examples of simple and compound sentences to make the distinction clear in your minds."

[Write the individual examples from **Cue Card #8** on the board, or use the transparency. Ask the students to identify verbs and subjects and decide which of the two formulas each sentence matches. For each pair of sentences, ask the students how the sentence meaning changes as a different formula is used even though the subjects and verbs are the same. Point out that in simple sentences the "and" comes between the subjects and between the verbs. In compound sentences, the "and" comes between the two independent clauses.]

"To summarize, we've seen that compound sentences differ from simple sentences with compound subjects and compound verbs. Compound

sentences contain at least two independent clauses that each can stand alone. Simple sentences have only one independent clause that can stand alone."

9. **Introduce the use of commas and coordinating conjunctions to join independent clauses.** "Have you noticed what elements these compound sentences have in common with regard to the way in which their independent clauses are joined?"

[Prompt the students to look at their notes on *Cue Card #7,* or show the transparency of *Cue Card #7* again. Ask them to identify what separates the two independent clauses in each sentence.]

"**That's right. A comma and a short word can separate the two independent clauses in a compound sentence. The short word is called a '**coordinating conjunction**.' ''**

[Show the title of the transparency of *Cue Card #9,* or write "Coordinating Conjunction" on the board.]

"**A coordinating conjunction is a word that is used to join two independent clauses.**"

[Show the definition on *Cue Card #9,* or write the definition on the board.]

"**There are seven coordinating conjunctions. They may be used, one at a time, with a comma to separate independent clauses.**"

[Write the seven coordinating conjunctions, each preceded by a comma, on the board, or use the transparency of *Cue Card #9.* Pronounce each conjunction.]

"**Do you see an easy way to remember these seven coordinating conjunctions?**"

[Elicit the mnemonic device, "FAN BOYS," and underline the initial letter of each conjunction.]

"**Let's look at some examples that show how each of the coordinating conjunctions is used.**"

[Show the examples by writing them on the board one by one or by sequentially revealing them on the transparencies of *Cue Cards #7* and *#9.* Ask the students to identify the coordinating conjunction in each example. Explain the meaning of each coordinating conjunction. For example, for the first example on *Cue Card #7,* explain that "and" is used to show that two ideas are equally important and connected. For the second example on *Cue Card #7,* explain that "so" is used to show the second clause is the result of the first clause. For the third example on *Cue Card #7,* explain that "for" means the same as "because" when it is used as a coordinating conjunction. "For" can also be used as a preposition as is also exemplified in this example sentence. Caution the students about confusing the two uses of this word. Remind them that they must follow any coordinating conjunction with a subject and a verb. For the first two examples on *Cue Card #9,* explain that "but" and "yet" are used to show contrast. For the third example, explain that "or" joins two ideas when there is a choice between them. For the fourth example on *Cue Card #9,* explain that "nor" is used to introduce the second clause of a negative statement and shows that the second clause is negative as well. Also explain that in sentences using the conjunction "nor," the verb will come before the subject in the second independent clause. In sentences with "nor" and helping verbs (as in the last example on *Cue Card #9*), the helping verb(s) will come before the subject, and the main verb will come after the subject in the second independent clause.]

10. Introduce the use of semicolons to join independent clauses.
"Another way of joining two independent clauses is to use a semicolon."

[Write the word, "Semicolon," on the board and put a semicolon (;) next to it, or use the transparency of *Cue Card #10.*]

"A semicolon is used whenever you don't want to use a coordinating conjunction. Maybe you've already written two compound sentences with coordinating conjunctions in a paragraph. To make the next compound sentence a little different, you can use a semicolon. Whenever you use a semicolon correctly, your reader will be impressed with your sophistication as a writer."

"Let's look at some examples. In the sentence, 'Susan loves to swim; her brother likes to dive,' the two independent clauses are joined by a semicolon."

[Write the sentence on the board, or uncover it on the transparency of *Cue Card #10.* Draw a circle around the semicolon. Have the students identify the two independent clauses, the subjects, and the verbs. In a similar manner, discuss the other examples on *Cue Card #10.* Provide feedback as necessary.]

11. Introduce the compound sentence formulas. "There are two formulas for compound sentences. To write these formulas, we will use a new symbol, a capital 'I,' which stands for 'Independent Clause.' "

"What are the four ways to make independent clauses?"

[Solicit the four simple sentence formulas. Write:

$$I = S \quad V$$
$$I = SS \quad V$$
$$I = S \quad VV$$
$$I = SS \quad VV$$

on the board as each formula is mentioned.]

"That's right, so each time you see an 'I' you can substitute in your mind any one of the four formulas."

"Using a capital 'I' for an independent clause and a small 'c' for a coordinating conjunction, what formula can we use for a compound sentence in which the independent clauses are joined by a comma and a coordinating conjunction?"

[Elicit the formula, "I,cI", and write it on the board.]

"Good. Using a capital 'I' for independent clause, what formula can we use for a compound sentence in which the independent clauses are joined by a semicolon?"

[Elicit the formula, "I;I", and write it on the board.]

"These are the two formulas we will use for compound sentences. Remember, each time you see an 'I,' you can substitute one of the simple sentence formulas."

12. **Expand the Formula Cards.** [Have the students add the heading "Compound Sentences" and the two compound sentence formulas to the lower-left quadrant of their Formula Cards. Show them your own card as a model. Check each student's card to ensure it is correct.]

13. **Add the formulas to the Cue Cards.** [Have the students locate their copies of *Cue Cards #9* and *#10*. Ask them to write the correct formula next to each example sentence on their Cue Cards. Explain that they can use these Cue Cards as Example Sheets.]

14. **Integrate compound sentences with the *Sentence Writing Strategy* steps.** "The *Sentence Writing Strategy*, 'PENS,' works with compound sentences just as it did with simple sentences. However, you need to attend to a few additional things when you write a compound sentence."**

a. **Step 1: Pick a formula.** "What's the first step?"

[Elicit the answer, "Pick a formula."]

"Right. Now, when you pick a formula, you have six to choose from—the four simple sentences and the two compound sentences. When you choose one of the compound sentence formulas, be sure to think of the kinds of independent clauses you want to write."

b. **Step 2: Explore words to fit the formula.** "What's the second step?"

[Elicit the answer, "Explore words to fit the formula."]

"Correct. When you explore words to fit a compound sentence formula, think of words for each independent clause. If you've chosen the I,cI formula, also think of an appropriate coordinating conjunction."

c. **Step 3: Note the words.** "What's the third step?"

[Elicit the answer, "Note the words."]

"Exactly. When you write a compound sentence, capitalize the first letter of the first word, and put a period at the end of the sentence."

"What other punctuation will you need to remember?"

[Elicit the answer, "A comma or semicolon."]

"That's right. A compound sentence must have a comma or a semicolon depending on the formula you've chosen. If you leave out the punctuation, you will not get full credit for the sentence in this class."

d. **Step 4: Search and check.*** "What's step 4?"

[Elicit the answer, "Search and check."]

"True. Be sure to search through your compound sentence to make sure you have all the subjects and verbs you need. To be complete, each independent clause must have at least one subject and one verb. Search through each independent clause separately. Then read through the whole sentence to check that it makes sense, that it has the needed capitalization and punctuation, and that you haven't left out any words."

15. **Give a post-organizer.** "Today we've discussed the requirements and formulas for compound sentences, and we've talked about how to apply the *Sentence Writing Strategy* steps to write compound sentences. Next, I'll model the process for you."

16. **Solicit and answer questions.**

17. **Record the completion date for Stage 2.** [Ask the students to turn to the *Compound Sentence Progress Charts* in their folders and record the day's date for completion of Stage 2 in the appropriate box under "Stage 2" and next to the words "Completion Date."

Instruct the students to put the Cue Cards they made and their Formula Cards in their folders. Have one student record the day's date under the Describe Stage on the *Management Chart* for each of the students in the group.]

Where to go from here:

After the students have written the completion date on their *Progress Charts* and on the *Management Chart,* immediately proceed to STAGE 3: MODEL, if time allows. Otherwise, begin the next instructional session with STAGE 3: MODEL.

---

* If the students have completed the *Fundamentals in the Sentence Writing Strategy* program, they will have learned the "MARK" Substeps that are subsumed under the Search and Check Step. Be sure to review those substeps here and to mention them each time the Search and Check Step is discussed in the remainder of this program.

PART II: COMPOUND SENTENCES
STAGE 3: MODEL

What your goal is:

- To demonstrate how to write compound sentences using the *Sentence Writing Strategy* while thinking aloud, so students can witness all the processes involved.

What you need:

- Chalkboard or other writing surface and appropriate writing implement
- Your own Formula Card
- *Cue Cards #7-10* (pp. 159-162)
- Student folders
- *Management Chart for Instruction in Compound Sentences*

How to prepare:

1. **Gather the needed materials.**

2. **Familiarize yourself with the instructions below.**

3. **Practice using the strategy.** Go through the demonstration yourself a few times to become fluent at using the *Sentence Writing Strategy* steps for compound sentences. Your demonstration should appear spontaneous, so be well prepared.

4. **Think of content for the last sentence in your demonstration.** Decide on a topic for the sentence you and your students will write together.

How much time to allow:

Allow approximately 5-10 minutes for the demonstration.

What to do:

1. **Review the *Sentence Writing Strategy*.*** [At the beginning of the lesson, ensure that student folders have been distributed, and conduct a quick review. Using the rapid-fire format, ask the students to define a simple sentence, a compound sentence, and an independent clause. Ask them to name the strategy steps, the four kinds of simple sentences, and the two kinds of compound sentences, to specify where they can use the strategy, and to explain how the strategy can help them. Refer them to their Cue Cards if necessary.]

2. **Give an advance organizer.** "Now I will show you how to use the *Sentence Writing Strategy* to write compound sentences. Listen and

---

* This review is not necessary if these activities are conducted on the same day as STAGE 2: DESCRIBE.

watch carefully because I will expect you to talk to yourself and do everything exactly as I do it."

3. **Demonstrate writing a compound sentence using the *Sentence Writing Strategy*.** "To begin I'll say, 'Sentence writing: PENS.' "

   a. **Step 1: Pick a formula:** " 'P' stands for 'Pick a formula,' so I'll look at my Formula Card . . ."

   [Look at your Formula Card.]

   " . . . and I'll choose the first kind of compound sentence: the one with the comma and coordinating conjunction."

   [Point to the I,cI formula.]

   "For each 'I,' I'll write an independent clause using the first simple sentence formula."

   [Point to the "S V" formula on your Formula Card.]

   b. **Steps 2 and 3: Explore words to fit the formula and note the words.** "Now I'm ready for the 'E' Step; I'll explore some words. Let's see, I want to write this sentence about two teams playing a game. For my first independent clause, I'll use 'teams' as my subject and 'were' as my verb. 'Both teams were exhausted.' Since this is going to be a long sentence and since I don't want to forget it, I'll skip to step 3 and note the words for the first independent clause right away."

   [Write the words, "Both teams were exhausted," on the board or transparency. As you write the clause, remind yourself to capitalize the first letter of the first word and to put a comma at the end of the clause.]

   "Now I need a coordinating conjunction. Since I want to say why they were exhausted, I'll use the coordinating conjunction 'for.' "

   "I'm ready to explore words for the second independent clause. I'll use 'game' as my subject and 'had lasted' as my verb: '. . . for the game had lasted too long.' "

   "I'll now go to step 3 and note the words for the second independent clause."

   [Write on the board, "for the game had lasted too long." Remind yourself to end the sentence with a period.]

   c. **Step 4: Search and check.** "Now I'll do the 'S' Step to check my sentence. First, I'll see if the sentence I wrote matches the formula for the compound sentence I chose. Do I have two groups of words separated by a comma and a coordinating conjunction? Yes. Next, I'll apply the Verb-Subject Identification Procedure* to the first independent clause made up of all the words in front of the comma. I need to look for the action or state-of-being word or words. It's 'were.' Next, I'll ask myself 'Who or what were?'; the answer is 'teams.' Are there any other subjects that answer the 'Who/What Question'? No. I have a subject and a verb in the first independent clause. Thus, it checks out against the formula I chose for it."

[Point to the "S V" formula on the Formula Card.]

"Now I'll apply the Verb-Subject Identification Procedure to the words that follow the coordinating conjunction. 'Had lasted' is the verb. Who or what had lasted? The game had lasted. I now have a subject and a verb for the second independent clause. It all checks out against the formulas I chose. Finally, I'll read through and check the whole sentence one last time. 'Both teams were exhausted, for the game had lasted too long.' Did I remember to use a capital letter? Yes. Did I remember a comma and a period? Yes. Are there any words left out? No. Does it make sense? Yes. Good, this is a complete sentence."

4. **Involve the students in the demonstration.** [For the remaining type of compound sentence (an I;I sentence), have the students state what should be done and suggest responses for each strategy step. Name a general topic for the sentence, but ask the students to choose the formula and come up with the subjects and verbs, and the final wording of the sentence. Have a student write the sentence on the board, and ask other students to check it. Provide corrective feedback as needed.]

5. **Give the post-organizer.** "Now we have learned about the requirements for compound sentences, and you have seen how we use the *Sentence Writing Strategy* to write the two kinds of compound sentences. Next we'll do some verbal practice."

6. **Solicit and answer questions.**

7. **Record the completion date for Stage 3.** [Ask the students to record the day's date for completion of Stage 3 on their *Compound Sentence Progress Charts* and on the *Management Chart.*]

Where to go from here:

After all questions have been answered and completion dates have been recorded, go to STAGE 4: VERBAL PRACTICE.

---

* If your students have completed the *Fundamentals in the Sentence Writing Strategy* program, use the words "MARK Steps" instead of the words "Verb-Subject Identification Procedure" here and throughout the remainder of this program.

PART II: COMPOUND SENTENCES
STAGE 4: VERBAL PRACTICE

What your goals are:
- To ensure that each student has memorized the requirements for compound sentences and understands the concepts involved in writing them.
- To review the steps of the *Sentence Writing Strategy* and ensure the students remember them.

What you need:
- Chalkboard or other writing surface and appropriate writing implement
- Student folders
- *Compound Sentence Verbal Practice Checklist* (p. 171) (one per student)
- *Compound Sentence Quiz* (in the *Student Lessons* volume) (one per student)
- *Cue Cards #7-10* (pp. 159-162)
- *Management Chart for Instruction in Compound Sentences*

How to prepare:
1. **Check your supply of *Compound Sentence Verbal Practice Checklists* and *Compound Sentence Quizzes*.** If necessary, make additional copies.

2. **Gather the other materials listed.**

3. **Familiarize yourself with the instructions below.**

How much time to allow:
Most students will reach mastery on the oral quiz within 25 minutes; some may need more time. The written quiz takes approximately 10-15 minutes to complete, and most students reach mastery on the first attempt.

What to do:
1. **Review.** [Using the rapid-fire format, ask the students to name the *Sentence Writing Strategy* steps, to define a compound sentence, an independent clause, and a coordinating conjunction, to explain how commas and semicolons are used in compound sentences, and to name the mnemonic device "FAN BOYS," the coordinating conjunctions, and the two kinds of compound sentences. Write their responses on the board.]

2. **Give an advance organizer.** "Today you will memorize the requirements for writing compound sentences and take an oral and a written quiz over compound sentences. If you know the requirements well, you will be able to tell yourself what to do when you write compound sentences."

3. Conduct rapid-fire verbal rehearsal of the strategy steps. "Before we begin, let's review the 'PENS' Steps using the rapid-fire technique."

[Erase the steps from the board and conduct rapid-fire verbal practice for several rounds following the instructions on pp. 42-43. Stop when most of the students can name the steps.]

4. Conduct a rapid-fire question-and-answer exercise to memorize the requirements for compound sentences.* "Now let's use the rapid-fire technique to memorize the definitions and the requirements for compound sentences. I will ask a question, and, if I point to you, you are to answer the question as quickly as you can. Here are the questions and the answers." **

1. **What's a compound sentence?**
   A sentence with two or more independent clauses.
2. **What's an independent clause?**
   A group of words with a subject and a verb that can stand alone.
3. **What's a coordinating conjunction?**
   A word used with a comma to join two independent clauses.
4. **Name one coordinating conjunction.*****
   For, and, nor, but, or, yet, so.
5. **How do you use a comma in a compound sentence?**
   In front of the coordinating conjunction.
6. **How do you use a semicolon in a compound sentence?**
   To join the two independent clauses.
7. **What's one kind of compound sentence? ******
   I,cl   I;I
8. **What's one way to make an 'I' (independent clause)? *******

S	**V**
SS	**V**
S	**VV**
SS	**VV**

[Solicit and answer questions.]

"O.K., let's begin."

[Conduct the rapid-fire exercise as you did for simple sentences. After several rounds with the answers remaining on the board, erase them. Start each new round with a different person. Continue until the students appear to have learned the requirements for writing compound sentences.]

---

* If you are working with one student, she may rehearse the questions and answers on her own or together with you using the list provided. Alternatively, the student can use 3" × 5" cards to practice remembering the definitions. Have the student put the question on one side of the card and the definition or answer on the other. Ask her to keep testing herself until she gets all the definitions correct three times in a row. See the footnote on p. 42 for suggestions for working with a large group of students.
** The answers should be similar to what you have written on the board for the review.
*** Ask this question seven times.
**** Ask this question twice.
***** Ask this question four times.

5. **Allow time for individual review.** [After the group verbal practice exercise, allow the students time for individual review. Explain that they must be able to define a compound sentence, an independent clause, and a coordinating conjunction, to name the two kinds of compound sentences, to name the seven coordinating conjunctions, and to explain how commas and semicolons are used in compound sentences. Inform the students that they must orally answer all your questions correctly and without help and that they must get at least 90% of their answers correct on the written quiz.]

6. **Conduct the oral quizzes.*** [Using the *Compound Sentence Verbal Practice Checklist,* conduct individual oral quizzes when students are ready. Determine the percentage of questions each student answers correctly.]

7. **Conduct the written quiz.** [When a student passes the oral quiz (see the mastery criterion below), have him complete the *Compound Sentence Quiz.* Determine the percentage of questions answered correctly using the chart on p. 149.]

8. **Provide feedback.** [Review the results of the oral and written quizzes with the student. Provide positive and corrective feedback as necessary. Have the student plot the percentage of questions answered correctly on the *Compound Sentence Quiz* on the *Compound Sentence Progress Chart* on the vertical line above the "Q."]

What to require for mastery:

To reach mastery, the student must correctly answer 100% of the questions on the oral quiz and at least 90% of the questions on the written quiz without referring to a Cue Card and without receiving other assistance.

Where to go from here:

If the student achieves mastery on both quizzes, ask her to record the completion date on her *Progress Chart* and on the *Management Chart.* Have her place the *Verbal Practice Checklist* and written quiz in her folder, and proceed to STAGE 5: CONTROLLED PRACTICE AND FEEDBACK.

If the student does not achieve mastery on the oral quiz, provide feedback and have him rehearse the definitions several times by himself or with a peer before giving him another oral quiz.

If the student does not achieve mastery on the written quiz, review the pertinent concepts with the student, and ask her to orally complete similar items. When the student appears to understand the concepts, have her take the written quiz again.

How to trouble-shoot:

Help students figure out ways to remember the definitions or answers they have forgotten. Prompt the use of memorization techniques to help students remember the required information (see pp. 45-46 for suggestions). The students must know the terms because the feedback process will be facilitated if they understand the vocabulary you use.

---

* See the footnote on p. 44 for an alternative to this procedure if you are working with a large class.

PART II: COMPOUND SENTENCES
STAGE 5: CONTROLLED PRACTICE AND FEEDBACK

What your goals are:

- To ensure the students master the skills involved in writing two types of compound sentences.
- To ensure the students can integrate the skills related to writing simple and compound sentences.

What you need:

- *Compound Sentence Lessons 1A, 1B, 1C, 1D* (the *#1 Series*), *2A, 2B, 2C, 2D* (the *#2 Series*), *3A, 3B, 3C, 3D* (the *#3 Series*), *4A, 4B, 4C, 4D* (the *#4 Series*), and *5A, 5B, 5C, 5D* (the *#5 Series*) (in the *Student Lessons* volume)
- *Evaluation Guidelines* and *Answer Keys* for the lessons listed above (in the *Student Lessons* volume)
- Twenty lesson folders for *Compound Lessons 1A-5D* (see p. 9 for description)
- Student folders
- Pencils
- *Cue Cards #1-10* (pp. 153-162)
- *Management Chart for Instruction in Compound Sentences*

How to prepare:

1. **Check lesson folders.** If necessary, make additional copies of the lessons (see p. 9 for a description of lesson folders).

2. **Gather the other materials listed.**

3. **Familiarize yourself with the instructions below.**

4. **Plan assignments.** Determine for each student the next lesson to be completed. Record the assignment on the Assignment Sheet in the student's folder.

How much time to allow:

Compound Sentence Lessons in the *#1* and *#4 Series* take about 10 minutes to complete. In the *#2, #3,* and *#5 Series,* lessons require approximately 15-25 minutes. Some students will finish in as few as five days; others may require up to 20 days.

What to do:

1. **Review the *Sentence Writing Strategy.*** [Distribute student folders. Using the rapid-fire format, ask the students to define a simple sentence, a compound sentence, and an independent clause, to name four kinds of simple sentences

and two kinds of compound sentences, and to list the *Sentence Writing Strategy* steps. Ask the students when and why they should use the strategy.]

2. **Give an advance organizer.** [After students have obtained their assigned lessons, give one of the following advance organizers, as appropriate, when a student begins a new type of lesson.]

   a. **Give an advance organizer for *Compound Sentence Lesson 1A.*** "*Lesson 1A* requires that you determine what kind of compound sentence has been written. You must mark each complete verb with a "V" and each main subject with an "S," and write the formula for the sentence on the blank to the left of the sentence. In order to do this, you will need to apply the Verb-Subject Identification Procedure to each clause in each sentence."

   "You will earn 1 point for each correct formula, 1 point for correctly identifying the subjects of a sentence, and 1 point for correctly identifying the verbs. You must earn 90% of the points possible in this lesson (27 points) to reach mastery and move on to a different lesson. You should finish this lesson in 10 to 15 minutes. You must master five different lessons for compound sentences before moving on to Advanced Practice."

   [Solicit and answer questions. Conduct guided practice as needed. Proceed to instructional step 3 below.]

   b. **Give an advance organizer for *Compound Sentence Lesson 2A.*** "In the next lesson, the formula and the coordinating conjunction have been picked for you and the first independent clause has been written. You must add the correct punctuation for the formula and the coordinating conjunction, if one is indicated, and write a second independent clause that goes with the first. That is, the second clause must make sense within the context of the first. Clauses will not be accepted unless they make sense when put together with the first clause. For example, to get full credit for the first sentence, you must add a comma, the coordinating conjunction 'and,' an independent clause that makes sense when connected with 'Scott rode his moped to school,' and a period. For the second sentence, you must add a semicolon, an independent clause, and a period. Use the Verb-Subject Identification Procedure to check your work. Mark each complete verb in the clause you have added with a 'V' and each main subject in the clause you have added with an 'S.'"

   "You will earn 1 point if your sentence matches the listed formula and includes any required conjunction and 1 point if your sentence is complete and correct. To be complete and correct, your sentence must include a capital letter and end punctuation, your added clause must make sense by itself and when attached to the first clause, and there can be no words missing. You will earn 1 point if you've identified the subjects and the verbs in your added clause correctly. Again, you must earn 27 points to reach mastery on this lesson. You should finish this lesson in about 20 minutes."

[Solicit and answer any questions. Conduct guided practice as needed. Proceed to instructional step 3 below.]

c. Give the advance organizer for *Compound Sentence Lesson 3A*. "For this lesson, you will write 10 compound sentences. For the first eight sentences, the formulas and needed coordinating conjunctions have been picked for you, so your job is to complete the remaining three strategy steps for each of these sentences. For the last two sentences, you should do all four 'PENS' Steps, including picking the formula. Write the formula on the blank to the left of the sentence. You can also choose any coordinating conjunction you'd like for these sentences. Be sure to check your work using the Verb-Subject Identification Procedure on each clause that you write. Your sentences can be about any topic, but they must be different from one another, and they must make sense. You will earn 2 points for each sentence that matches the formula and 1 point for each sentence that is complete and correct. Remember, to be complete and correct, your sentence must include beginning capitalization and end punctuation, must make sense, and must have no words missing. You must earn at least 27 points to reach mastery. You should finish this lesson in about 20 minutes."

[Solicit and answer questions. Conduct guided practice as needed. Proceed to instructional step 3 below.]

d. Give the advance organizer for *Compound Sentence Lesson 4A*. "This lesson requires that you determine the kind of sentence that has been written. Some of the sentences are simple sentences; others are compound sentences. You must apply the Verb-Subject Identification Procedure and mark the subjects and verbs to figure out the formula. Mark each complete verb with a 'V' and each main subject with an 'S.' Write the correct formula on the blank to the left of the sentence. You can earn 1 point for the correct formula, 1 point for identifying all the subjects, and 1 point for identifying all the verbs. You must earn at least 27 points to reach mastery. You should finish this lesson in 10 to 15 minutes."

[Solicit and answer any questions. Conduct guided practice as needed. Proceed to instructional step 3 below.]

e. Give the advance organizer for *Compound Sentence Lesson 5A*. "In this lesson, you will write both simple and compound sentences. For the first eight sentences, the formulas and coordinating conjunctions have been picked for you, but you must complete the remaining three 'PENS' Steps yourself. When you check your work, mark the subjects with an 'S' and the verbs with a 'V.' Your sentences can be about any topic, but they must be different from one another and make sense. For the last two sentences, the type of sentence has been indicated. For #9, you must write a simple sentence. For #10, you must write a compound sentence. For each sentence, you must complete all the 'PENS' Steps yourself, including picking a formula. Write the formula to the left of the sentence on the blank."

"You will earn 2 points for matching the formula and 1 point for a complete and correct sentence. Remember, a complete and correct sentence includes a beginning capital letter and end punctuation, makes sense, and has no words missing. You must earn at least 27 points to reach mastery. You should finish this lesson in about 20 to 25 minutes."

[Solicit and answer questions. Conduct guided practice as needed.]

3. Direct the students to begin practicing.-9. File completed products. [Follow the instructions on pp. 50-51 for these instructional steps. Provide feedback individually to each student after each practice attempt.]

What to require for mastery:

The student must earn at least 90% (27 points) of the 30 points possible on one lesson in each of the *#1, #2, #3, #4,* and *#5 Series.*

Where to go from here:

Progress through the lessons as specified on p. 52. Provide individual feedback after each lesson. Repeat instructional steps 1 through 9 above as appropriate with each new lesson.

When the student completes a lesson in the *#5 Series* at or above the mastery level, congratulate her, and ask her to record the day's date on her Progress Chart and the Management Chart. Then proceed to STAGE 6: ADVANCED PRACTICE/ POSTTEST AND FEEDBACK with that student.

How to trouble-shoot:

If a student continues to make the same error on more than one lesson, have him write a goal *before* he starts each subsequent lesson that reflects his intention to correct the error (e.g., "I will not lose points today for leaving out commas."). Also, have him write a one-sentence plan for ensuring he does not make the error (e.g., "I will check each sentence to make sure it has a comma before the coordinating conjunction.").

If a student continues to make a certain type of grammatical error (e.g., does not make the subject and verb agree in number), provide instruction to the student regarding this error. Tell the student that points earned for complete and correct sentences will now be contingent on the student not making this type of error as well as on capitalizing and punctuating the sentence correctly and making sure it makes sense.

By this time, the students should be able to complete 10 sentences in one sitting. If not, follow the instructions on p. 53 when they are working on lessons in the *#3* and *#5 Series.*

If a student has difficulty thinking of content for sentences in the *#3* and *#5 Series,* provide pictures or other stimuli to prompt ideas.

PART II: COMPOUND SENTENCES
STAGE 6: ADVANCED PRACTICE/POSTTEST AND FEEDBACK

What your goal is:
- To ensure that students can write simple and compound sentences in response to a grade-appropriate assignment.

What you need:
- *Compound Sentence Lessons 6A, 6B, 6C, 6D* (the *#6 Series*) (in the *Student Lessons* volume)
- Four lesson folders
- Pictures and other stimuli
- Student folders
- *Cue Cards #1-10* (pp. 153-162)
- Pencils
- *Sentence Score Sheet* (p. 174) (one per student per lesson)
- *Sentence Scoring Instructions* (pp. 137-143)
- *Compound Sentence Checklist* (p. 181) (two per student per lesson)
- *Management Chart for Instruction in Compound Sentences*
- Stapler or paper clips

How to prepare:
1. **Check lesson folders.** Make sure each folder contains sufficient copies of the lessons and stimulus items for your group of students (see p. 54 for a description).
2. **Gather the other materials listed.**
3. **Read the instructions below.**
4. **Plan assignments.** Specify on each student's Assignment Sheet the lesson she is to complete and the stimulus item to be used.

How much time to allow:
Students usually take from 20-30 minutes to complete one lesson in the *#6 Series*. Allow additional time if students must read something first.

What to do:
1. **Review.** [Ensure the student folders are distributed. Using the rapid-fire format, ask the students to define a simple sentence, a compound sentence, and an independent clause, to name four kinds of simple sentences and two kinds of compound sentences, and to list the *Sentence Writing Strategy* steps. Ask the students when and why they should use the strategy. Then distribute *Lesson 6A*.]

2. Give an advance organizer. "You have practiced the skills of writing simple and compound sentences in isolation. Now we will practice them while writing a group of sentences about the same topic. For this next lesson, therefore, you will write at least six sentences about the topic listed on the Assignment Sheet in your folder. Include at least two simple sentences and two compound sentences. Use all four 'PENS' Steps. You may use your Formula Card as you work. Use a *Compound Sentence Checklist* to be sure you've included enough simple and compound sentences. Attach your *Checklist* to your paper before you hand it in to me."

"In order for you to reach mastery, all sentences must address the topic and must be complete and correct. Two sentences must be simple sentences and two must be compound."

3. Direct the students to begin practicing.-9. File completed products. [Follow the instructions provided for steps 3-9 under STAGE 5: CONTROLLED PRACTICE AND FEEDBACK (pp. 50-51). Encourage students to refer to their Formula Cards as they work. Use the *Sentence Scoring Instructions* (pp. 137-143), a *Sentence Score Sheet*, and a *Compound Sentence Checklist* to evaluate each student's product. Provide individual feedback after each lesson.]

What to require for mastery:

Percentage of complete sentences. One hundred percent (100%) of the sentences must address the topic and be complete. To be considered complete, all sentences must include a subject and a verb, have no missing words, and be designated as sentences with beginning capitalization and end punctuation.

Percentage of complicated sentences. At least two of the six sentences (33%) must be compound sentences. The compound sentences must be punctuated correctly in order to be considered acceptable.

Where to go from here:

If the student meets the mastery requirement on any lesson in the *#6 Series,* congratulate him, and ask him to record the day's date on his *Compound Sentence Progress Chart* and on the *Management Chart.* Proceed to STAGE 7: MAKE COMMITMENTS FOR GENERALIZATION (p. 117).

If the student meets the mastery requirements, wants to learn more about compound sentences, and has the instructional time available, proceed to APPENDIX C: ENRICHMENT ACTIVITIES (p. 183), and then to STAGE 7: MAKE COMMITMENTS FOR GENERALIZATION.

If the student does not meet mastery, provide feedback, and assign the next lesson in the *#6 Series.* Make sure a different topic is provided for each lesson. Repeat instructional steps 1-9 above with each new lesson.

How to trouble-shoot:

See pp. 52-53 for instructions.

PART III: COMPLEX SENTENCES
STAGE 2: DESCRIBE

What your goals are:

To provide students a description of:
- Requirements for complex sentences.
- Formulas to be used in writing complex sentences.
- Application of the *Sentence Writing Strategy* to the writing of complex sentences.

What you need:

- Chalkboard or other writing surface and appropriate writing implement
- Overhead projector and screen (if using overhead transparencies)
- *Sentence Writing Cue Cards #11-13* (pp. 163-165)
- Student folders (containing such items as Formula Cards and Cue Cards)
- Paper for student notes
- Pencils
- Large calendar
- *Complex Sentence Progress Chart* (p. 177) (one per student)
- *Management Chart for Instruction in Complex Sentences* (p. 180)
- Your own Formula Card

How to prepare:

1. **Make a copy of the *Cue Cards* on paper or overhead transparencies.**
2. **Gather the other listed materials.** Make additional copies of the *Complex Sentence Progress Charts* (p. 177) if necessary. Expand your own Formula Card to include the complex sentence formulas. Fill in the title and the students' names on the *Management Chart for Instruction in Complex Sentences.*
3. **Familiarize yourself with the instructions below.**

How much time to allow:

Allow approximately 20-30 minutes for the presentation of the information, depending on whether you are presenting to an individual or a group of students.

What to do:

1. **Review.** [Using the rapid-fire format, ask the students to define a simple sentence, a compound sentence, and an independent clause, to name four kinds of simple sentences and two kinds of compound sentences, and to list the *Sentence Writing Strategy* steps. Ask the students when and why they should use the strategy.]

2. Give an advance organizer. "You've mastered the skills involved in writing simple and compound sentences. Today we are going to begin a unit on the _complex sentence,_ the third type of sentence you will learn."

[Write "Complex Sentence" on the board or show only the title on the transparency of **_Cue Card #11._**]

"We will review why you need to vary the sentences you write, you'll set some goals, and we'll go over the requirements and formulas for complex sentences. Finally, we'll talk about using the 'PENS' Steps to write complex sentences."

3. Review rationales for using a variety of sentences. "Just like using both simple and compound sentences makes a passage more interesting to read, adding a third kind of sentence, the complex sentence, makes a passage even more interesting. Let's review why we want to make our writing interesting. What are the benefits to you if your writing appears interesting and sophisticated?"

[Elicit a variety of rationales related to a number of settings: school, community, and employment.]

4. Set goals. "We'll be following the same procedures for learning complex sentence writing as we did for simple and compound sentences. Let's write down some goals on your new **_Progress Charts_** for how fast you want to learn complex sentences."

[Distribute student folders, _Complex Sentence Progress Charts,_ and pencils. Follow the instructions on p. 20 to guide the students through the goal-setting process. Suggest the following number of days for each stage:

STAGE 2:	DESCRIBE	1 day
STAGE 3:	MODEL	1 day
STAGE 4:	VERBAL PRACTICE	1-2 days*
STAGE 5:	CONTROLLED PRACTICE AND FEEDBACK	5-20 days*
STAGE 6:	ADVANCED PRACTICE/POSTTEST AND FEEDBACK	1-4 days*
STAGE 7:	MAKE COMMITMENTS FOR GENERALIZATION	1 day
STAGE 8:	GENERALIZATION	10-15 days*]

5. Define a complex sentence. "Let's go over the components or parts of a complex sentence. A complex sentence consists of one independent clause and one or more dependent clauses."

[Write the definition on the board, or uncover the definition on the transparency of **_Cue Card #11._** Prompt the students to make their own Cue Cards throughout the remainder of the lesson as needed.]

---

* The students should choose the number of days that fits their individual learning rates on previous activities. Help them review their learning rates and choose accordingly.

6. Review the definition of an independent clause and define a dependent clause. "What's an independent clause?"

[Elicit the correct definition.]

"That's right. An independent clause is a group of words with a subject and a verb that can stand alone. In contrast, a _dependent_ _clause_ is a group of words including a subject and a verb that cannot stand alone."

[Write the definition of a dependent clause on the board, or uncover it on the transparency of *Cue Card #11.*]

"In the sentence, 'I like Sally because she is funny', . . ."

[Write the sentence on the board, or uncover the example on the transparency of *Cue Card #11.*]

". . . the clause 'I like Sally' is the independent clause; it can stand alone. The clause 'because she is funny' is the dependent clause; it cannot stand alone. It does not make sense by itself."

[Underline the independent clause with two lines and the dependent clause with one line. Ask the students to identify the verb and subject in each clause. Write the other examples on the board, or show them on the transparency, and ask the students to identify the independent clause and the dependent clause in each. Underline the independent clauses with two lines and the dependent clauses with one line. Ask the students to identify the verb and subject in each clause.]

7. Define subordinating conjunctions. "As we have discussed previously, both independent and dependent clauses have a subject and a verb. The main difference between the two types of clauses is that the dependent clause starts with a word showing the relationship between the dependent clause and the independent clause. These relating words are called _subordinating_ _conjunctions_."

[Write "Subordinating Conjunctions" and the definition on the board, or show the transparency of *Cue Card #12.*]

"Let's look at the following sentences and find the word that relates the dependent clause to the independent clause."

[Have the students find the subordinating conjunction in each of the example sentences on the board or on the transparency of *Cue Card #11.* Draw a circle around each to highlight it.]

"Here are some other subordinating conjunctions that you can use to build complex sentences."

[List the subordinating conjunctions on the board, or point to them on the transparency of *Cue Card #12* as you say them aloud. Have the students make their own Cue Card of the definition and the list.]

8. Explain how to sequence and punctuate independent and dependent clauses. "You can sequence the clauses in complex sentences in two ways. We will limit our discussion to complex sentences with two clauses (one dependent clause and one independent clause) because this is the type of complex sentence you must master. After you have learned this kind, we can talk about complex sentences with three or more clauses if you are interested. The independent and the dependent clauses in a complex sentence with two clauses can be sequenced in two major ways."

a. Explain that the dependent clause can come first. "You can make the dependent clause come *before* the independent clause. Here's an example, 'When I get to Phoenix, you will be sleeping.' "

[Write this sentence and the next two examples on the board, or uncover them one by one on the transparency of *Cue Card #13*. Ask the students to identify the independent clause, the dependent clause, the subordinating conjunction, and the subjects and verbs. Underline the independent clause with two lines and the dependent clause with one line.]

"What do these three sentences have in common with regard to how the two clauses are joined?"

[Elicit the response, "A comma."]

"That's right. A comma is required to join the two clauses when the dependent clause comes *before* the independent clause."

b. Explain that the independent clause can come first. "In the second way of sequencing the clauses in a complex sentence, the dependent clause comes *after* the independent clause."

[Write the remaining examples from *Cue Card #13* on the board, or uncover them one by one on the transparency of *Cue Card #13*. Have the students identify the independent clause, the dependent clause, the subjects and verbs, and the subordinating conjunction in each example. Underline the independent clauses with two lines and the dependent clauses with one line.]

"What is different about the way in which the clauses are joined in these three sentences compared to the way they are joined in the sentences where the dependent clause comes first?"

[Elicit the response, "There are no commas."]

"That's right. A comma is *not* required when the independent clause comes before the dependent clause."

"In summary, a comma is used when the dependent clause comes first. A comma is not used when the independent clause comes first."

9. Introduce the formulas for complex sentences. "We've talked about two kinds of complex sentences: one in which the dependent clause comes *before* the independent clause, the other where it comes *after* the independent clause. Two formulas can help us remember the two types of complex sentences."

"We'll use an 'I' to represent an independent clause and a 'D' to represent a dependent clause. Since we always use a subordinating conjunction at the start of a dependent clause, the 'D' stands for a subordinating conjunction and the rest of the dependent clause."

"Using the letters, 'I' and 'D,' what should the formula be when the dependent clause comes before the independent clause?"

[Elicit the formula, "D,I." Write it on the board or on a transparency.]

"What is the formula when the dependent clause comes *after* the independent clause?"

[Elicit the formula, "ID." Write it on the board or on a transparency.]

"Can you think of an easy way to remember when a comma is needed?"

[Elicit a response like, "When the formula is ID, like an 'I.D.' (for identification), it's fine as it is. When it's backwards, DI, you need a comma in it."]

10. **Expand the Formula Cards.** [Ask the students to take out their Formula Cards. Have them add the heading "Complex Sentences" and the two complex sentence formulas to the upper-right quadrant of their cards. Show them your own card as a model. Check each student's card to ensure it is correct.]

11. **Add the formulas to the Cue Cards.** [Have the students add the correct formula next to each example on their copies of *Cue Cards #11* and *#13.*]

12. **Integrate complex sentences with the *Sentence Writing Strategy* steps.** "Let's discuss how to use the 'PENS' Steps when writing complex sentences."

    a. **Step 1: Pick a formula.** "What's the first step?"

    [Elicit "Pick a formula."]

    "Good. Now you have eight formulas to choose from on your card. You really are learning how to vary your sentences."

    b. **Step 2: Explore words to fit the formula.** "What's the second step?"

    [Elicit "Explore words to fit the formula."]

    "Right. Think of words for both the dependent and the independent clause and choose an appropriate subordinating conjunction."

    c. **Step 3: Note the words.** "What's the third step?"

    [Elicit "Note the words."]

"Correct. When you write your sentence, what must you remember to do?"

[Elicit the response that you must capitalize the first letter of the first word, insert a comma where needed, and put a period at the end of the sentence.]

"Exactly. Remember, you will not get full credit for the sentence in this class if you leave out a comma when it is required."

d. **Step 4: Search and check.** "What's the last step?"

[Solicit "Search and check."]

"Correct. Search through your complex sentence to make sure you have a verb and a subject in each clause. Do each clause separately. Then read the sentence one last time to make sure it makes sense and that all the needed words have been included. Also make sure you have a capital letter, a comma if one is needed, and end punctuation."

13. **Give a post-organizer.** "Today we've discussed the requirements and formulas for writing complex sentences and have talked about using the 'PENS' Steps to write complex sentences. Next, I'll demonstrate how to write complex sentences."

14. **Solicit and answer questions.**

15. **Record the completion dates and file Cue Cards, Formula Cards, and *Examples Sheets* in student folders.**

Where to go from here:

After the students have written the completion date on their *Complex Sentence Progress Charts* and on the *Management Chart,* proceed immediately to STAGE 3: MODEL, if time allows. Otherwise, begin the next instructional session with STAGE 3: MODEL.

How to trouble-shoot:

If you expect that your students will have difficulty with the underlining system, explain that they can make an arch above each clause and label the arch with an 'I' (for independent clause) and a 'D' (for dependent clause).

PART III: COMPLEX SENTENCES
STAGE 3: MODEL

What your goal is:
- To demonstrate how to write complex sentences using the *Sentence Writing Strategy* while thinking aloud, so students can witness all the processes involved.

What you need:
- Chalkboard or other writing surface and appropriate writing implement
- Your own Formula Card
- *Cue Cards #11-13* (pp. 163-165)
- Student folders
- *Management Chart for Instruction in Complex Sentences*

How to prepare:
1. **Gather the needed materials.**
2. **Familiarize yourself with the instructions below.**
3. **Practice using the strategy.** Go through the demonstration yourself a few times to become fluent at using the steps of the *Sentence Writing Strategy* for complex sentences. Your demonstration should appear spontaneous, so be well prepared.
4. **Think of content for the last sentence in your demonstration.** Select a topic for the sentence that you and the students will write together.

How much time to allow:
Allow approximately 5-10 minutes for the demonstration.

What to do:
1. **Review the *Sentence Writing Strategy*.*** [At the beginning of the lesson, ensure that the student folders have been distributed, and conduct a quick review. Using the rapid-fire format, ask the students to define a simple sentence, a compound sentence, a complex sentence, an independent clause, and a dependent clause. Ask them to name the strategy steps, the four kinds of simple sentences, the two kinds of compound sentences, the two types of complex sentences, to specify where they can use the strategy, and to explain how the strategy can help them. Refer them to their Cue Cards if necessary.]

---

* This review is not necessary if you conduct these activities on the same day as STAGE 2: DESCRIBE.

2. **Give an advance organizer.** "Now I will show you how to use the *Sentence Writing Strategy* to write complex sentences. Listen and watch carefully because I expect you to talk to yourself and do everything exactly as I do it."

3. **Demonstrate writing a complex sentence using the *Sentence Writing Strategy.*** "To begin I'll say, 'Sentence Writing: PENS.' "

   a. **Step 1: Pick a formula:** " 'P' stands for 'Pick a formula,' so I'll look at my Formula Card . . ."

   [Look at your 3″ × 5″ Formula Card.]

   " . . . and choose the first kind of complex sentence; the one with the dependent clause first."

   [Point to the "D,I" formula.]

   b. **Steps 2 & 3: Explore words to fit the formula and note the words.** "Now I'm ready for the 'E' step; I'll explore some words. Let's see, I want to write this sentence about what you have to do before making a sandwich. That's good! I'll use the word, 'before,' as my subordinating conjunction and the first word of the sentence. For my dependent clause, I'll use, 'Before you make a sandwich.' Since this is going to be a long sentence, I'll skip ahead to step 3 and note those words right away before I forget them."

   [Write, "Before you make a sandwich," on the board. Remind yourself to capitalize the first letter of the first word and to put a comma after the word, "sandwich."]

   "Now I need to go back to step 2 and explore some words for the independent clause. Let's see, before you make a sandwich, you need to find a clean surface. That's good! Now I'll write that down."

   [Write "you need to find a clean surface." after the dependent clause on the board. Remind yourself to put a period at the end of the sentence.]

   c. **Step 4: Search and check .** "Now I'll do the 'S' step. First, I'll check the sentence against the formula for the complex sentence I chose. Do I have two groups of words separated by a comma? Yes. Do I have a subordinating conjunction at the beginning of the dependent clause? Yes, the subordinating conjunction is 'before.' "

   "Next, I'll apply the Verb-Subject Identification Procedure to the dependent clause which is made up of all the words in front of the comma. I have to look for the action or state-of-being word. It's 'make.' Next, I'll ask myself, 'Who or what makes?' The answer is 'you.' I have a subject and a verb in the dependent clause."

   "Now I'll apply the Verb-Subject Identification Procedure to the words that follow the comma. 'Need' is the verb. Who or what needs? You need.

Thus, I have a subject and a verb in the independent clause. It all checks out."

"Finally, I'll read the sentence one last time. 'Before you make a sandwich, you need to find a clean surface.' That makes sense. Did I remember a capital letter, a comma, and a period? Yes. Are there any words left out? No. Good, this is a complete sentence."

4. **Involve the students in the demonstration.** [For the remaining type of complex sentence (an ID sentence), ask the students to state what should be done next and to suggest responses for each step of the strategy. Provide a general topic about which the sentence is to be written, but ask the students to choose the formula and come up with the subjects and verbs, the subordinating conjunction, and the final wording of the sentence. Have a student write the sentence on the board, and ask other students to check it. Provide corrective feedback as needed.]

5. **Give the post-organizer.** "We have now learned about the requirements for complex sentences and seen how to use the *Sentence Writing Strategy* to write complex sentences. Tomorrow we'll do verbal practice."

6. **Solicit and answer questions.**

7. **Record the completion date for Stage 3.** [Ask the students to record the day's date for completion of Stage 3 on their *Complex Sentence Progress Charts* and on the *Management Chart.*]

Where to go from here:

After all questions have been answered and completion dates have been recorded, go to STAGE 4: VERBAL PRACTICE.

PART III: COMPLEX SENTENCES
STAGE 4: VERBAL PRACTICE

What your goals are:
- To ensure that students have memorized the requirements for complex sentences and understand the concepts involved in writing them.
- To review the steps of the *Sentence Writing Strategy* and ensure that students still remember them.

What you need:
- Chalkboard or other writing surface and appropriate writing implement
- Student folders
- *Complex Sentence Verbal Practice Checklist* (p. 172) (one per student)
- *Complex Sentence Quiz* (in the *Student Lessons* volume) (one per student)
- *Cue Cards #11-13* (pp. 163-165)
- *Management Chart for Instruction in Complex Sentences*

How to prepare:
1. **Check your supply of *Complex Sentence Verbal Practice Checklists* and *Complex Sentence Quizzes.*** If necessary, make additional copies.
2. **Gather the other materials listed.**
3. **Familiarize yourself with the instructions below.**

How much time to allow:
Most students will reach mastery on the definitions within 25 minutes. Some students may need more time. The written quiz takes approximately 10-15 minutes to complete, and most students reach mastery on the first attempt.

What to do:
1. **Review.** [Using the rapid-fire format, ask the students to state the *Sentence Writing Strategy* steps, to define a complex sentence, an independent clause, a dependent clause, and a subordinating conjunction, and to name the two kinds of complex sentences. Write their responses on the board.]

2. **Give an advance organizer.** "Today you will memorize the requirements for writing complex sentences and take an oral and a written quiz over complex sentences. If you know the requirements well, you will be able to tell yourself what to do when you write a complex sentence."

3. **Conduct rapid-fire verbal rehearsal of the strategy steps.** "Be-

fore we begin, let's review the 'PENS' Steps using the rapid-fire technique."

[Erase the steps from the board, and conduct rapid-fire verbal practice for several rounds following the instructions on pp. 42-43. Stop when most of the students can name the steps.]

4. Conduct a rapid-fire question-and-answer exercise to learn the requirements for complex sentences. * "Now let's use the rapid-fire technique to memorize the definitions and requirements for complex sentences. I'll ask a question, and, if I point to you, you are to answer the question as quickly as possible. Here are the questions and the answers." **

1. **What's a complex sentence?**
    A sentence containing one independent clause and one or more dependent clauses.
2. **What's an independent clause?**
    A group of words with a subject and a verb that can stand alone.
3. **What's a dependent clause?**
    A group of words with a subject and a verb that cannot stand alone.
4. **What's a subordinating conjunction?**
    The word that relates the 'D' clause to the 'I' clause.
5. **What's one kind of complex sentence?** ***
    D,I
    ID

[Solicit and answer questions.]

"O.K., let's begin."

[Conduct the rapid-fire exercise as for compound sentences. After several rounds with the answers on the board, erase them. Start each new round with a different person. Continue until the students appear to have learned the requirements.]

5. Allow time for individual review. [After the group verbal practice exercise, allow the students time for individual review. Explain that they must be able to orally define a complex sentence, an independent clause, a dependent clause, and a subordinating conjunction, name the kinds of complex sentences, and explain the punctuation rules for commas in complex sentences without help. Finally, they must get at least 90% of their answers correct on the written quiz.]

---

* If you are working with one student, she can rehearse the questions and answers independently using either the list provided here or 3" × 5" cards with the questions and answers on them. See the footnote on p. 42 for suggestions on how to work with a large class.
** The answers should be similar to what you have written on the board for the review.
*** Ask this question twice.

6. **Conduct the oral quizzes.*** [Using the *Complex Sentence Verbal Practice Checklist,* conduct individual oral quizzes when students are ready. Determine the percentage of questions they answer correctly.]

7. **Conduct the written quiz.** [After a student passes the oral quiz (see the mastery criterion below), have him complete the *Complex Sentence Quiz.* Determine the percentage of questions answered correctly using the table on p. 149.]

8. **Provide feedback.** [Review the results of the oral and written quizzes with the student. Provide positive and corrective feedback as necessary. Have the student plot the percentage of questions answered correctly on the *Complex Sentence Quiz* on the *Complex Sentence Progress Chart* on the vertical line above the "Q."]

What to require for mastery:

To reach mastery, the student must correctly answer 100% of the questions on the oral quiz and at least 90% of the questions on the written quiz without referring to a Cue Card and without receiving other assistance.

Where to go from here:

If the student achieves mastery on both quizzes, have her record the completion date for Stage 4 on her *Complex Sentence Progress Chart* and on the *Management Chart.* Have her place the *Verbal Practice Checklist* and quiz in her folder, and proceed to STAGE 5: CONTROLLED PRACTICE AND FEEDBACK.

If the student does not reach mastery on the oral quiz, provide feedback, and have him rehearse by himself or with a peer the items missed. Give him additional oral quizzes until he reaches mastery.

If the student does not reach mastery on the written quiz, review the pertinent concepts that were missed. Present new but similar items to her orally or on the board until you are certain she understands the concepts. Ask her to complete the written quiz again. Give additional quizzes until the student reaches mastery.

How to trouble-shoot:

Help students figure out ways to remember the definitions or answers they have forgotten. Prompt the students to use a memorization technique to help them remember the required information (see p. 45 for suggestions). Students must know the terms to facilitate the feedback process.

---

* See the footnote on p. 44 for an alternative procedure to be used in place of the oral quiz for a large class.

PART III: COMPLEX SENTENCES
STAGE 5: CONTROLLED PRACTICE AND FEEDBACK

What your goals are:

- To ensure students master the skills involved in writing four types of complex sentences.
- To ensure students can integrate the skills required to write simple, compound, and complex sentences.

What you need:

- *Complex Sentence Lessons 1A, 1B, 1C, 1D* (the *#1 Series*), *2A, 2B, 2C, 2D* (the *#2 Series*), *3A, 3B, 3C, 3D* (the *#3 Series*), *4A, 4B, 4C, 4D* (the *#4 Series*), and *5A, 5B, 5C, 5D* (the *#5 Series*) (in the *Student Lessons* volume)
- *Evaluation Guidelines* and *Answer Keys* for the lessons listed above (in the *Student Lessons* volume)
- Twenty lesson folders for *Complex Sentence Lessons 1A-5D* (see p. 9 for description)
- Student folders
- Pencils
- *Cue Cards #1-13* (pp. 153-165)
- *Management Chart for Instruction in Complex Sentences*

How to prepare:

1. **Check lesson folders.** If necessary, make additional copies of the lessons (see p. 9 for a description of the lesson folders).
2. **Gather the other materials listed.**
3. **Familiarize yourself with the instructions below.**
4. **Plan assignments.** Determine for each student the next lesson to be completed. Record the assignment on the Assignment Sheet in the student's folder.

How much time to allow:

Complex Sentence Lessons in the *#1* and *#4 Series* take about 10 minutes to complete. In the *#2, #3,* and *#5 Series,* they require approximately 15-25 minutes. Some students will finish in as few as five days; others may take up to 20 days.

What to do:

1. **Review the *Sentence Writing Strategy.*** [Ensure that student folders are distributed. Using the rapid-fire format, ask the students to define a simple sentence, a compound sentence, a complex sentence, an independent clause,

and a dependent clause, to name four kinds of simple sentences, two kinds of compound sentences, and two kinds of complex sentences, and to list the *Sentence Writing Strategy* steps. Ask the students when and why they should use the strategy.]

2. **Give an advance organizer.** [Give one of the following advance organizers, as appropriate, when students begin a new type of lesson after they have obtained a copy of the lesson.]

   a. **Give an advance organizer for *Complex Sentence Lesson 1A.*** "*Lesson 1A* requires that you determine what kind of complex sentence has been written. All these sentences contain an independent and a dependent clause. Underline the independent clause with two lines and the dependent clause with one line, and write the formula for the sentence on the blank to the left of the sentence. You will earn 2 points for each correct formula and 1 point for correctly underlining the clauses. You must earn 90% of the points possible on this lesson (27 points) to reach mastery and move on to a different lesson. You should finish this lesson in 10-15 minutes."

   [Solicit and answer questions. Conduct guided practice as needed. Proceed to instructional step 3 below.]

   b. **Give the advance organizer for *Complex Sentence Lesson 2A.*** "In this next lesson, the formula and the subordinating conjunction have been picked for you and one clause of the sentence has been written. Your job is to write another clause that goes with the first and to add any needed punctuation. The clause you add must make sense within the context of the clause that is already written. Clauses will not be accepted unless they make sense when put together with the clause that's already written. For the first sentence on this sheet you must add a dependent clause at the end. The independent clause has already been written. To the second sentence, add an independent clause at the end. The dependent clause has already been written. Mark each complete verb in each clause that you add with a 'V' and each main subject with an 'S.' "

   "You will earn 1 point if your sentence matches the listed formula and includes the indicated subordinating conjunction, 1 point if the sentence is complete and correct, and 1 point if you've identified the subjects and verbs in your added clause correctly. To be complete and correct, your sentence must include end punctuation, your added clause must make sense by itself and when attached to the first clause, and there can be no words missing. Again, you must earn 90% (27 points) of the points possible to reach mastery on this lesson. You should finish this lesson in about 20 minutes."

   [Solicit and answer any questions. Conduct guided practice as needed. Proceed to instructional step 3 below.]

   c. **Give the advance organizer for *Complex Sentence Les-***

son 3A. "For this lesson, you will write 10 complex sentences. For the first eight sentences, the formulas and subordinating conjunctions have been picked for you, so you must complete the remaining three strategy steps for each sentence. For the last two sentences, you should do all four 'PENS' Steps, including picking a formula. Write the formula on the blank to the left of the sentence. You will also have to choose a subordinating conjunction for these two sentences. Be sure to check your work by using the Verb-Subject Identification Procedure on each clause that you write."

"Your sentences can be about any topic, but they must be different, and they must make sense. You will earn 2 points for each sentence that matches the formula and 1 point for each sentence that is complete and correct. Remember, to be complete and correct, your sentence must include beginning capitalization and end punctuation, must make sense, and must have no missing words. You must earn at least 27 points to reach mastery. You should finish this lesson in about 25 minutes."

[Solicit and answer questions. Conduct guided practice as needed. Proceed to instructional step 3 below.]

d. Give the advance organizer for *Complex Sentence Lesson 4A.* "This lesson requires that you determine the kind of sentence that has been written. Some of the sentences are simple, some are compound, and others are complex. Underline independent clauses with two lines and dependent clauses with one line; write the correct formula in the blank to the left of the sentence. You can earn 2 points for the correct formula and 1 point for correctly underlining the clauses in each sentence. You must earn at least 27 points for mastery. You should finish this lesson in about 10 to 15 minutes."

[Solicit and answer any questions. Conduct guided practice as needed. Proceed to instructional step 3 below.]

e. Give the advance organizer for *Complex Sentence Lesson 5A.* "For this lesson you must write simple, compound, and complex sentences. For each of the first six sentences, the formula and the needed conjunctions have been picked for you. Your job is to complete the remaining three 'PENS' Steps. For the last four sentences, the type of sentence is indicated. You must do all four 'PENS' Steps, including picking the formula. Write the formula on the blank to the left of the sentence. You can earn 2 points for matching the formula and 1 point if the sentence is complete and correct. To be complete and correct, your sentence must include beginning capitalization and end punctuation, must make sense, and must have no words missing. You must earn at least 27 points to reach mastery. You should finish this lesson in 25 minutes."

[Solicit and answer any questions. Conduct guided practice as needed.]

3. Direct the students to begin practicing.-9. File completed products. [Follow the instructions on pp. 50-51 for these instructional steps.]

What to require for mastery:
The student must earn at least 90% (27 points) of the 30 points possible on one lesson in each of the *#1, #2, #3, #4,* and *#5 Series.*

Where to go from here:
Progress through the lessons as specified on p. 52. Provide individual feedback after each lesson. With each new lesson, repeat instructional steps 1 through 9 above as appropriate.

When the student completes a lesson in the *#5 Series* at or above the mastery level, congratulate her, and ask her to record the day's date on her *Progress Chart* and the *Management Chart.* Then proceed to STAGE 6: ADVANCED PRACTICE/ POSTTEST AND FEEDBACK with the student.

How to trouble-shoot and respond to inquiries:
If a student continues to make the same error on more than one lesson, have him write a goal *before* he starts each subsequent lesson that reflects his intention to correct the error (e.g., "I will earn all the points for matching the formula today."). Also have him write a one-sentence plan for ensuring that he does not make a particular kind of error (e.g., "I will check each complex sentence to make sure it contains a subordinating conjunction.").

If a student has difficulty thinking of content for sentences in the *#3* and *#5 Series,* provide pictures or other stimuli to generate ideas.

Often, students leave a verb out of the dependent clause. They might write a sentence like, "Before the storm, the sky was gray." Explain that this is not a complex sentence; a verb is needed in the first phrase to form a dependent clause. Usually, students making this type of error are not using the Verb-Subject Identification Procedure on each clause in the sentence. Have the students practice doing the procedure aloud with you listening. Provide feedback as necessary.

PART III: COMPLEX SENTENCES
STAGE 6: ADVANCED PRACTICE/POSTTEST AND FEEDBACK

What your goal is:
- To ensure that students can write simple, compound, and complex sentences in response to a grade-appropriate assignment.

What you need:
- *Complex Sentence Lessons 6A, 6B, 6C, 6D* (the *#6 Series*) (in the *Student Lessons* volume)
- Four lesson folders
- Pictures and other stimuli
- Student folders
- *Cue Cards #1-13* (pp. 153-165)
- Pencils
- *Sentence Scoring Instructions* (pp. 137-143)
- *Sentence Score Sheet* (p. 174) (one per student per lesson)
- *Complex Sentence Checklist* (p. 181) (two per student per lesson)
- *Management Chart for Instruction in Complex Sentences*
- Stapler or paper clips

How to prepare:
1. **Check lesson folders.** Make sure each folder contains sufficient copies of the lessons and stimulus items for your group of students (see p. 54 for a description).
2. **Gather the other materials listed.**
3. **Read the instructions below.**
4. **Plan assignments.** Specify on each student's Assignment Sheet the lesson she is to complete and the stimulus item to be used.

How much time to allow:
Students usually take from 20-30 minutes to complete one lesson in the *#6 Series*. Allow additional time if students must read something first.

What to do:
1. **Review.** [Ensure that student folders are distributed. Using the rapid-fire format, ask students to define a simple sentence, a compound sentence, a complex sentence, an independent clause, and a dependent clause, to name four kinds of simple sentences, two kinds of compound sentences, and two kinds of complex sentences, and to list the *Sentence Writing Strategy* steps. Ask the students when and why they should use the strategy. Then distribute *Lesson 6A*.]

2. **Give an advance organizer.** "You have practiced the isolated skills involved in writing simple, compound, and complex sentences. Now you must practice them while writing a group of sentences about the same topic. For this lesson, write at least six sentences about the topic listed on the Assignment Sheet in your folder. Include at least one compound and two complex sentences in the six sentences. Use all four 'PENS' Steps to write each sentence. You may use your Formula Cards as you work. Use a *Complex Sentence Checklist* to be sure you've included enough simple, compound, and complex sentences. Turn in your *Checklist* with your sentences."

"In order for you to reach mastery, all sentences must address the topic and must be complete and correct; one sentence must be compound, and two must be complex. All must be punctuated correctly."

3. **Direct the students to begin practicing.-9. File completed products.** [Follow the instructions provided for steps 3-9 under STAGE 5: CONTROLLED PRACTICE AND FEEDBACK (pp. 50-51). Encourage students to refer to their Formula Cards as they work. Use the *Sentence Scoring Instructions* (pp. 137-143), a *Sentence Score Sheet,* and a *Complex Sentence Checklist* to evaluate each student's product. Provide individual feedback after each lesson.]

What to require for mastery:

Percentage of complete sentences. One hundred percent (100%) of the sentences must address the topic and be complete, including beginning capitalization and end punctuation.

Percentage of complicated sentences. At least fifty percent (50%) of the sentences must be complicated sentences.

Percentage of correctly punctuated sentences. At least sixty-six percent (66%) of the complicated sentences must be punctuated correctly.

Sentence mix. One sentence must be a compound sentence; two must be complex.

Where to go from here:

If the student meets the mastery requirement on a lesson in the *#6 Series,* congratulate him, and ask him to record the day's date on his *Complex Sentence Progress Chart* and on the *Management Chart.* Proceed to STAGE 7: MAKE COMMITMENTS FOR GENERALIZATION (p. 117).

If the student meets the mastery requirements, wants to learn more about complex sentences, and has the instructional time available, proceed to APPENDIX C: ENRICHMENT ACTIVITIES (p. 183), and then to STAGE 7: MAKE COMMITMENTS FOR GENERALIZATION.

If the student does not meet mastery, assign the next lesson in the series after providing feedback. Make sure a different stimulus or topic is provided for each lesson. Repeat instructional steps 1-9 above with each new lesson.

How to trouble-shoot:

See pp. 52-53 for instructions.

PART IV: COMPOUND-COMPLEX SENTENCES
STAGE 2: DESCRIBE

What your goals are:
To provide students with a description of:
- Requirements for compound-complex sentences.
- Formulas to be used in writing compound-complex sentences.
- Application of the *Sentence Writing Strategy* to the writing of compound-complex sentences.

What you need:
- Chalkboard or other writing surface and appropriate writing implement
- Overhead projector and screen (if using overhead transparencies)
- *Sentence Writing Cue Cards #14-15* (pp. 166-167)
- Student folders (containing Formula Cards and Cue Cards)
- Paper for student notes
- Pencils
- Large calendar
- *Compound-Complex Sentence Progress Chart* (p. 178) (one per student)
- *Management Chart for Instruction in Compound-Complex Sentences* (p. 180)
- Your own Formula Card

How to prepare:
1. **Make a copy of the *Cue Cards* on paper or overhead transparencies.**
2. **Gather the other listed materials.** Make additional copies of the *Compound-Complex Sentence Progress Charts* (p. 178) if necessary. Fill in the words "Compound-Complex" in the blank in the title of the *Management Chart,* and fill in the students' names. Expand your own Formula Card to include the compound-complex sentence formulas.
3. **Familiarize yourself with the instructions below.**

How much time to allow:
Allow approximately 20-30 minutes for presenting the information, depending on whether you are presenting to an individual or a group of students.

What to do:
1. **Review.** [Using the rapid-fire format, ask the students to: (a) define a simple, a compound, and a complex sentence; (b) name four kinds of simple sentences,

two kinds of compound sentences, and two kinds of complex sentences; and (c) list the *Sentence Writing Strategy* steps. Ask them to state when and why they should use the strategy.]

2. Give an advance organizer. "Now that you have mastered the skills involved in writing simple, compound, and complex sentences, you are ready for the fourth type of sentence, the *compound-complex* *sentence*."

[Write "Compound-Complex Sentence" on the board, or show only the title on the transparency of *Cue Card #14*.]

"We will now review why varying the sentences you write is important, set your goals for the coming weeks, go over the requirements for compound-complex sentences, and talk about using the 'PENS' Steps to write compound-complex sentences."

3. Review rationales for using a variety of sentences. "Just like using simple, compound, and complex sentences makes a written product more interesting to read, adding another kind of sentence, the compound-complex sentence, makes it even more interesting. Let's review why we want to make our writing interesting. What benefits could result if your writing appears interesting and sophisticated?"

[Elicit a variety of rationales related to a number of settings: school, community, and employment.]

4. Set goals. "We'll follow the same procedures for learning compound-complex sentences as for the other sentence types. Let's set some goals on your new *Progress Charts* for how fast you want to learn to write compound-complex sentences."

[Distribute student folders, *Compound-Complex Sentence Progress Charts,* and pencils. Follow the instructions on p. 20 to guide the students through the goal-setting process. Suggest the following number of days for each stage:

STAGE 2:	DESCRIBE	1 day
STAGE 3:	MODEL	1 day
STAGE 4:	VERBAL PRACTICE	1-2 days*
STAGE 5:	CONTROLLED PRACTICE AND FEEDBACK	6-24 days*
STAGE 6:	ADVANCED PRACTICE/POSTTEST AND FEEDBACK	1-4 days*
STAGE 7:	MAKE COMMITMENTS FOR GENERALIZATION	1 day
STAGE 8:	GENERALIZATION	10-15 days*]

5. Define a compound-complex sentence. "Sometimes when we write long sentences, they get so long that they turn into run-on sentences. Compound-complex sentences allow us to write long sentences that work and make sense."

---

* The students should choose the number of days that fits their individual learning rates on previous activities. Help them review their learning rates and choose accordingly.

"As the name implies, compound-complex sentences are a combination of compound and complex sentences. They consist of two or more independent clauses and at least one dependent clause."

[Write the definition on the board, or reveal the definition on the transparency of *Cue Card #14*. Prompt the students to make their own Cue Cards from this point on.]

"Most of the compound-complex sentences you are going to write will consist of two independent clauses and one dependent clause."

[Ask the students to provide the definitions of independent and dependent clauses.]

6. **Provide an example of a compound-complex sentence with a coordinating conjunction.** "Let's look now at an example in which independent and dependent clauses are combined to make a compound-complex sentence. In the sentence, 'When you are ready, I will call the store, and we can talk to Reed,'. . . ."

[Write the sentence on the board, or uncover the example on *Cue Card #14.*]

". . . what is the dependent clause?"

[Elicit the answer, "When you are ready," and underline the clause with one line.]

"Right. Name one of the independent clauses in this sentence."

[Elicit one of the remaining clauses as the answer, and underline it with two lines.]

"Good. What is the other independent clause?"

[Elicit the remaining independent clause as the answer, and underline it with two lines.]

"Great. This sentence contains **two independent clauses** (point to them) **and one dependent clause** (point to it)."

[Ask the students to identify the coordinating conjunction, the subordinating conjunction, and the subjects and verbs in each clause.]

7. **Provide an example of a compound-complex sentence with a semicolon.** "The example we just looked at had a coordinating conjunction in it. What's another way to join two independent clauses?"

[Elicit the answer, "With a semicolon."]

"Right. Using a semicolon is another way of making a compound-complex sentence. In the sentence, 'Before the trick-or-treaters came, Jill made candied apples; they were delicious,' . . ."

[Write the sentence on the board, or uncover it on the transparency of *Cue Card #14.*]

". . . we have a dependent clause followed by two independent clauses. The two independent clauses are joined by a semicolon."

[Ask the students to identify the dependent and independent clauses and the subordinating conjunction. Underline the dependent clause with one line and the independent clause with two lines.]

8. **Review the symbols and formulas.** [Ask the students to name the symbols for independent and dependent clauses and the formulas for compound sentences and complex sentences. Write them on the board.]

9. **Explain the sequencing of clauses in compound-complex sentences.** "As you will see, the process of making several kinds of compound-complex sentences consists of putting the formulas for compound sentences and complex sentences together in different combinations. Let's limit our discussion to compound-complex sentences with three clauses (two independent clauses and one dependent clause) because that is the kind of compound-complex sentence you will be required to master. If you want to work on other compound-complex sentence types, you may do so later. Compound-complex sentences with three clauses may be sequenced in a number of ways."

   a. **Explain how the dependent clause can come first.** "Can you design two formulas for compound-complex sentences in which the dependent clause comes first and is followed by two independent clauses?"

   [Prompt the students to design the following formulas complete with punctuation: D,I,cI and D,I;I. Write the formulas on the board.]

   "Good. The example sentences we've looked at fit these formulas."

   [Point to the sentences and ask the students to link each sentence with a formula. Write the formula next to the sentence, and ask the students to write the formulas next to the sentences on their Cue Cards.]

   "Let's look at two more examples."

   [Write the first two sentences from *Cue Card #15* on the board, or reveal them on the transparency of *Cue Card #15*. Ask the students to identify the dependent clause, the independent clauses, the subordinating conjunction, and, if present, the coordinating conjunction. Underline the dependent clause with one line and the independent clause with two lines. Ask the students to link each sentence to a formula. Write the correct formula next to each sentence, and ask them to do the same on their Cue Cards.]

   b. **Explain how the dependent clause can occur between the independent clauses.** "You can also write a compound-complex sentence in which the dependent clause is placed between the two independent clauses. Let's look at some examples of this kind of compound-complex sentence."

   [Write the four sentences that appear on *Cue Card #15* under the heading "Dependent Clause Second" on the board one by one, or uncover them sequentially on the transparency of *Cue Card #15.* For each sentence, ask the students to identify the independent clauses, the dependent clause, the subordinating conjunction, and, if present, the coordinating conjunction. Underline the dependent clause with one line and the independent clauses with two lines.]

"Notice, in this kind of a sentence, a comma and a coordinating conjunction or a semicolon are used between the dependent clause and the independent clause that follows it."

[Point to the comma and coordinating conjunction in the first two sentences and the semicolon in the last two sentences in the examples under the heading "Dependent Clause Second."]

"This is the only time you will see a coordinating conjunction or a semicolon between a dependent clause and an independent clause. They are used here to join the second independent clause to the rest of the sentence in a compound-complex sentence just like they would be used to join the second independent clause to the rest of the sentence in a compound sentence."

"Let's design some formulas for this kind of compound-complex sentence where the dependent clause comes between the two independent clauses."

[Prompt the students to design the following formulas complete with punctuation: ID,cI and ID;I. Write the formulas on the board. Ask the students to link each example sentence on *Cue Card #15* with a formula. Write the appropriate formula next to each example sentence.]

c. **Explain how the dependent clause can come after the two independent clauses.** "The dependent clause can also come after the two independent clauses in a compound-complex sentence. Let's look at some examples of this kind of sentence."

[Write the four sentences that appear on *Cue Card #15* under the heading "Dependent Clause Third" on the board one by one, or uncover them sequentially on the transparency of *Cue Card #15.* For each sentence, ask the students to identify the dependent clause, the independent clauses, the subordinating conjunction, and, if present, the coordinating conjunction. Underline the dependent clause with one line and the independent clauses with two lines.]

"Let's design some formulas for compound-complex sentences in which the dependent clause comes after both independent clauses."

[Prompt the students to design the following formulas complete with punctuation: I,cID and I;ID. Write the formulas on the board. Ask the students to link each example sentence with a formula, and write the appropriate formula next to the sentence.]

d. Summarize the formulas and the punctuation rules. "Notice that we have six formulas: two for sentences where the dependent clause is first, two for sentences where the dependent clause is second, and two for sentences in which the dependent clause comes third. The punctuation rules we learned for compound and complex sentences apply to compound-complex sentences as well."

"What are two ways of connecting two independent clauses?"

[Elicit the responses, "With a comma and coordinating conjunction." and "With a semicolon."]

"Right. What do we use to join a dependent clause in the first position to an independent clause in the second position?"

[Elicit the response, "A comma."]

"What are two ways of joining a dependent clause in the second position to an independent clause in the third position?"

[Elicit the responses, "With a comma and a coordinating conjunction." and "With a semicolon."]

10. **Expand the Formula Cards.** [Ask the students to take out their Formula Cards. Have them add the heading "Compound-Complex Sentences" and the compound-complex sentence formulas to the lower right quadrant of their cards. Show your card as a model. Check each student's card to ensure it is correct.]

11. **Add the formulas to the Cue Cards.** [Have the students add the correct formula next to each example on their copies of the Cue Cards.]

12. **Integrate compound-complex sentences with the *Sentence Writing Strategy* steps.** "Let's discuss how to use the 'PENS' Steps when writing compound-complex sentences."

   a. **Step 1: Pick a formula.** "What's the first step?"

   [Solicit "Pick a formula."]

   "Good. Now you have 14 formulas to choose from on your card. With these 14 formulas you can be a very versatile writer."

   b. **Step 2: Explore words to fit the formula.** "What's the second step?"

   [Elicit the response, "Explore words to fit the formula."]

   "Right. Think of words for both the dependent and the two independent clauses and choose appropriate subordinating and coordinating conjunctions."

   c. **Step 3: Note the words.** "What's the third step?"

[Elicit the response, "Note the words."]

"Correct. When you write your sentence, what do you need to remember to do?"

[Solicit the response, "Capitalize the first letter of the first word, put in commas or a semicolon where needed, and add a period at the end of the sentence."]

"Exactly. Remember, you will not get full credit for the sentence in this class if you leave out the punctuation when it is required."

d. **Step 4: Search and check.** "What's the last step?"

[Elicit the response, "Search and check."]

"Correct. Search through your compound-complex sentence to make sure you have a subject and a verb in each clause. Check to make sure you have a capital letter at the beginning, correct punctuation throughout, and a period at the end. Also be sure to read over the whole sentence one last time to ensure that it makes sense and that no words have been left out."

13. **Give a post-organizer.** "Today we've discussed the requirements and formulas for writing compound-complex sentences and talked about using the 'PENS' Steps for writing complex sentences. Next, I'll model the process for you."

14. **Solicit and answer questions.**

15. **Record the completion dates and file Cue Cards and Formula Cards appropriately in student folders.**

Where to go from here:

After the students have recorded the completion date on their *Compound-Complex Sentence Progress Charts* and on the *Management Chart,* immediately proceed to STAGE 3: MODEL, if time allows. Otherwise, begin the next instructional session with STAGE 3: MODEL.

PART IV: COMPOUND-COMPLEX SENTENCES
STAGE 3: MODEL

What your goal is:
- To demonstrate the writing of compound-complex sentences using the *Sentence Writing Strategy* while thinking aloud, so students can witness all the processes involved.

What you need:
- Chalkboard or other writing surface and appropriate writing implement
- Your own Formula Card
- *Cue Cards #14-15* (pp. 166-167)
- Student folders
- *Management Chart for Instruction in Compound-Complex Sentences*

How to prepare:
1. **Gather the needed materials.**
2. **Familiarize yourself with the instructions below.**
3. **Practice using the strategy.** Go through the demonstration yourself a few times to become fluent at using the *Sentence Writing Strategy* steps for compound-complex sentences. Your demonstration should appear spontaneous, so be well prepared.
4. **Think of content for the sentences in your demonstration.** Select some topics for the sentences you and your students will write together.

How much time to allow:
Allow approximately 10-15 minutes for the demonstration.

What to do:
1. **Review the *Sentence Writing Strategy.*** * [Ensure that the student folders have been distributed, and conduct a quick review. Using the rapid-fire format, ask the students to: define a simple sentence, a compound sentence, a complex sentence, a compound-complex sentence, an independent clause, and a dependent clause; name the strategy steps, the four kinds of simple sentences, the two kinds of compound sentences, the two kinds of complex sentences, and six kinds of compound-complex sentences; specify where they can use the strat-

---

* This review is not necessary if you conduct these activities on the same day as STAGE 2: DESCRIBE.

egy; and explain how the strategy can help them. Refer them to their Cue Cards if necessary.]

2. **Give an advance organizer.** "Now I will show you how to use the *Sentence Writing Strategy* in writing complex sentences. Listen and watch carefully because I will expect you to talk to yourself and do everything exactly as I do it."

3. **Demonstrate writing a compound-complex sentence using the *Sentence Writing Strategy.*** "To begin I'll say, 'Sentence writing: PENS.' "

   a. **Step 1: Pick a formula:** " 'P' stands for 'Pick a formula', so I'll look at my Formula Card . . ."

   [Look at your Formula Card.]

   ". . . and I'll choose the first kind of compound-complex sentence: the one with the dependent clause first and a comma and a coordinating conjunction between the independent clauses."

   [Point to the "D,I,cI" formula.]

   b. **Steps 2 and 3: Explore words to fit the formula and note the words.** "Now I'm ready for the 'E' Step; I'll explore some words. Let's see, I want to write a sentence about what you have to do to be a safe traveler in a snowstorm. I'll use the word 'when' for my subordinating conjunction. For the dependent clause, I'll say 'When a snowstorm is raging'. Since this is going to be a long sentence, I'll skip ahead to Step 3 and note the words for the first clause right away, so I won't forget them."

   [Write the words "When a snowstorm is raging," on the board or on a transparency. As you write the clause, remind yourself at the appropriate time to capitalize the first word and put a comma at the end of the clause.]

   "Now I must explore words for an independent clause. Hmm . . . how about 'you should drive very slowly'? That sounds good. So I'll write those words down."

   [Write "you should drive very slowly" on the board or on a transparency following the first clause.]

   "Now I need to think of a coordinating conjunction and another independent clause. I'll use the word 'and' and add, 'you should stop regularly to clean snow off the windows.' I'll write that down."

   [Write, ", and you should stop regularly to clean snow off the windows." on the board or on the transparency following the first two clauses. As you write the clause, remind yourself at the appropriate times to add the comma before the coordinating conjunction and the period at the end of the sentence.]

   c. **Step 4: Search and check.** "Now I'll do the 'S' Step to check my sentence. First, I'll compare the sentence to the formula for the compound-complex sentence I chose. Do I have three groups of words separated by commas? Yes. Do I have a subordinating conjunction at the beginning and a coordinating conjunction between the last two clauses? Yes."

"Next, I'll use the Verb-Subject Identification Procedure on the dependent clause which is made up of all the words in front of the first comma. I need to look for the action or state-of-being word or words. They are 'is raging.' Next, I'll ask myself, 'Who or what is raging?'; the answer is 'snowstorm.' I have a subject and a verb in the dependent clause."

"Now I'll apply the Verb-Subject Identification Procedure to the words occurring *between* the two commas. Hmm . . . 'should drive' is the verb. Who or what should drive? You. 'You' is the subject. Thus, I have a subject and a verb in the first independent clause."

"Next, I need to check the last independent clause. Hmm . . . 'should stop' is the verb. Who or what should stop? You. 'You' is the subject. Thus, I have a subject and a verb in each of the three clauses. It all checks out."

"Finally, I'll read the whole sentence through one last time. I see that I have a capital letter at the beginning, commas where I need them, and a period at the end. I haven't left out any words, and it makes sense. Great."

4. **Involve the students in the demonstration.** [For two or three of the remaining types of compound-complex sentences, ask the students what to do next and to suggest responses for each strategy step. Assign a general topic about which the sentence is to be written, but ask the students to choose the formulas and come up with the subjects and verbs, the subordinating and coordinating conjunctions, and the final wording of the sentence. Have a student write the sentence on the board; ask other students to check it. Provide corrective feedback as needed.]

5. **Give the post-organizer.** "Now we have learned about the requirements for compound-complex sentences, and you have seen how to use the *Sentence Writing Strategy* to write several kinds of compound-complex sentences. Tomorrow we'll do verbal rehearsal."

6. **Solicit and answer questions.**

7. **Record the completion date for Stage 3.** [Ask the students to record the day's date for completion of Stage 3 on their *Compound-Complex Sentence Progress Charts* and on the *Management Chart.*]

Where to go from here:

After all questions have been answered and completion dates have been recorded, go to STAGE 4: VERBAL PRACTICE.

PART IV: COMPOUND-COMPLEX SENTENCES
STAGE 4: VERBAL PRACTICE

What your goals are:
- To ensure that students have memorized the requirements for compound-complex sentences and understand the concepts involved in writing them.
- To review the steps of the *Sentence Writing Strategy* and ensure that students still know them.

What you need:
- Chalkboard or other writing surface and appropriate writing implement
- Student folders
- *Compound-Complex Sentence Verbal Practice Checklist* (p. 178) (one per student)
- *Compound-Complex Sentence Quiz* (in the *Student Lessons* volume) (one per student)
- *Cue Cards #14-15* (pp. 166-167)
- *Management Chart for Instruction in Compound-Complex Sentences*

How to prepare:
1. **Check your supply of *Compound-Complex Sentence Verbal Practice Checklists* and *Compound-Complex Sentence Quizzes.*** If necessary, make additional copies.
2. **Gather the other materials listed above.**
3. **Familiarize yourself with the instructions below.**

How much time to allow:
Most students will reach mastery on the definitions within 25 minutes of instructional time. Some students may need more time. The written quiz takes approximately 10-15 minutes to complete, and most students reach mastery on the first attempt.

What to do:
1. **Review.** [Using the rapid-fire format, ask the students to name the *Sentence Writing Strategy* steps, to define a compound-complex sentence, an independent clause, a dependent clause, a coordinating and a subordinating conjunction, and to name the six kinds of compound-complex sentences. Write their responses on the board.]

2. **Give an advance organizer.** "Today you will memorize the requirements for writing compound-complex sentences and take an oral and a

written quiz over compound-complex sentences. If you know the requirements well, you will be able to tell yourself what to do when you write a compound-complex sentence."

3. Conduct rapid-fire verbal rehearsal of the strategy steps. "Before we begin, let's review the 'PENS' Steps using the rapid-fire technique."

[Erase the steps from the board and conduct rapid-fire verbal rehearsal for several rounds following the instructions on pp. 42-43. Stop when most of the students can name the steps.]

4. Conduct a rapid-fire question-and-answer exercise to memorize the requirements for compound complex-sentences.* "Now let's use the rapid-fire technique to memorize the definitions and requirements for compound-complex sentences. I'll ask a question, and, if I point to you, you are to answer that question as quickly as possible. Here are the questions and the answers."**

1. What's a compound-complex sentence?
   A sentence with two or more independent clauses and at least one dependent clause.
2. What's an independent clause?
   A group of words with a subject and a verb that can stand alone.
3. What's a dependent clause?
   A group of words with a subject and a verb that cannot stand alone.
4. What's a coordinating conjunction?
   A word that connects two "I" clauses.
5. What's a subordinating conjunction?
   The word that relates the "D" clause to the "I" clause.
6. Name one kind of compound-complex sentence.***

D,Icl	ID,cI	I,cID
D,I;I	ID;I	I;ID

7. What punctuation goes between two "I" clauses that are connected with a coordinating conjunction?
   A comma.
8. What punctuation goes between two "I" clauses that are not connected with a coordinating conjunction?
   A semicolon.
9. What punctuation goes between a dependent clause and an independent clause if the dependent clause is first and the independent clause is second?
   A comma.

---

* If you are working with one student, she can rehearse the questions and answers on her own using either the list provided here or 3″ × 5″ cards for self-testing. See the footnote on p. 42 for suggestions on how to work with a large class.
** The answers should be similar to what you have written on the board for the review.
*** Ask this question six times.

If the independent clause is first and the dependent clause is second?
No comma.
If the dependent clause is second and the independent clause is third?
A comma or a semicolon.

[Solicit and answer questions.]

"O.K., let's begin."

[Conduct the rapid-fire exercise as for complex sentences. After several rounds with answers on the board, erase them. Start each new round with a different person. Continue until the students appear to have learned the requirements.]

5. **Allow time for individual review.** [After the group verbal-rehearsal exercise, allow the students time for individual review. Explain that they must be able to: define a compound-complex sentence, an independent clause, a dependent clause, a coordinating conjunction, and a subordinating conjunction; name six kinds of compound-complex sentences; and explain the punctuation rules without help. Finally, they have to get at least 90% of their answers correct on the written quiz.]

6. **Conduct the oral quizzes.*** [Using the *Compound-Complex Sentence Verbal Practice Checklist,* conduct individual oral quizzes when the students are ready. Determine the percentage of questions they answer correctly.]

7. **Conduct the written quiz.** [When a student passes the oral quiz (see the mastery criterion below), have him complete the *Compound-Complex Sentence Quiz.* Determine the percentage of questions answered correctly by using the table on p. 149.]

8. **Provide feedback.** [Review the results of the oral and written quizzes with the student. Provide positive and corrective feedback as necessary. Have the student plot the percentage of questions answered correctly on the *Compound-Complex Sentence Quiz* on the *Compound-Complex Sentence Progress Chart* on the vertical line above the "Q."]

What to require for mastery:

To reach mastery, the student must correctly answer 100% of the questions on the oral quiz and at least 90% of the questions on the written quiz without referring to a Cue Card and without receiving other assistance.

Where to go from here:

If the student achieves mastery, ask her to record the completion date on her *Compound-Complex Sentence Progress Chart* and on the *Management Chart.* Have her place the *Verbal Practice Checklist* and quiz in her folder, and proceed to STAGE 5: CONTROLLED PRACTICE AND FEEDBACK.

If the student does not achieve mastery on the oral quiz, provide feedback, and ask him to rehearse the correct definitions alone or with a peer. Give the student additional oral quizzes until he reaches mastery.

---

* See p. 44 for an alternative procedure for large classes.

If the student does not achieve mastery on the written quiz, review the pertinent concepts with the student orally. Ask her to answer oral questions similar to those on the written quiz until it is clear that she understands the concepts. Have her retake the written quiz.

How to trouble-shoot:

Help students figure out ways to remember the definitions or answers they have forgotten. Prompt the students to use memorization techniques to help them remember the required information (see p. 45 for some suggestions). Students must know the terms to facilitate the feedback process.

PART IV: COMPOUND-COMPLEX SENTENCES
STAGE 5: CONTROLLED PRACTICE AND FEEDBACK

What your goals are:

- To ensure the students master the skills involved in writing six types of compound-complex sentences.
- To ensure the students can integrate the skills of writing simple, compound, complex, and compound-complex sentences.

What you need:

- *Compound-Complex Sentence Lessons 1A, 1B, 1C, 1D* (the *#1 Series*), *2A, 2B, 2C, 2D* (the *#2 Series*), *3A, 3B, 3C, 3D* (the *#3 Series*), *4A, 4B, 4C, 4D* (the *#4 Series*), *5A, 5B, 5C, 5D* (the *#5 Series*), and *6A, 6B, 6C, 6D* (the *#6 Series*) (in the *Student Lessons* volume)
- *Evaluation Guidelines* and *Answer Keys* for the lessons listed above (in the *Student Lessons* volume)
- Twenty-four lesson folders for *Compound-Complex Lessons 1A-6D* (see p. 9 for description)
- Student folders
- Pencils
- *Cue Cards #1-15* (pp. 153-167)
- *Management Chart for Instruction in Compound-Complex Sentences*

How to prepare:

1. **Check your lesson folders.** If necessary, make additional copies of the lessons (see p. 9 for a description of the lesson folders).
2. **Gather the other materials listed.**
3. **Familiarize yourself with the instructions below.**
4. **Plan assignments.** Determine for each student the next lesson to be completed. Record the assignment on the Assignment Sheet in the student's folder.

How much time to allow:

Compound-Complex Sentence Lessons in the *#1* and *#5 Series* take about 10 minutes to complete. In the *#2, #3, #4,* and *#6 Series,* lessons require approximately 15-25 minutes. Some students will finish in as few as six days; others may take up to 24 days.

What to do:

1. Review the *Sentence Writing Strategy.* [Ensure that student folders are distributed. Using the rapid-fire format, ask the students to: define a simple sentence, a compound sentence, a complex sentence, a compound-complex sentence, and an independent clause; name four kinds of simple sentences, two kinds of compound sentences, two kinds of complex sentences, and six kinds of compound-complex sentences; and list the *Sentence Writing Strategy* steps. Ask them when and why they should use the strategy.]

2. Give an advance organizer. [Give one of the following advance organizers, as appropriate, when a student begins a new type of lesson and after the student has obtained a copy of the lesson.]

a. Give an advance organizer for *Compound-Complex Sentence Lesson 1A.* *"Lesson 1A* requires that you determine what kind of a compound-complex sentence has been written. Underline the independent clauses with two lines and the dependent clause with one line, and write the formula for the sentence on the blank to the left of the sentence. You can earn 2 points for each formula and 1 point for identifying the clauses correctly. You must earn 90% of the points possible on this lesson (27 points) to reach mastery and move to a different lesson. You must master six different kinds of lessons for compound-complex sentences before moving on to Advanced Practice. You should finish this lesson in 10 to 15 minutes."

[Solicit and answer questions. Conduct guided practice as needed. Proceed to instructional step 3 below.]

b. Give the advance organizer for *Compound-Complex Sentence Lesson 2A.* "In this next lesson, the formula and the needed conjunction have been picked for you, and two clauses of the sentence have been written. Your job is to write a clause to make the sentence match the listed formula and to add any needed punctuation. The clause you add must make sense within the context of the clauses that are already written. No clauses will be accepted that do not make sense when put together with the clause that's already written. For the first sentence on this sheet, you must add a comma, the coordinating conjunction 'but,' and an independent clause at the end. One independent clause and a dependent clause have already been written. For the second sentence, you must add the subordinating conjunction 'after' and a dependent clause at the end. Be sure to check your work. Use the Verb-Subject Identification Procedure, and mark the verbs in your added clause with a 'V' and the subjects in your added clause with an 'S'."

"You will earn 1 point if your sentence matches the listed formula and includes the required conjunction, 1 point if it is complete and correct, and 1 point if you mark the verbs and subjects in your added clause correctly. To be complete and correct, your sentence must include end punctuation, your added clause must make sense by itself and when attached to the other clauses, and there can be no words missing. Again, you must earn 90% (27 points) of the points possible to reach mastery on this lesson. You should finish in about 15 minutes."

[Solicit and answer any questions. Conduct guided practice as needed. Proceed to instructional step 3 below.]

c. **Give the advance organizer for *Compound-Complex Sentence Lesson 3A.*** "In this lesson, the formula and the subordinating and coordinating conjunctions have been picked for you, and the first clause of the sentence has been written. Write two clauses that go with the first, and add any needed punctuation. The clauses you add must make sense within the context of the clause that is already written. For the first sentence, the dependent clause has been written. You need to add two independent clauses separated by the conjunction 'for.' For the second sentence, an independent clause has been written. Therefore, you need to add an independent clause that starts with the coordinating conjunction 'nor,' the subordinating conjunction 'unless,' and a dependent clause. Be sure to check your work using the Verb-Subject Identification Procedure. Mark each complete verb in your added clauses with a 'V' and each main subject with an 'S.' "

"You will earn 1 point if your sentence matches the listed formula and includes the required conjunctions, 1 point if the sentence is complete and correct, and 1 point if you mark the verbs and subjects in your added clauses correctly. To be complete and correct, your sentence must include beginning capitalization and end punctuation, your added clauses must make sense when attached to the first clause and each other, and there can be no words missing. You must earn at least 27 points for mastery. You should finish this lesson in 15 to 20 minutes."

[Solicit and answer any questions. Conduct guided practice as needed. Proceed to instructional step 3 below.]

d. **Give the advance organizer for *Compound-Complex Sentence Lesson 4A.*** "For this lesson, you will write 10 compound-complex sentences. For the first eight sentences, the formulas and conjunctions have been picked for you, so your job is to complete the remaining three strategy steps. For the last two sentences, you should do all four 'PENS' Steps, including picking the formula. Write the formula on the blank to the left of the last two sentences. You will also have to choose the conjunctions for these two sentences. Your sentences can be about any topic, but they must be different, and they must make sense."

"You will earn 2 points for each sentence that matches the formula and 1 point for each sentence that is complete and correct. To be complete and correct, your sentence must include beginning capitalization and end punctuation, must make sense, and must have no words missing. You must earn at least 27 points to reach mastery. You should finish this lesson in about 25 minutes."

[Solicit and answer questions. Conduct guided practice as needed. Proceed to instructional step 3 below.]

e. Give the advance organizer for *Compound-Complex Sentence Lesson 5A*. "This lesson requires that you determine the kind of sentence that has been written. Some of the sentences are simple, some are compound, some are complex, while others are compound-complex. Underline the independent clauses with two lines and the dependent clause with one line; write the correct formula in the blank to the left of the sentence. You can earn 2 points for the correct formula and 1 point for underlining the clauses correctly. You must earn at least 27 points for mastery. You should finish this lesson in 10 to 15 minutes."

[Solicit and answer any questions. Conduct guided practice as needed. Proceed to instructional step 3 below.]

f. Give the advance organizer for *Compound-Complex Sentence Lesson 6A*. "For this lesson, you are to write simple, compound, complex, and compound-complex sentences. For each of the first six sentences, the formula and the necessary conjunctions have been picked for you. You need to complete the remaining three 'PENS' Steps yourself. For the last four sentences, the type of sentence has been indicated. You will need to do all four 'PENS' Steps for these four sentences. Write the formula that you choose in the blank to the left of the sentence. Your sentences can be about any topic, but they must be different from each other. You will earn 2 points if your sentence matches the formula and 1 point if the sentence is complete and correct. To be complete and correct, your sentence must include beginning capitalization and end punctuation, must make sense, and must have no words missing. You must earn at least 27 points to reach mastery. You should finish this lesson in about 25 minutes."

[Solicit and answer any questions. Conduct guided practice as needed.]

3. Direct the students to begin practicing.-9. File completed products. [Follow the instructions on pp. 51-52 for these instructional steps.]

What to require for mastery:

The student must earn at least 90% (27 points) of the 30 points possible on one lesson in each of the *#1, #2, #3, #4, #5,* and *#6 Series.*

Where to go from here:

Progress through the lessons as specified on p. 52. Provide individual feedback after each lesson. Repeat instructional steps 1 through 9 above, as appropriate, with each new lesson.

When the student completes a lesson in the *#6 Series* at or above the mastery level, congratulate her, and ask her to record the day's date on her *Progress Chart* and the *Management Chart*. Then proceed to STAGE 6: ADVANCED PRACTICE/ POSTTEST AND FEEDBACK with the student.

How to trouble-shoot:

If a student continues to make the same error on more than one lesson, have him write a goal *before* he starts each subsequent lesson that reflects his intention to correct the error (e.g., "I will earn all the points for matching the formula today."). Also have him write a one-sentence plan for reaching the goal (e.g., "I will check each compound-complex sentence to make sure it contains both a subordinating conjunction and a coordinating conjunction.").

If a student has difficulty thinking of content for sentences in the *#4* and *#6 Series,* provide pictures or other stimuli to generate ideas.

If a student has difficulty thinking of content for a sentence with the provided conjunctions in the *#4 Series,* allow her to choose her own conjunctions.

PART IV: COMPOUND-COMPLEX SENTENCES
STAGE 6: ADVANCED PRACTICE/POSTTEST AND FEEDBACK

What your goal is:

- To ensure that students can write simple, compound, complex, and compound-complex sentences in response to a grade-appropriate assignment.

What you need:

- *Compound-Complex Sentence Lessons 7A, 7B, 7C, 7D (the #7 Series)* (in the *Student Lessons* volume)
- Four lesson folders
- Pictures and other stimuli
- Student folders
- *Cue Cards #1-15* (pp. 153-167)
- Pencils
- *Sentence Scoring Instructions* (pp. 137-143)
- *Sentence Score Sheet* (p. 174) (one per student per lesson)
- *Sentence Checklist* (p. 181) (two per student per lesson)
- *Management Chart for Instruction in Compound-Complex Sentences*
- Stapler or paper clips

How to prepare:

1. **Check your lesson folders.** Make sure each folder contains sufficient copies of the lessons and stimulus items for your group of students (see p. 54 for a description).
2. **Gather the other materials listed.**
3. **Read the instructions below.**
4. **Plan assignments.** Specify on each student's Assignment Sheet the lesson she is to complete and the stimulus item to be used.

How much time to allow:

Students usually take from 20-30 minutes to complete one lesson in the *#7 Series*. Allow additional time if they must read something first.

What to do:

1. **Review.** [Ensure that student folders are distributed. Using the rapid-fire format, ask the students to: define a simple sentence, a compound sentence, a com-

114

plex sentence, a compound-complex sentence, and an independent and a dependent clause; name four kinds of simple sentences, two kinds of compound sentences, two kinds of complex sentences, and six kinds of compound-complex sentences; and list the *Sentence Writing Strategy* steps. Ask students to specify when and why they should use the strategy. Then distribute *Lesson 7A*.]

2. **Give an advance organizer.** "You have practiced writing simple, compound, complex, and compound-complex sentences in isolation. Now you must practice these skills while writing a group of sentences about the same topic. For the next lesson, write at least six sentences about the topic listed on the *Assignment Sheet* in your folder. Include at least one compound, one complex, and one compound-complex sentence. You must use all the 'PENS' Steps as you write each sentence. You may use your Formula Card as you work. Use a *Sentence Checklist* to be sure you've included enough compound, complex, and compound-complex sentences. Attach your *Checklist* to your product before you turn it in to me."

"In order for you to reach mastery, your sentences must address the topic, be complete, and make sense. One sentence must be a compound sentence, one must be a complex sentence, and one must be a compound-complex sentence. You should finish this task in about 20 to 25 minutes."

3. **Direct the students to begin practicing.-9. File completed products.** [Follow the instructions provided for steps 3-9 under Stage 5: Controlled Practice and Feedback (pp. 50-51). Encourage students to refer to their Formula Cards as they work. Use the *Sentence Scoring Instructions* (pp. 137-143), a *Sentence Score Sheet,* and a *Sentence Checklist* to evaluate each student's product. Provide individual feedback after each lesson.]

What to require for mastery:

Percentage of complete sentences. One hundred percent (100%) of the sentences must be complete; they must all be about the topic and make sense. To be accepted, sentences must have beginning capitalization and end punctuation.

Percentage of complicated sentences. At least fifty percent (50%) of the sentences must be complicated sentences.

Percentage of correctly punctuated complicated sentences. At least sixty-six percent (66%) of the complicated sentences must be punctuated correctly.

Sentence mix. One sentence must be a compound sentence, one must be a complex sentence, and one must be a compound-complex sentence.

Where to go from here:

If the student meets the requirements on any given lesson in the *#7 Series,* congratulate him and ask him to record the day's date cn his *Compound-Complex Sentence Progress Chart* and on the *Management Chart.* Proceed to STAGE 7: MAKE COMMITMENTS FOR GENERALIZATION (p. 117).

If the student meets the mastery requirements, wants to learn more about compound-complex sentences, and has the instructional time available, proceed to APPENDIX C: ENRICHMENT ACTIVITIES (p. 183), and then to STEP 7: MAKE COMMITMENTS FOR GENERALIZATION.

If the student does not meet mastery, assign the next lesson in the series after providing feedback. Assign a different stimulus or topic for each lesson. Repeat instructional steps 1-9 above with each new lesson.

How to trouble-shoot:
See pp. 52-53 for instructions.

STAGE 7: MAKE COMMITMENTS FOR GENERALIZATION

What your goals are:
- To review individual student progress.
- To obtain student commitment to use the strategy in a wide variety of situations and circumstances.
- To make a commitment to help the student generalize the strategy.

What you need:
- Student's pretest and most recent Advanced Practice assignment (these writing samples should be in the student's folder)
- Student's IEP file
- Paper
- Pencil

How to prepare:
1. **Review the student's work to date.** Compare the pretest to the student's most recent writing sample. Think of several ways in which the writing has improved.
2. **Gather the other needed materials.**
3. **Familiarize yourself with the instructions below.**

How much time to allow:
Allow approximately 5-10 minutes to speak individually with each student.

What to do:
1. **Give an advance organizer.** "Now that you have mastered writing several kinds of sentences, we need to review your progress and determine where we go from here."
2. **Contrast the writing samples.*** [Ask the student to take out her pretest and her most recent writing assignment. Ask her to contrast the two samples and to point out some ways in which her writing has improved. If necessary, prompt the student to name at least three ways in which her writing has improved.]
3. **Obtain the student's commitment to generalize.** "You have done a wonderful job learning to use the *Sentence Writing Strategy* to write cer-

---

* If you have a large group of students who have met mastery at the same time, ask them to list at least three ways their writing has improved on a sheet of paper. Circulate among the students, and provide help and feedback as they complete this task.

tain kinds of sentences. You now have a tool for writing down your thoughts wherever and whenever you are required or want to do so. You have worked hard and invested several weeks to acquire this tool. Such an investment should be used in a way that pays off. How do you intend to use your investment?"

[Elicit a response from the student regarding when or where he intends to use the strategy.]

"Great! I'm glad to see you're already thinking of ways to use the strategy. That means you are ready to begin STAGE 8: GENERALIZATION where you will learn to use the *Sentence Writing Strategy* in a variety of situations. Before we move on to that stage, however, you need to write a goal for your IEP file about where you plan to use the *Sentence Writing Strategy*."

[Help the student write a goal specifying where she will use the strategy to write the kind(s) of sentences she has learned and the intended outcome (e.g., improved grades). Have the student sign the goal and place the goal sheet in her IEP folder.]

4. **Make your commitment.** "I'm glad you're committed to making a further investment in your writing, and you know what? I'm committed to working with you to help you reach this goal."

[Write a statement to that effect on the student's goal sheet, and sign it.]

5. **Record the completion date and adjust goals.** [Have the student record the day's date on his current *Progress Chart* under Stage 7. Ask him whether he needs to adjust the goal date for Stage 8 (he should allow about 2-3 weeks for this stage). If necessary, have him change the goal date. Ask him to refile his pretest and most recent writing sample in his folder. Have him record the day's date on the *Management Chart* under "Make Commitments for Generalization." Ask him to bring his notebooks from all his regular classes to your next meeting.]

What to require:

The student must write a goal specifying the situations in which he will use the *Sentence Writing Strategy* and the kinds of sentences he has learned. The goal should also specify the intended outcome of using the newly acquired skills.

Where to go from here:

Proceed to STAGE 8: GENERALIZATION, PHASE I: ORIENTATION.

STAGE 8: GENERALIZATION
PHASE I: ORIENTATION

What your goal is:
- To make the students aware of situations and circumstances in which the *Sentence Writing Strategy* can be used.

What you need:
- Chalkboard or other writing surface and writing implement
- 4" × 6" cards
- A selection of assignment sheets and tests from regular classes, job applications, accident reports, and other materials that require the respondent to write sentences
- Students' notebooks from current courses
- Tape for affixing 4" × 6" Cue Cards to notebook covers
- Student folders
- Paper
- Pencils
- *Sentence Checklist* (p. 181) (several per student)
- 5" or 6" envelopes (2 or 3 per student)
- Current *Management Chart*

How to prepare:
1. **Ask the students to bring their notebooks to class.** Remind students to bring their notebooks from current courses to class.
2. **Gather the other materials.** In addition to materials from a variety of settings that require sentence writing, gather the other materials listed. Copy additional *Sentence Checklists* (p. 181) that correspond to the types of sentences your students have learned (e.g., if your students have learned to write simple sentences, prepare *Simple Sentence Checklists*). Prepare at least 30 checklists per student.
3. **Familiarize yourself with the instructions below.**

How much time to allow:
Allow approximately 25-30 minutes for a group discussion or about 10 minutes for a discussion with an individual.

What to do:
1. **Give an advance organizer.** "You have invested a lot of time in learning to write new kinds of sentences using the *Sentence Writing Strategy*. Now you're going to learn how to use that investment wisely. Today we'll discuss situations where you might write the kinds of sentences you have learned; we're going to get ready to recognize those situations and use the strategy."

2. Discuss situations where the strategy is applicable. [Distribute the materials you have gathered. Ask the students how and where they might apply the *Sentence Writing Strategy* and the kind(s) of applicable sentences they have learned. Ask them to name other situations in their present or future lives (e.g., home, school, employment, community, work) where they could make use of the strategy. Ask them if they've already tried using the strategy and, if so, how it worked for them.]

3. Discuss using the strategy in a flexible manner. [Ask the students how they might use the *Sentence Writing Strategy* in combination with other strategies they have learned. Explore the sequences they would use in combining various strategies to complete a task.

Explain how, even during a test, the students can write down the formulas in the margin of the test paper to help them write their sentences. Ask them if they have any other suggestions about how to use the strategy flexibly.]

4. Discuss current courses and cues in those courses for strategy use. [Distribute a sheet of paper to each student. Ask students to list on the paper their current courses, leaving a space under each course name. Have them think about each course and list the kinds of assignments, tests, and other requirements for which sentence writing is necessary. Also ask them to list next to each requirement the cues they should listen for to determine whether or not to use the *Sentence Writing Strategy* (e.g., the teacher says, "Today I want you to write a paragraph about the war" or "For this week's assignment, you'll need to write a book report"). Ask the students to also generate cues to listen for in other settings and to add them to their list. Have them keep their lists in their notebooks. Suggest that they expand their lists as they recognize additional cues.]

5. Have the students make Cue Cards. [Distribute 4" × 6" cards to the students, and ask them to take their previously made Formula Cards out of their student folders. Have the students make a Cue Card with the 'PENS' Steps and a Formula Card for each current course that requires sentence writing. If they have already done this, ask them to add new formulas to previously made Formula Cards. Have the students affix the Cue Card and the Formula Card to the inside cover of their respective notebooks. Point out that each time they open their notebooks to get paper for a writing assignment, the cards should cue them to use the *Sentence Writing Strategy.*]

6. Have the students insert *Sentence Checklists* in their notebooks. [Distribute envelopes and *Sentence Checklists*. Have students affix an envelope to the inside cover of the notebooks they use for classes in which writing is required. Have them insert several *Sentence Checklists* in each envelope. (If they have already done so, have them replace any extra *Sentence Checklists* for a previous unit with new checklists from the most recent unit.) Stress to the students that each time they write something, they should use a *Sentence Checklist* to check whether they have used a variety of sentences.]

What to require:

Each student should have compiled a list of situations and cues for using the *Sentence Writing Strategy* and should have attached a Cue Card, a Formula Card, an envelope, and *Sentence Checklists* to the inside cover of each of his notebooks.

Where to go from here:

Once the requirements are met, have the student record the day's date on the current *Management Chart* under "Generalization: Orientation." Proceed to STAGE 8: GENERALIZATION, PHASE II: ACTIVATION.

STAGE 8: GENERALIZATION
PHASE II: ACTIVATION

What your goal is:

- To ensure that students apply the *Sentence Writing Strategy* in a variety of settings and circumstances.

What you need:

- A variety of stimulus materials, including job applications, regular class assignments, etc.
- "Report of Strategy Use" forms (see instructions below) (at least 4 per student)
- Student folders
- *Sentence Score Sheets* (p. 174) (several per student)
- *Sentence Scoring Instructions* (pp. 137-143)
- *Sentence Checklists* (p. 181) (several per student)
- *Generalization Progress Chart* (p. 179) (one per student)

How to prepare:

1. **Gather and familiarize yourself with the requirements of the assignments or other tasks.** Obtain job applications from a variety of sources in your community. Identify some that require the applicant to respond in sentences and make copies. Speak to several of each student's teachers about upcoming writing assignments. Become familiar with the requirements for these writing assignments and obtain stimulus materials and due dates from the teachers involved.

2. **Obtain a sample of the student's writing in other classes.** As you talk with the student's other teachers, explain the need to check whether the student is generalizing her use of sentence-writing skills. Obtain a sample of the student's writing from at least one class.

3. **Plan assignments.** Plan an assignment for each student that requires the student to write at least 6 sentences. If an assignment in one of the student's classes is due soon, use that. If not, create an assignment based on a job application or some other stimulus material (e.g., a newspaper article, a questionnaire you received in the mail, a letter the student must answer). Require that the student use other mastered strategies in combination with the *Sentence Writing Strategy.* For example, ask the student to use the *Paraphrasing Strategy* on a magazine article and write a letter to the editor of the magazine about her thoughts on the article. Write the student's assignment on the Assignment Sheet (see p. 47 for a description of an Assignment Sheet) in her folder. Specify on the Assignment Sheet where the assignment is to be completed. Put stimulus materials needed for an assignment in the student's folder.

4. Make "Report of Strategy Use" forms. Make a form with the title "Report of Strategy Use" at the top and places for recording the student's name, date, setting in which the strategy was used, and title of the assignment. Make the necessary number of copies of these forms (at least 4 per student).

5. Gather the other listed materials. Check your supplies of *Sentence Score Sheets, Sentence Checklists,* and *Generalization Progress Charts.* If necessary, make additional copies. Fill in the student's name and the title on each *Progress Chart.* A new *Generalization Progress Chart* is to be used each time a student masters one of the sentence types.

How much time to allow:

For the first day, allow about 10-15 minutes to explain the nature of the assignments you will be giving. Thereafter, allow about 5-10 minutes per day to review the previous day's assignment with each student individually and about 2-3 minutes to give a new assignment. Since the purpose of these activities is to encourage students to use the *Sentence Writing Strategy* in other settings and with a variety of materials, assignments should not be completed in your instructional setting under your supervision. Thus, you do not need to schedule instructional time for completion of the assignments.

What to do:

1. Give an advance organizer. "Yesterday, we talked about how you are going to make your investment in learning the *Sentence Writing Strategy* pay off. Today, we will begin making sure it pays off. Name some situations in which you intend to use the *Sentence Writing Strategy.*"

[Elicit responses.]

"That's good. You should begin using it every time you are required to write one or more sentences."

2. Review the writing sample. [Using a *Sentence Checklist,* review with each student at least one product from the student's other classes. Evaluate the product jointly. Discuss whether or not the student is using all the skills he has learned. Congratulate the student if he is. If not, encourage him to apply the *Sentence Writing Strategy* to future products. Explain that you will be reviewing products from other classes on a regular basis.]

3. Explain assignments. "For the next several days, I am going to give you a daily writing assignment to be completed somewhere other than here. You are to complete the assignment using the *Sentence Writing Strategy* and a mixture of the sentence types you have learned. I will not remind you to use the *Sentence Writing Strategy.* You must remind yourself to use both the strategy and a *Sentence Checklist* to check your work. On the day after I have given you an assignment, I will check your written product and your *Sentence Checklist.* Your sentence writing grade for the day will depend on how well you've used a mixture of the sentence types you know."

"To reach mastery, you must write at least six sentences and use at least _____ * sentence types; all your sentences must be complete sentences for you to get full credit for an assignment."

"I expect you to make the assignment as neat as you would if it were to be handed in to one of your regular teachers. Each sentence should be capitalized and punctuated correctly, and everything should be neatly written. You must complete six assignments at the mastery level to finish this step in the strategy-learning process."

[Conduct a comprehension check to ensure the students understand your instructions.]

4. **Explain the "Report of Strategy Use" forms.** "Also, as we've discussed, from now on, you must use the *Sentence Writing Strategy* whenever you think it is appropriate. Each time you use the *Sentence Writing Strategy,* I want you to tell me about the situation in which you found it appropriate. I will give you credit toward finishing this part of the strategy each time you report having used the strategy and show me the product to which you've applied it. You must use the strategy at least four times in situations other than the assignments I give you to finish this part of the program. For example, to get credit for one instance of strategy use, you might use it to write a letter to a friend or to write an essay answer on a test. Each time you use the strategy, fill out one of these forms."

[Display a "Report of Strategy Use" form.]

"There's a place on the form for your name, the date on which you used the strategy, the title of the product to which you applied the strategy (e.g., "a letter to Kathy," or "a book report on *Animal Farm* for English"), and the place where you used it (e.g., at home, in study hall, in class). Each time you fill out a form, bring it and your paper to me. If you have to hand the paper in to one of your teachers first, that's okay. Bring me the paper after it has been graded and returned to you. We will evaluate your work together using the *Sentence Checklist.* You must use a variety of the sentence types you now know in order to get credit for the assignment. You need to complete four reports and get them approved by me in order to reach mastery."

[Explain the mastery requirement as specified below in the "What to require for mastery" section (pp. 125-126). Solicit and answer questions. Distribute report forms.]

"I'm giving each of you some report forms. A stack of them will also be available (explain where) in case you need more. Put the forms in the envelopes in your course notebooks for easy access."

---

* After the student has learned simple sentences, require three kinds of simple sentences; after compound sentences, require two kinds of simple sentences and two kinds of compound sentences; after complex sentences, require one simple, one compound, and one complex sentence; after compound-complex sentences, require one of each of the four sentence types.

[Conduct a comprehension check to ensure the students understand the instructions.]

5. **Give assignments.** [Refer the students to their assignment for the day on their Assignment Sheets. Explain that they will not be given time in your class to do the assignments. They must complete each assignment in the place specified on the Assignment Sheet. If they need to change the place, they must check with you. Explain that they must complete and hand in a *Sentence Checklist* each time they do an assignment to show that they've checked their work.

Explain that the sooner they finish their six assignments and four reports, the sooner they can concentrate all their energies on learning a new kind of sentence (or a new strategy, if they've learned all four sentence types). Thus, if their goal is to finish this part of the *Sentence Writing Strategy* in 2 weeks, they need to complete an assignment or use the strategy elsewhere almost every day. Remind the students to turn in their assignments to you the next day.]

6. **Evaluate the student's work.** [Each time a student brings you a product based on one of your assignments or a self-initiated product, jointly evaluate it. Also, jointly evaluate products that teachers give you. Together with the student, determine what kinds of sentences were included in the product using a *Sentence Checklist* and a *Sentence Score Sheet*. Calculate the percentage of complete sentences, the percentage of complicated sentences, and the percentage of correctly punctuated complicated sentences used. Have the student plot these data on his *Generalization Progress Chart*. Data for your assignments should be plotted above the label "Assignments;" data for self-initiated products should be plotted above the label "Reports." Compare the student's *Sentence Checklist* to the one you have completed together. Review any problems the student has encountered in applying the strategy by itself or in combination with other strategies.]

7. **Provide feedback.** [Give the student positive and corrective feedback after each joint evaluation. Have the student record the completion date for assignments or reports that meet the mastery requirements on his *Generalization Progress Chart* to keep track of how many required tasks he has completed satisfactorily. Provide the student with another assignment, when necessary. Record new assignments on the Assignment Sheet, and remind the student how many more assignments and/or reports are due.]

8. **Record progress and adjust goals.** [Ask the student to evaluate her progress with respect to her goal date for Stage 8. If necessary, she should adjust the goal date. Have the student record the completion date under "Stage 8" on the most recent *Progress Chart* and under "Activation" on the current *Management Chart* when she has satisfactorily completed all the required assignments and reports.]

What to require for mastery:

The student must complete six writing assignments and hand in four self-initiated products that meet the following requirements. (The products need not represent consecutive successes.)

After simple sentences. The product must contain 100% complete sentences. At least one third of the sentences must be structured *differently* from the basic simple sentence (S V).

After compound sentences. The product must contain 100% complete sentences. At least 33% of the sentences must be complicated sentences. The product must contain at least two compound sentences. At least 66% of the complicated sentences must be punctuated correctly.

After complex sentences. The product must contain 100% complete sentences. At least 33% of the sentences must be complicated sentences. The product must include at least one compound sentence and one complex sentence. At least 66% of the complicated sentences must be punctuated correctly.

After compound-complex sentences. The product must contain 100% complete sentences. At least 50% of the sentences must be complicated sentences. There must be at least one compound, one complex, and one compound-complex sentence in the product. At least 66% of the complicated sentences must be punctuated correctly.

Where to go from here:

After the student has begun the Activation assignments and is making progress (i.e., is handing in completed assignments), proceed to STAGE 2: DESCRIBE for the next sentence type. That is, once the student shows he is generalizing his use of simple sentences, you can begin teaching compound sentences. Once he is generalizing his use of compound sentences, you can begin teaching complex sentences, and so forth. After the student begins generalizing compound-complex sentences, proceed to the pretest of a new strategy.

After the student reaches the mastery requirements for the Activation Stage, she should record the completion of her generalization goal in her IEP folder. Have her write the completion date and any comments on the sheet inserted in her IEP folder. Proceed to STAGE 8: GENERALIZATION, PHASE III: ADAPTATION about one week after the Activation Phase has been completed if you do not plan to teach the student an additional sentence type immediately.

Although a student may begin a new sentence type or a new strategy before completing the Activation, Adaptation, and Maintenance activities on mastered skills, these activities *must* be completed if the student is to be expected to generalize his newly learned writing skills.

How to trouble-shoot:

If you have difficulty getting a student to complete assignments elsewhere, you may have to begin the Activation Phase by asking the student to complete several assignments in your instructional setting and then gradually increase the distance from you on each subsequent assignment as indicated by the student's progress. For example, have the first assignment completed in your room, the next in a room nearby, the third in the school library, and so forth. You can also ask the student's other teachers to cue him to use the *Sentence Writing Strategy* whenever they assign a writing task. Give them a supply of *Sentence Checklists,* and ask them to hand a checklist to the student each time a writing assignment is given. This will help the student remember to use the strategy.

If you have difficulty getting a student to bring in self-initiated assignments (e.g., those completed for other teachers), ask the teachers to give you the products after they have graded them. Sometimes teachers do not return products to students; in other instances, they do not allow students to keep the products. In such cases, ask to borrow the products for a short time so you can give feedback to the student.

If necessary, contract with the student to complete each assignment or report by a certain time for a certain reward, or have the student write her own contract to complete the work by a certain time for a certain reward to be delivered to herself by herself.

STAGE 8: GENERALIZATION
PHASE III: ADAPTATION

What your goals are:

- To ensure that students are aware of the cognitive strategies imbedded in the *Sentence Writing Strategy.*
- To ensure that the students become aware of situations and circumstances in which parts of the *Sentence Writing Strategy* can be adapted for use.
- To give the students practice in adapting the *Sentence Writing Strategy.*
- To build the students' confidence in themselves as generalized strategic learners.

What you need:

- Large writing surface and writing implement
- Student folders
- Paper
- Pencils
- *Management Chart*

How to prepare:

1. **Gather the needed materials.**
2. **Familiarize yourself with the instructions below.**

How much time to allow:

Allow approximately 25-50 minutes for the initial discussion. Allow several days for the students to practice adaptations of the *Sentence Writing Strategy.*

What to do:

1. **Give an advance organizer.**

   a. **Review previous lessons.** "You have become aware of how and where you might generalize the *Sentence Writing Strategy.* You have also begun actually using the *Sentence Writing Strategy* outside of this classroom."

   b. **State the purpose of this lesson.** "Today, we begin the Adaptation Phase of Generalization instruction. That means that we will be discussing the different parts of the *Sentence Writing Strategy* and how you might adapt them for use in a variety of situations. What does 'adapt' mean?"

   [Elicit a definition like "Change," or have someone look up "adapt" in a dictionary.]

"That's right. 'Adapt' means to change something to fit it to your needs. I think you'll find that you can now change parts of the *Sentence Writing Strategy* to help you meet your needs in a variety of ways."

c. **State your expectations.** "As we discuss how you will be adapting the strategy, I expect you to pay attention, take notes, and contribute to the discussion. Later, you'll practice adapting the *Sentence Writing Strategy*. As we discuss the different adaptations you might make, consider which of them you would like to try first, so you'll be ready with an idea when the time comes."

2. **Review the "PENS" Steps.** [Ask the students to name the steps of the *Sentence Writing Strategy*. As they are named, write the steps on the board. Leave plenty of space between the steps.]

3. **Discuss the cognitive features of the parts of the *Sentence Writing Strategy*.** "You could say that there are four main mental functions that you are performing as a learner when you use the *Sentence Writing Strategy*: the formula part, . . . "

[Write "Using formulas" to the left of Step 1.]

". . . the planning part, . . ."

[Write "Planning" to the left of Step 2.]

" . . . the writing part, . . ."

[Write "Writing" to the left of Step 3.]

". . . and the checking part."

[Write "Checking" to the left of Step 4.]

"The three actions that you can adapt to use in a variety of situations are those related to Steps 1, 2, and 4. Let's discuss what you are doing and thinking as you complete each of these actions."

a. **Discuss the "Using formulas" part.** "Let's start by thinking about using formulas. A formula is really a pattern. A formula or pattern tells you exactly what to do and the order in which to do it. How can formulas or patterns help you?"

[Elicit responses like, "They make your life easier because you know what to do" and "You don't have to think very hard because you have a formula to follow."]

"Yes, you don't have to make a lot of decisions or think very hard about what to do because the formula or pattern is there for you to follow. That way, you can concentrate on other things in your life. For example, if you have a formula to follow for writing a sentence, you can concentrate all your thinking on what the sentence is going to say. You don't have to worry about how you will structure it."

(1.) Discuss making new sentence formulas. "Now that you know the basic parts of sentences, you can start to make your own formulas. You can create formulas that will help you make your writing more and more interesting. What are some of the basic parts of sentences?"

[Elicit the parts such as subjects, verbs, prepositional phrases, infinitives, adjectives, adverbs, independent clauses, and dependent clauses. Write them on the board. Assign each part a code letter. Create one new formula as a group. Write it on the board, and ask the students to write it on their formula cards. Then ask the students to work in pairs or individually to create some new formulas and to write at least one example sentence for each formula. Circulate among the students as they work, and provide feedback. Have the students share their formulas and examples with the group and write their favorite new formulas on their Formula Cards.]

(2.) Discuss making other types of formulas. "You can also make formulas for other activities in your life. You can use letters or pictures in your formulas, whatever works best for you. Each symbol in the formula will represent one action you will take. For example, you might make a formula for all the activities you need to remember to do before you go to school. What are some activities you might include in your formula for getting ready for school?"

[Elicit some activities like eating breakfast, feeding the dog, taking a shower, gathering books together, etc. Write them on the board. Then ask for a code letter for each activity. Have the students then arrange the letters in the order in which the activities should be done. Help them create acronyms or other mnemonic devices to help them remember their formula.]

"There are other tasks or routines for which you may need a formula. I think you'll find that if you create formulas for some of the routines in your life, your life will go smoothly and you can relax and think about meaningful things that are going on in your life. What are some examples of sets of activities you do every day for which you could create formulas?"

[Elicit some examples related to work or school or even driving the car. Write them on the board.]

(3.) Conduct formula-making practice. "Take a few minutes now to create at least one formula for a group of activities in your life. You can choose one of the examples written on the board or something else."

[Circulate among the students, and provide help and feedback.]

b. Discuss the planning part. "Now, let's think for a few minutes about the planning part. What are you planning when you do the 'Explore words to fit the formula' step?"

[Elicit a response like, "I'm planning what words I want to include in the sentence."]

"**Exactly! You are focusing your mind on the words you will include in your sentence. What might happen if you just started writing without thinking?**"

[Elicit responses like, "You might leave out something important," or "The sentence might not match the formula."]

"**Yes. Planning something before you actually do it can help you a great deal. If you think before you write, think before you speak, or think before you act, what you actually do will be much better. Can you think of situations where planning might help you?**"

[Elicit several responses related to school, home, and community settings. Write them on the board. Responses might relate to planning a picnic, planning a date, planning how to get homework done, planning the order in which several errands will be done, planning what to say to invite someone to go to a movie, planning what to say to a parent before asking for a curfew extension. Ask the students to explain how planning helps in each instance.]

(1.) Conduct planning practice. "These are excellent examples of situations where planning will help you. When you make a plan, you typically list what you will do in the order in which you will do it. You can make the list on paper or in your mind. Today, you will make a plan by listing it on paper so I can see it. Take a minute to choose one of the situations we've listed on the board or something else of interest to you that you want to plan. Then list everything you will do for that activity."

[Circulate among the students, and provide help and feedback.]

c. Discuss the checking part. "Now let's talk for a few minutes about the checking part of the Sentence Writing Strategy. Basically, what you are doing here is looking at your work very carefully to make sure that you have done a high-quality job. What does a high-quality job mean to you?"

[Elicit responses like, "It's correct," "It looks neat," "It includes everything you want to include," and "It's complete."]

"**Yes. You can check whether you have done a high quality job on just about anything that you do. What are some of the things that you need to do every day?**"

[Elicit responses related to situations in school, at home, and in the community. Write them on the board. Examples might include: chores, sports, work, math homework, cooking, yard work. Ask the students what a high quality job might entail for one or two examples and how they might check whether they did a high-quality job.]

"Great. You've seen that you can check for quality on just about anything that you do. Why might checking for quality be a good thing to do?"

[Elicit reasons such as, "It will help us get better grades," "People will think we're responsible," and "People will think we care about what we do."]

(1.) Conduct checking practice. **"Exactly! You'll feed good about yourself, too, if you consistently do quality work. Take a couple of minutes now to think about something that you do often that you could check for quality. Write the name of the activity at the top of a piece of paper and then list everything you can check to make sure that you have done quality work."**

[Circulate among the students, and provide help and feedback.]

d. Discuss other ideas. **"Can you think of any other ways you might use the mental actions involved in the *Sentence Writing Strategy*?"**

[Elicit and discuss any ideas the students have. Present any additional ideas you have.]

4. Ensure student use the strategy adaptations in other settings. [After the students have practiced using a strategy adaptation and seem to be proficient at using it, initiate activation activities with it. (See pp. 122-125 for a full description of activation activities. Explain that the students should begin using the strategy adaptations in other settings. Ask them to plan where they will use the adaptations on their own, make assignments to use the adaptations, and encourage use of the strategy report forms in reporting use of the adaptations. Explain that they must complete four assignments in which they use an adaptation of the *Sentence Writing Strategy* and that they must hand in four "Report of Strategy Use" forms indicating where they have used an adaptation on their own in order to reach mastery on this phase of generalization instruction.]

5. Provide feedback. [When a student completes an assignment or hands in a "Report of Strategy Use" form, review the task and any products connected with the task with the student. Provide positive and corrective feedback as appropriate.]

What to require for mastery:

The student must demonstrate that she is readily using adaptations of the *Sentence Writing Strategy* in a variety of settings. Require each student to complete at least four adaptation assignments (which you create in partnership with the student) in settings other than your learning setting. Also require the student to complete and hand in at least four "Report of Strategy Use" forms related to applications of adaptations and to explain to you how he used adaptations of the strategy in each case.

Where to go from here:

When the student completes this phase of instruction, have him record the day's date on the *Management Chart* under "Generalization, Adaptation."

Once a student has completed the Adaptation Phase, proceed to STAGE 8: GENERALIZATION, PHASE IV: MAINTENANCE.

How to trouble-shoot:

Refer to pp. 126-127 for instructions on how to help students become activated.

STAGE 8: GENERALIZATION
PHASE IV: MAINTENANCE*

What your goals are:
- To ensure that students do not forget the *Sentence Writing Strategy.*
- To ensure that students continue to use the *Sentence Writing Strategy* correctly over time.

What you need:
- *Cue Cards #1-15* (pp. 153-167)
- Student journals (see description below)
- Occasional products from students' classes
- *Sentence Checklists* (p. 181)
- *Sentence Score Sheets* (p. 174)
- *Sentence Scoring Instructions* (pp. 137-143)
- Student folders
- Current *Generalization Progress Chart*
- Current *Management Chart*
- Stapler or paper clips

How to prepare:
1. **Gather the needed materials.** If you do not have student journals, make some out of notebooks and paper. Have students decorate the covers of their journals with their names and the word "Journal." Check your supplies of *Sentence Score Sheets* and *Sentence Checklists,* and make additional copies if necessary.

2. **Collect products from other teachers.** Once a month, ask the student's other teachers for a written product the student has completed. Obtain at least one product.

3. **Familiarize yourself with the instructions below.**

4. **Plan maintenance probe assignments.** Determine what topics are to be assigned each student and the dates on which the assignments are to be given. Topics should be related to current or past events in the student's life or to current world events. Write the student's assignment and the due date on the Assignment Sheet in his folder.

How much time to allow:
Students will take approximately 20-25 minutes to write each maintenance assign-

---

* This step is used only when the student is not receiving instruction in any additional sentence types or when the student has mastered all four sentence types.

134

ment in their journals. You may decide to use class time for this activity or to assign it as homework, depending on how reliable and independent each student is.

Each time you review a product with a student, plan to use about 5-10 minutes of instructional time.

The first maintenance probe should occur about a week after the student meets the requirements of the most recent Activation Phase. Subsequent probes should be scheduled about 2 weeks apart. That is, any time the student is not receiving writing instruction, a maintenance probe should be conducted at least twice a month. For each student, obtain a product from another teacher at least once a month.

What to do:

1. **Give an advance organizer.** "Today we will review and use the *Sentence Writing Strategy.* It's important that you refresh your memory about the strategies you have learned, just to remind yourself about the steps and how to best use a given strategy."

   "Tell me how you've been using the *Sentence Writing Strategy.* What products have you written lately?"

   [Solicit responses.]

   "Good. I'm glad to hear you've been using this strategy because you put a lot of work into learning it."

   "How has the strategy helped you?"

   [Solicit responses.]

   "Great. I'm glad to hear you're doing better/well in your classes."

2. **Review the steps and sentence types.** [Ask the student(s) to name the steps of the *Sentence Writing Strategy* and define the types of sentences they have learned. Have the student(s) name the formulas they have learned. Ask them where and why they should use the strategy.]

3. **Distribute materials, and provide instructions.** [Ensure that each student has a journal, a *Sentence Checklist,* and his folder. Ask the student to write at least six sentences on the topic listed on the Assignment Sheet in his folder on a page in his journal. Explain when the product is due. Remind the student of the mastery requirements (see pp. 125-126) and about using the *Sentence Checklist* to check his written work.

   Inform the student(s) that you will score the product. Explain that if the product meets the mastery requirements, the student can return to work on a new strategy. Also explain that if a student's performance indicates that she needs to review the *Sentence Writing Strategy,* additional time will be spent on that.]

4. **Monitor the students' work.** [If students are to complete the task in your instructional setting, circulate among them to ensure that they are proceeding as instructed.]

5. **Collect the materials.** [When a student indicates he has completed the task, have him staple or paper clip the completed *Sentence Checklist* to the product and give both to you.]

6. **Evaluate the student's product.** [Each time a student makes a journal entry or whenever you receive a product from a mainstream teacher, evaluate it using a *Sentence Score Sheet* and the *Sentence Scoring Instructions*. Calculate the percentage of complete sentences, complicated sentences, and correctly punctuated complicated sentences.]

7. **Provide feedback.** [Give the student feedback on her performance. (See pp. 50-51 for specific guidelines on how to give feedback.) Ask the student to put the *Score Sheet* in her folder and to plot the new data points on her current *Generalization Progress Chart*. Have the student write in the date under the appropriate maintenance probe number on her current *Generalization Progress Chart* and on the current *Management Chart* each time a probe is satisfactorily completed.]

What to require for mastery:

Use the same mastery requirements as for the Activation Phase (pp. 125-126).

Where to go from here:

If a student does not achieve mastery on a maintenance probe, return to STAGE 6: ADVANCED PRACTICE/POSTTEST AND FEEDBACK for the most recently completed sentence type. (If necessary, have the student complete the last three lesson series of the most recently completed STAGE 5: CONTROLLED PRACTICE.) Work with the student until he reaches mastery again. Then repeat STAGE 7: MAKE COMMITMENTS FOR GENERALIZATION and STAGE 8: GENERALIZATION.

If the student achieves mastery on a maintenance probe, congratulate her, and resume instruction on another strategy.

APPENDIX A: EVALUATION GUIDELINES
SENTENCE SCORING INSTRUCTIONS
Scoring Steps

Each product will consist of one or more sentences written on a piece of paper. Review the products carefully to score each sentence. The evaluation process for a product containing six sentences should take no more than 2-3 minutes once you understand the scoring process and the definitions. You may train a paraprofessional or volunteer to do the scoring. If so, be sure to train the person as you were trained to score products. Have the person read these instructions. Then have the person score a product, receive feedback from you, score another product, receive feedback from you, and so forth, until the person's scoring agrees perfectly with yours on two or three consecutive products. Thereafter, check the person's scoring periodically to determine whether he continues to apply the definitions appropriately.

Regardless of who scores the product, the same five-step procedure is used.

1. **Number the lines of writing.** In the left-hand margin of the student's paper, place a number next to each line of writing. Place the #1 on the line on which the first sentence begins, the #2 on the next line, and so forth. These line numbers will help you give quick and efficient feedback to your students. In addition, they will allow you to quickly match up your scores with another person's scores.

2. **Determine where a sentence begins and ends.** The beginning of a sentence can be designated through the use of (a) a capital letter in the first letter of the first word of the sentence, (b) an end punctuation mark after the last word of the previous sentence, or (c) both punctuation and capitalization. The end of a sentence can be designated through the use of (a) end punctuation after the last word of the sentence, (b) a capital letter of the first letter of the first word of the next sentence, or (c) both punctuation and capitalization. *Whatever appears on the paper is evaluated as it stands.* For example, if a period appears in what you would think should be the middle of a sentence, treat it as an end punctuation mark, and evaluate the words in front of the period as if they were supposed to be a sentence. Never second-guess the student.

3. **Read a sentence and determine the category to which it belongs.** Once you have determined where a sentence begins and ends, read the sentence carefully. Use the definitions and examples below to determine what kind of a sentence it is.

4. **Record the sentence on the *Sentence Score Sheet*.** After you have determined the type of sentence that has been written, record it on the *Sentence Score Sheet*. Place a checkmark (✓) or appropriate code (see below) in the box under the number that corresponds to the line number of the first word of the sentence and next to the correct category. For example, if a complex sentence starts on line 5 of the paper, place your checkmark in the box that appears under the number 5 and next to the label "Complex Sentence."

5. Repeat steps 2 through 4 for each sentence.

Sentence Definitions

The definitions for each type of sentence are as follows. (For more information and examples, see the *Instructional Methods* or read the chapters in an English textbook on sentence writing.)

Simple Sentence

A **simple sentence** is a group of words with one independent clause. A simple sentence may contain a single subject and a single verb, a compound subject and a single verb, a single subject and a compound verb, or a compound subject and a compound verb. The sentence must be complete (no words left out) in order to be scored as a simple sentence.

Examples*	Explanations
S V The boy ran to the store.	(Simple sentence with single subject, single verb.)
S S V The boy and girl ran in a relay race.	(Simple sentence with compound subject, single verb.)
S V V Kevin went to the party and had a wonderful time.	(Simple sentence with single subject, compound verb.)
S S V V Sally and Susan are friends and play together often.	(Simple sentence with compound subject, compound verb.)

Compound Sentence

A **compound sentence** consists of *two* or more independent clauses. In order to be scored as a compound sentence, two independent clauses must be joined *either* by a comma and a coordinating conjunction *or* by a semicolon. Sentences with three or more independent clauses must have commas separating the initial independent clauses and a comma and a coordinating conjunction separating the final two independent clauses *or* semicolons separating all the independent clauses. The sentence must be complete (no words left out). If a comma is missing, but the coordinating conjunction is present, place "NP" ("not punctuated correctly") in the appropriate compound sentences box. If the comma *and* the conjunction are missing *or* if a semicolon is missing, the sentence will be scored as a run-on sentence (see below).

Coordinating Conjunctions:

for	but
and	or
nor	yet
	so

Examples	Explanations
The boy ran to the store, and he bought some apples.	(Compound sentence with a comma and a coordinating conjunction separating the two independent clauses.)
Angels and devils came to the costume party; they got along fine.	(Compound sentence with a semicolon separating the two independent clauses.)
The baker wore chef's hat, the firefighter wore a helmet, but the farmer wore no hat at all.	(Compound sentence with three independent clauses separated by commas and a coordinating conjunction [but].)
The baker wore a chef's hat; the firefighter wore a helmet; the farmer wore a straw hat.	(Compound sentence with three independent clauses separated by semicolons.)

Note: Sometimes conjunctive adverbs are used in a compound sentence in which the independent clauses are joined with a semicolon.

Common Conjunctive Adverbs:

accordingly	however	otherwise
also	instead	similarly
anyhow	likewise	still
besides	meanwhile	then
consequently	nevertheless	therefore
furthermore	next	thus

Examples	Explanations
Angels and devils came to the costume party; however, they got along fine.	(Compound sentence with the conjunctive adverb at the beginning of the second clause.)
Angels and devils came to the costume party; they, however, got along fine.	(Compound sentence with the conjunctive adverb in the middle of the second clause.)
Angels and devils came to the costume party; they got along fine, however.	(Compound sentence with the conjunctive adverb at the end of the second clause.)

---

* Subjects are marked by an 'S' and verbs by a 'V.'

Complex Sentence

A **complex sentence** consists of one independent clause and *one or more* dependent clauses. Each clause *must* have a subject and a verb. A dependent clause *must* include a subordinating word, a subject, and a verb. (See Notes 1 and 2 below for allowed exceptions to this requirement.) In order to be scored as a complex sentence, the sentence must be complete (no words left out).

Common Subordinating Conjunctions:

after	even if	since
although	even though	so that
as	if	than
as if	in order that	though
as long as	just as	unless
as soon as	like	until
as though	once	when
because	provided	whenever
before	rather than	while

The dependent clause in a complex sentence may be an adverb clause, an adjective clause, or a noun clause.

Complex sentences with adverb clauses.* An **adverb clause** tells when, why, how, where, under what conditions, or with what result an action took pace. The adverb clause may come before or after the independent clause. If it precedes the independent clause, a comma must be used to separate it from the independent clause. If the dependent clause follows the independent clause, a comma is not required. For this type of complex sentence, record a checkmark next to "Complex Sentence" on the score sheet. It the student omits a comma where it is required, place "NP" in the appropriate box on the *Sentence Score Sheet*.

Examples**	Explanations
Because baseball involves so much strategy, it is my dad's favorite game.	(Complex sentence with the dependent clause first and a comma separating the clauses.)
Baseball is my dad's favorite game because it involves so much strategy.	(Complex sentence with the dependent clause after the independent clause. No comma is required to separate the clauses.)
Because you are my friend, I will support you unless you have lied to me.	(Complex sentence with one independent clause and two dependent clauses. A comma is used to separate the dependent clause only when it comes *before* the independent clause.)

Complex sentences with adjective clauses. An **adjective clause** modifies or tells more about a noun or a pronoun in the independent clause. The relative pronouns who, whom, whose, whoever, whomever, that, which, whichever, what, and whatever are used as the subordinating words in this type of clause as are some of the subordinating conjunctions (e.g., when, whenever, where, wherever). The adjective clause should immediately follow the word(s) it modifies. Thus, it can appear in the middle of an independent clause or at the end of the clause, depending on where the modified word occurs.

A comma (or commas) must be used to separate nonrestrictive adjective clauses from the rest of the sentence. That is, if the adjective clause is merely used to give additional explanatory detail about a noun or pronoun, it should be set off with commas. If the clause is restrictive (i.e., used to identify a particular person, place or thing) no commas should be used. That is, when the dependent clause is important to the meaning of the independent clause, no commas are needed because the dependent clause is an integral part of the independent clause. For this type of complex sentence, record a checkmark next to "Complex Sentence" on the *Sentence Score Sheet*. *** If the comma (or commas) is missing in a sentence where the adjective clause is nonrestrictive, put "NP" in the scoring box.

---

* This is the type of complex sentence that is taught in the *Instructional Methods* section of this manual.

** Independent clauses are underlined with two lines; dependent clauses are underlined with one line.

*** If you want to keep track of this type of complex sentence separately from the type of complex sentence that you are teaching (the complex sentence with an adverb clause), you can use a different symbol than a checkmark. For example, you can use an "A."

Examples*	Explanations
The dog that Jim kept tied to his garage barked at us.	(The adjective clause modifies "dog" and is restrictive [it identifies a particular dog]; therefore, commas are not used. The adjective clause is inside the independent clause.)
Jane likes the boy whom Kathy despises.	(The adjective clause modifies "boy" and is restrictive [it identifies a particular boy]; therefore, commas are not used. The adjective clause appears after the independent clause since the word it modifies is the last word of the independent clause.)
Shovels, which workers use for digging, come in many shapes and sizes.	(The adjective clause modifies "shovels" and is non-restrictive [it just adds information to the sentence]; therefore, commas are used. The adjective clause is inside the independent clause; thus, two commas are needed.)
The shovels which Paul painted brown are drying outside.	(The adjective clause modifies "shovels" and is restrictive [it identifies particular shovels]; therefore, commas are not used. The adjective clause is inside the independent clause.)
Karen went to the prom with Steve Jones, whose family recently moved here.	(The adjective clause modifies "Steve Jones" and is not restrictive [Steve Jones is already clearly identified, so the clause merely adds information to the sentence]; therefore, a comma is used. The adjective clause is at the end of the sentence.)
Paul used one of the shovels which he had painted brown.	(The adjective clause modifies "shovels" and is restrictive [it identifies particular shovels]; therefore, a comma is not used. The adjective clause is at the end of the sentence.)

Note 1: Sometimes the subordinating conjunction serves as the subject of the adjective clause. This is acceptable, and sentences using this form should be scored as complex sentences.

Examples	Explanations
Jill, who has long blond hair, often wears pigtails.	(In the adjective clause, "who" serves as the subordinating conjunction *and* as the subject of the clause.)
Jesse could not wait to see Dakota, who had been away for a year.	(In the adjective clause, "who" serves as the subordinating conjunction *and* as the subject of the clause.)
The storm, which had been raging for 4 hours, began to abate.	(In the adjective clause, "which" serves as the subordinating conjunction *and* as the subject of the clause.)

Complex sentences with noun clauses. A **noun clause** takes the place of a noun in the independent clause. Thus, it is a part of the independent clause; it can serve as the subject, direct object, indirect object, predicate nominative, or as the object of the preposition in the independent clause. For complex sentences with noun clauses, record a checkmark next to "Complex Sentence" on the *Sentence Score Sheet.***

Examples	Explanations
Why Mike wants to run a marathon is unclear to me.	(The dependent clause, "Why Mike wants to run a marathon," is the subject of the independent clause.)

---

* Independent clauses are underlined with two lines; dependent clauses are underlined with one line.

** If you want to keep track of complex sentences with noun clauses separately from other types of complex sentences, you can use a different symbol like an "N."

Examples (cont.)	Explanations (cont.)
Jane wanted to know when she could see her children.	(The dependent clause, "when she could see her children," serves as the direct object of the independent clause.)
Helen will give whoever wins the contest a wonderful prize.	(The dependent clause, "whoever wins the contest," serves as the indirect object of the independent clause.)
One possibility is that he has hidden under the stairs.	(The dependent clause, "that he has hidden under the stairs," serves as the predicate nominative of the independent clause.)
Scott had no idea about what he would say.	(The dependent clause, "what he would say," serves as the object of the preposition "about.")

Note 2: Often students leave out the subordinating the subordinating conjunction "that" when writing complex sentences. If the subordinating conjunction "that" is missing, score the sentence as a complex sentence with an adjective clause or a noun clause and encircle the checkmark. Give feedback to the student regarding this omission. This is the only omission of a word that is acceptable.

Examples	Explanations
Baseball has several rules you have to know.	(In this sentence, the subordinating conjunction "that" has been left out between the words "rules" and "you." ["you have to know" is an adjective clause])
I think soccer is a more active sport.	(In this sentence, the subordinating conjunction "that" has been left out between the words "think" and "soccer." ["soccer is a more active sport" is a noun clause])
Some women feel they deserve more out of life.	(In this sentence, the subordinating conjunction "that" has been left out between the words "feel" and "they." ["they deserve more out of life" is a noun clause])

Complex sentences with more than one dependent clause.

A complex sentence can have two or even three dependent clauses. The dependent clauses can be different kinds of dependent clauses or the same kind. A sentence of this type is still scored as a complex sentence. Put a checkmark next to "Complex Sentence" on the *Sentence Score Sheet*. The punctuation rules for adjective clauses and adverb clauses also apply here. Put "NP" in the box if the student has not used commas appropriately.

Examples	Explanations
Baseball has several rules that you should know before you begin to play.	(A complex sentence with an independent clause, a restrictive adjective clause, and an adverb clause.)
Before you begin to play baseball, you need to learn some rules from Floyd because he's the expert.	(A complex sentence with an adverb clause, an independent clause, and an adverb clause.)
What Jesse said surprised Jean, who is his mother.	(A noun clause serving as the subject of the independent clause which is followed by a nonrestrictive adjective clause.)

Compound Complex Sentence

A **compound-complex sentence** consists of two or more independent clauses and at least one dependent clause. In order to be scored as a compound-complex sentence, the sentence must be complete (no words left out), logical, and must make sense. Any compound-complex sentence that does not make sense should be scored as a nonsentence (see below). Record "NP" in the box if the sentence has not been punctuated correctly with commas (i.e., if a comma or commas have been left out). If a semicolon has been left out, score the sentence as a run-on sentence.

Examples*	Explanations
After the party was over, Jean had a headache, so Paul cleaned up the mess.	(A dependent clause followed by two independent clauses.)
Jean had a headache after the party was over, so Paul cleaned up the house.	(An independent clause followed by a dependent clause and an independent clause.)
Jean had a headache, so Paul cleaned up the house after the party was over.	(An independent clause followed by an independent clause and a dependent clause.)
Although it was snowing, Floyd planned to go to the game; Helen wanted to stay home.	(A dependent clause followed by two independent clauses.)
Floyd planned to go to the game even though it was snowing; Helen wanted to stay home.	(An independent clause followed by a dependent clause and an independent clause.)
Helen wanted to stay home; Floyd wanted to go to the game even though it was snowing.	(Two independent clauses followed by a dependent clause.)
Kevin, who had been late many times before, came late to class today; his teacher bawled him out after class was over.	(A nonrestrictive adjective clause imbedded in the first independent clause, another independent clause, and a dependent clause.)
Trin, whose family lives in Thailand, graded tests until her eyes hurt; she may need glasses.	(A nonrestrictive adjective clause imbedded in the first independent clause, an adverb clause, and another independent clause.)
The players who had been invited came to our house after the game was over; they celebrated the win.	(A restrictive adjective clause imbedded in the first independent clause, an adverb clause, and another independent clause.)
How she survived is a mystery to us; while the war was in progress, she had no food or other resources.	(A noun clause imbedded in the first independent clause [as its subject], an adverb clause, and another independent clause.)

Non Sentence

A **non-sentence** is scored when a student has designated one of the following as a sentence: a sentence fragment, a comma splice, a run-on sentence, or an illogical group of words. The definitions for each of these nonsentences appear below.

Sentence fragments. A **sentence fragment** is a part of a sentence that is set off through capitalization and/or punctuation as if it were a whole sentence. A sentence fragment may be missing a subject or a verb or both. It can be an independent clause that starts with a coordinating conjunction, a dependent clause that starts with a subordinating conjunction, or any other part of a sentence that has been set apart as a sentence (e.g., a prepositional phrase).

Examples	Explanations
The cow eating the grass.	(This sentence is missing a helping verb.)
Eats the grass.	(This sentence needs a subject.)
Eating the grass.	(This sentence needs a subject and a helping verb.)

---

* Independent clauses are underlined with two lines and dependent clauses with one line.

Examples (cont.)

And we will come, too.

Because she is sick.

Not in my wildest dreams.

Explanations (cont.)

(This is the second clause of a compound sentence.)

(This is a dependent clause that has no connection to an independent clause.)

(This is a sentence fragment consisting mostly of a prepositional phrase.)

Comma splices. A **comma splice** is a sentence in which two independent clauses are joined by a comma.

Examples

Danny was an excellent basketball player, he was recruited by several major universities.

The wind howled, the rain beat down on the roof.

Explanations

(In this sentence, only a comma separates the two independent clauses; the coordinating conjunction is omitted.)

(In this sentence, only a comma separates the two independent clauses; the coordinating conjunction has been omitted.)

Run-on sentences. A **run-on sentence** refers to a group of words in which two or more independent clauses are joined without punctuation or conjunctions.

Examples

The wind howled the rain beat down.

Danny was an excellent player he was recruited by several schools he chose the University of Kansas.

Explanations

(This sentence has no punctuation and no conjunction separating the two independent clauses.)

(This sentence has three independent clauses; the semicolons are omitted.)

Illogical/nonsensical sentences. Other groups of words are often designated as sentences but because of poor syntax, words being mixed up, clauses being mixed up or placed inappropriately, or a word being left out, they don't make sense. These should also be scored as non-sentences.

Examples

Sally made candied apples; they were delicious before the trick-or-treaters came.

Jason and Jane went the store.

The carpenters worked all day who put in our cabinets.

Explanations

(In this sentence the adverb clause, "before the trick-or-treaters came" modifies the verb "made." Thus, the dependent clause is misplaced, and the sentence does not make sense.)

(In this sentence, the word "to" was left out between the words "went" and "the." Thus, the sentence does not make sense.)

(The adjective clause, "who put in our cabinets" modifies "carpenters" and should have been placed immediately following "carpenters.")

For two samples of a student's writing and illustrations of how the sentences within those samples should be scored, see the samples on p. 146, the *Example Score Sheets* on p. 147, and the *Scoring Explanation* on pp. 148-149.

CALCULATION PROCEDURES

Refer to the section on the *Example Score Sheet II* (p. 147) for the *Practice Sample* (p. 146) labeled "Calculating the Scores" as you read this section. The procedures for calculating three scores, the Percentage of Complete Sentences, the Percentage of Complicated Sentences, and the Percentage of Complicated Sentences Punctuated Correctly, are as follows.

Percentage of Complete Sentences

Count the total number of sentences tallied for each sentence type, and record each total in the appropriate box in the column labeled "Totals." On *Example Score Sheet II*, one simple sentence, three compound sentences, four complex sentences, one compound-complex sentence, and no non-sentences were recorded. Add these totals to arrive at the total number of sentence attempts and record this sum in the box labeled "Total Sentence Attempts." On *Example Score Sheet II,* a total of 9 sentence attempts were recorded.

To calculate the Percentage of Complete Sentences, add up the total number of simple, compound, complex, and compound-complex sentences. Put this total in the numerator box on the top of the fraction under the label "Percentage of Complete Sentences." Then put the total number of sentence attempts in the denominator box of the same fraction. Divide the fraction to obtain a percentage score. Write the percentage score on the blank in front of the percentage sign (%).

On *Example Score Sheet II,* a total of 9 simple, compound, complex, and compound-complex sentences were recorded. There were 9 sentence attempts. These numbers were recorded in the appropriate boxes and the calculations carried out (9 was divided by 9 and the answer was multiplied by 100) to obtain a percentage score of 100%. This percentage score is one of the scores graphed on the student's *Progress Chart.* This score must be 100% for the student to reach mastery.

Percentage of Complicated Sentences

To calculate the Percentage of Complicated Sentences, add up the total number of compound, complex, and compound-complex sentences. Place this total in the numerator box on the top of the fraction under the label "Percentage of Complicated Sentences." Put the total number of sentence attempts in the denominator box of the same fraction. Divide the denominator into the numerator and multiply by 100 to obtain a percentage score. Write the percentage score on the blank in front of the percentage sign (%).

On *Example Score Sheet II,* a total of 8 compound, complex, and compound-complex sentences were recorded. There were 9 sentence attempts. These numbers were recorded in the appropriate boxes, and the calculations were carried out (8 was divided by 9 and the answer was multiplied by 100) to obtain a percentage score of 89%. This percentage score is one of the scores graphed on the student's *Progress Chart.* This score must equal or exceed 33% for the student to reach mastery after instruction in compound sentences, and must equal or exceed 50% for the student to reach mastery after instruction in complex and compound-complex sentences.

Percentage of Complicated Sentences Punctuated Correctly

To calculate the Percentage of Complicated Sentences Punctuated Correctly, count the total number of compound, complex, and compound-complex sentences for which "NP" is *not* recorded in the box along with the checkmark. Place this total in the numerator box of the fraction under the label "Percentage of Complicated Sentences Punctuated Correctly." Put the total number of compound, complex, and compound-complex sentences in the denominator box of the same fraction. Divide the fraction to obtain a percentage score. Write the percentage score on the blank in front of the percentage sign.

On *Example Score Sheet II,* 7 compound, complex, and compound-complex sentences were punctuated correctly. A total of 8 compound, complex, and compound-complex sentences were recorded. These numbers were entered in the appropriate boxes and the calculations were carried out (7 was divided by 8 and the answer was multiplied by 100) to obtain a percentage score of 87%. This percentage score is one of the scores graphed on the student's *Progress Chart.* This score must equal or exceed 66% for the student to reach mastery after instruction in compound, complex, and/or compound-complex sentences.

PROGRESS CHART EXPLANATION

Eight progress charts must be completed: one for each of the four sentence types and one for each set of generalization activities. Plot on each of the sentence *Progress Charts* the student's scores on: the pretest, the written quiz, controlled practice attempts, and advanced practice attempts. For example, the data from both *Example Sentence Score Sheets* (p. 147) are plotted on the *Example Progress Chart* (p. 145). The student, Kathy, earned the following percentage scores on the pretest: 25% complete sentences, 0% complicated sentences, and 0% correctly punctuated complicated sentences. The 25% is plotted on the vertical line above the label "Pretest" with a dot. The 0% for complicated sentences is plotted on the same vertical line with a star. The 0% for correctly punctuated complicated sentences is plotted on the same vertical line with a square.

Kathy earned the following scores on Compound-Complex Sentence Lesson 7B: 100% complete sentences, 89% complicated sentences, and 87% correctly punctuated complicated sentences. The 100% is plotted on the vertical line above 7B with a dot. The 89% is plotted on the same vertical line with a star; and the 87% is plotted on the same vertical line with a square. Scores from consecutive practice attempts within the same lesson series should be connected as shown in the *Example Progress Chart.*

EXAMPLE PROGRESS CHART

Student's Name: _Kathy Barker_

COMPOUND-COMPLEX SENTENCE PROGRESS CHART

Stages

GOAL-SETTING SECTION	2	3	4	5	6	7	8
Goal Date:	3/20	3/23	3/24	4/3	4/10	4/11	4/24
Date Completed:	3/20	3/23	3/24	4/7	4/10	4/12	

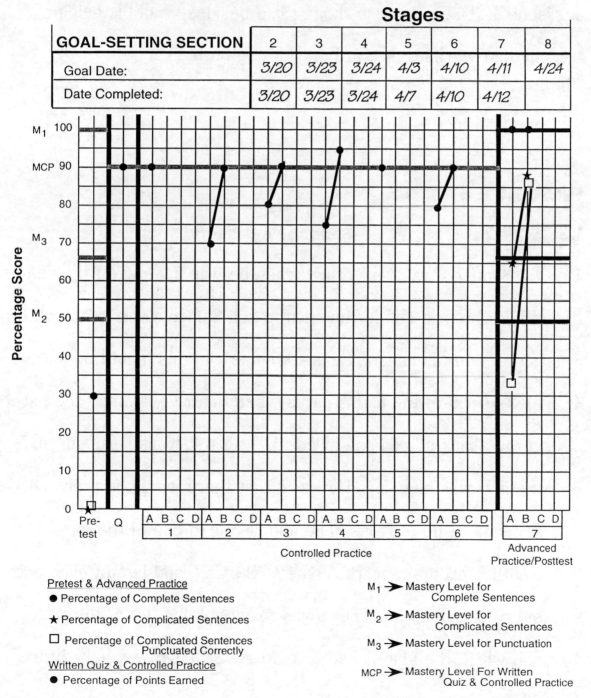

Pretest & Advanced Practice
● Percentage of Complete Sentences

★ Percentage of Complicated Sentences

☐ Percentage of Complicated Sentences
   Punctuated Correctly

Written Quiz & Controlled Practice
● Percentage of Points Earned

M₁ ➤ Mastery Level for
        Complete Sentences

M₂ ➤ Mastery Level for
        Complicated Sentences

M₃ ➤ Mastery Level for Punctuation

MCP ➤ Mastery Level For Written
         Quiz & Controlled Practice

PRETEST SAMPLE

Why I Love Weekends

1   I love weekends. so I can get away from school for a will.

2   Mainly so I can do some homework that I did not get dun at

3   school. There are also thens I like besides school is helping

4   my dad working the yard or working on the car.

PRACTICE SAMPLE

LESSON 7B   **Santiago's Bravery**

1   Santiago was very brave when he was fighting off the sharks.

2   When the first shark came at the fish Santiago was ready with the

3   harpoon in his hand. The shark came with his mouth open, and he

4   took 40 lbs of the fish. That is when Santiago jammed the harpoon

5   in the shark's head and killed it. He had lost his harpoon, and

6   the fish was bleeding. He knew that there would be more sharks

7   coming, so he took his knife and lash it to one of the oars.

8   Another group of sharks came at the fish, and he got each and

9   every one of them. There was really nothing left of the large

10   fish which the sharks had torn apart. Santiago was very brave

11   during his moment of truth.

EXAMPLE SENTENCE SCORE SHEET I

Student Name: _Kathy Barker_   Pretest/Posttest: _✔_

Date: _Jan. 21_   Practice: _____

Sentence Type	1	2	3	4	5	6	7	8	9	10	11	12	13	14	15	Totals
Simple	✔															1
Compound																
Complex																
Compound-Complex																
Non-Sentence	✔(2)	✔	✔													3

Total Sentence Attempts → 4

Calculating the Scores

Percentage of Complete Sentences

$$\frac{\text{No. Simple + Comp. + Complex + Comp./Complex}}{\text{Total No. Sentence Attempts}} = \frac{1}{4} \times 100 = 25\,\%$$

Mastery = 100%

Percentage of Complicated Sentences

$$\frac{\text{No. Comp. + Complex + Comp./Complex}}{\text{Total No. Sentence Attempts}} = \frac{0}{4} \times 100 = 0\,\%$$

Mastery = 33%, 40%, or 50%
(see criterion for each part)

Percentage of Complicated Sentences Punctuated correctly

$$\frac{\text{No. Comp. + Complex + Comp./Complex Punc. Corr.}}{\text{Total No. Complicated Sentences}} = \frac{0}{0} \times 100 = 0\,\%$$

Mastery = at least 66%

EXAMPLE SENTENCE SCORE SHEET II

Student Name: _Kathy Barker_   Pretest/Posttest: _____

Date: _April 10_   Practice: _C-C G.A. #7B_

Sentence Type	1	2	3	4	5	6	7	8	9	10	11	12	13	14	15	Totals
Simple										✔						1
Compound			✔		✔			✔								3
Complex	✔	✔NP		✔					✔							4
Compound-Complex					✔											1
Non-Sentence																0

Total Sentence Attempts → 9

Calculating the Scores

Percentage of Complete Sentences

$$\frac{\text{No. Simple + Comp. + Complex + Comp./Complex}}{\text{Total No. Sentence Attempts}} = \frac{9}{9} \times 100 = 100\,\%$$

Mastery = 100%

Percentage of Complicated Sentences

$$\frac{\text{No. Comp. + Complex + Comp./Complex}}{\text{Total No. Sentence Attempts}} = \frac{8}{9} \times 100 = 89\,\%$$

Mastery = 33%, 40%, or 50%
(see criterion for each part)

Percentage of Complicated Sentences Punctuated correctly

$$\frac{\text{No. Comp. + Complex + Comp./Complex Punc. Corr.}}{\text{Total No. Complicated Sentences}} = \frac{7}{8} \times 100 = 87\,\%$$

Mastery = at least 66%

SCORING EXPLANATION

PRETEST SAMPLE

Line No.	Sentence
1	I love weekends.

Explanation of Record Made on
Example Sentence Score Sheet I

Place a checkmark in the box under Line 1 and next to "Simple Sentence." (This sentence fits the formula S V.)

Line No.	Sentence
1	so I can get away from school for a will.

This is designated as a sentence by the period that occurs at the end of the first sentence and the period after the word "will." Place a checkmark in the box under Line 1 and next to "Non-Sentence." (This is a sentence fragment, the second clause of a compound sentence.) Since this is the second sentence that starts on Line 1, place a (2) in the box as well.

Line No.	Sentence
2	Mainly so I can do some home work that I did not get dun at school.

Place a checkmark in the box under Line 2 and next to "Non-Sentence." (This is also a sentence fragment.)

Line No.	Sentence
3	There are also thens I like be sides school is helping my dad working the yard or working the car.

Place a checkmark in the box under Line 3 and next to the "Non-Sentence." (This sentence does not make sense primarily due to words being left out.)

PRACTICE SAMPLE

Explanation of Record Made on
Example Sentence Score Sheet II

Line No.	Sentence
1	Santiago was very brave when he was fighting off the sharks.

Place a checkmark in the box under Line 1 and next to "Complex Sentence." (This sentence has an adverb clause and fits the formula, ID.)

Line No.	Sentence
2	When the first shark came at the fish Santiago was ready with the harpoon in his hand.

Place a checkmark in the box under Line 2 and next to "Complex Sentence." Also put "NP" in the box since the comma is missing. (This sentence has an adverb clause and fits the formula, D,I.)

Line No.	Sentence
3	The shark came with his mouth open, and he took 40 lb. of the fish.

Place a checkmark in the box under Line 3 and next to "Compound Sentence." (This sentence fits the formula, I,cI.)

Line No.	Sentence
4	That is when Santiago jammed the harpoon in the shark's head and killed it.

Place a checkmark in the box under Line 4 and next to "Complex Sentence." (This is a complex sentence that has a noun clause serving as the predicate nominative within the independent clause.)

Line No.	Sentence
5	He had lost his harpoon, and the fish was bleeding.

Place a checkmark in the box under Line 5 and next to "Compound Sentence." (This sentence fits the formula I,cI.)

SCORING EXPLANATION (cont.)

Line No.	Sentence	Explanation of Record Made on *Example Sentence Score Sheet II*
6	He knew that there would be more sharks coming, so he took his knife and lash it to one of the oars.	Place a checkmark in the box under Line 6 and next to "Compound-Complex Sentence." (This sentence has an independent clause, an adjective clause, and another independent clause.)
8	Another group of sharks came at the fish, and he got each and every one of them.	Place a checkmark in the box under Line 8 and next to "Compound Sentence." (This sentence fits the formula, I,cI.)
9	There was really nothing left of the large fish which the sharks had torn apart.	Place a checkmark in the box under Line 9 and next to "Complex Sentence." (This sentence is a complex sentence with a restrictive adjective clause.)
10	Santiago was very brave during his moment of truth.	Place a checkmark in the box under Line 10 and next to "Simple Sentence." (This sentence fits the formula S V.)

PERCENTAGE TABLE
For Controlled Practice Lessons*

No. Correct	%	No. Correct	%	No. Correct	%
1	3%	11	37%	21	70%
2	7%	12	40%	22	73%
3	10%	13	43%	23	77%
4	13%	14	47%	24	80%
5	17%	15	50%	25	83%
6	20%	16	53%	26	87%
7	23%	17	57%	27	90%
8	27%	18	60%	28	93%
9	30%	19	63%	29	97%
10	33%	20	67%	30	100%

*This table is to be used to quickly obtain the percentage correct on the controlled practice lessons and on the written quizzes.

APPENDIX B: INSTRUCTIONAL MATERIALS *

TOPIC LIST
SENTENCE WRITING STRATEGY

My Favorite Meal

Summer Activities

The Best Things About School

Life as a Teenager

The Best Place to Live

My Favorite Sport

The Best Job in the World

My New Year's Resolutions

UNIVERSITY OF KANSAS CENTER FOR RESEARCH ON LEARNING

SIMPLE SENTENCE

A sentence that has
one independent clause

INDEPENDENT CLAUSE

A group of words that
(1) makes a complete statement
(2) has a subject and a verb

THE SUBJECT OF A SENTENCE

The subject is the
person
place
thing
quality
or
idea

Nouns

that the sentence is about.

Examples:

John went for a walk.	(Person)
Towns are quiet after snowfalls.	(Place)
Eggs rolled off the counter.	(Things)
Silence is golden.	(Quality)
Peace is at hand.	(Idea)

VERB

A verb is a word that shows the
action
or
state of being
of the subject of the sentence.

Examples:

Sally sneezed.   (Physical action)

John thinks.   (Mental action)

Jesse is my friend.   (State of being)

VERB–SUBJECT IDENTIFICATION PROCEDURE

Step 1: Look for the action or state-of-being word to find the verb.

> **Example:** Kevin reported the theft.

Step 2: Ask yourself "Who or what (<u>verb</u>)?" to find the subject.

> **Example:** Paula is an astronaut.

HELPING VERBS

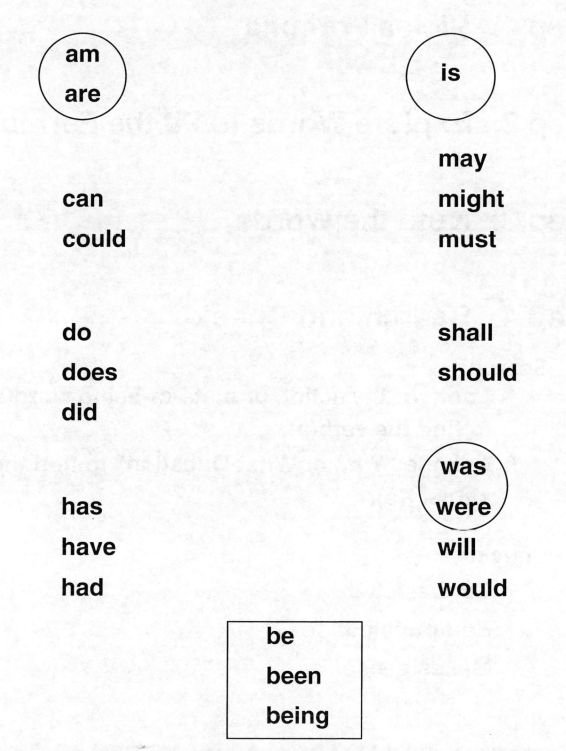

am
are

is

can
could

may
might
must

do
does
did

shall
should

has
have
had

was
were

will
would

be
been
being

STEPS FOR SENTENCE WRITING

Step 1: Pick a Formula

Step 2: Explore Words to Fit the Formula

Step 3: Note the Words

Step 4: Search and Check

Search:
- Look for the action or state-of-being word(s) to find the verb(s).
- Ask the "Who or What Question" to find the subject(s).

Check:
- Capital letter
- End punctuation
- Makes sense

<u>COMPOUND SENTENCE</u>

A compound sentence has two or more independent clauses.

<u>Examples:</u>

> The students finished class, and they went
>   to lunch.

> Kevin did not want to hurt Kathy's feelings,
>   so he said nothing about her mistake.

> I want to see my sister soon, for she has
>   been in Switzerland for two years.

COMPARING COMPOUND SENTENCES TO SIMPLE SENTENCES WITH COMPOUND SUBJECTS AND COMPOUND VERBS

SIMPLE SENTENCE:

The men and women met at the station and went to dinner.

COMPOUND SENTENCE:

The men met at the station, and the women went to dinner.

SIMPLE SENTENCE:

The ducks and geese squawked and fluttered their wings.

COMPOUND SENTENCE:

The ducks squawked, and the geese fluttered their wings.

SIMPLE SENTENCE:

Harry and Joe ate ice cream and drank pop.

COMPOUND SENTENCE:

Harry ate ice cream, and Joe drank pop.

COORDINATING CONJUNCTION

A word that is used with a comma to join two independent clauses.

, for	, but
, and	, or
, nor	, yet
	, so

Examples:

Baseball is my favorite sport to watch, but football Is my favorite sport to play.

The children ran all the way to school, yet they were late anyway.

You will have to finish the project, or your group will get a failing grade.

Hanni was not at the game, nor was she at the party.

We did not see Mike at the movie, nor did we see him at the restaurant.

SEMICOLONS

Semicolons (;) can also be used to join the two independent clauses of a compound sentence.

Examples:

Susan loves to swim; her brother likes to dive.

Jason was highly respected; he was always such a responsible person.

The meeting was over; it was already midnight.

COMPLEX SENTENCE

A complex sentence has one independent clause and one or more dependent clauses.

DEPENDENT CLAUSE

A dependent clause is a group of words with a subject and verb that cannot stand alone.

Examples:

I like Sally because she is funny.

Kathy will be late for dinner since the meeting is still in progress.

The game will end when one team scores.

SUBORDINATING CONJUNCTIONS

Subordinating conjunctions are words that show the relationship of the dependent clause to the independent clause.

Some words that can be used as subordinating conjunctions are:

after	even if	since
although	even though	so that
as	if	than
as if	in order that	though
as long as	just as	unless
as soon as	like	until
as though	once	when
because	provided	whenever
before	rather than	while

SEQUENCING COMPLEX SENTENCES

Dependent Clause First (comma needed)

When I get to Phoenix, you will be sleeping.

After the players practiced, they went out for a pizza.

Until the storm is over, we will not know about the damage.

Independent Clause First (comma not needed)

You will be sleeping when I get to Phoenix.

The players went out for a pizza after they practiced.

We will not know about the damage until the storm is over.

COMPOUND-COMPLEX SENTENCE

A compound-complex sentence has two or more independent clauses and at least one dependent clause.

Examples:

When you are ready, I will call the store, and we can talk to Tim.

Before the trick-or-treaters came, Megan made candied apples; they were delicious.

SEQUENCING COMPOUND-COMPLEX SENTENCES

Dependent Clause First

After the party was over, Jean had a headache, so Paul cleaned up the house.

When Jennifer feels sad, she calls Chris; he cheers her up.

Dependent Clause Second

Jean had a headache after the party was over, so Paul cleaned up the house.

Chad hates to sleep while his parents are awake, for he might miss something.

Jennifer calls Chris whenever she feels sad; he cheers her up.

The sky was gray when the volcano erupted; ash was falling everywhere.

Dependent Clause Third

Jean had a headache, so Paul cleaned up the house after the party was over.

The boss made Pat a good offer, and she accepted as long as he gave her a travel allowance.

The doctors were busy with the serious cases; the slightly wounded soldier quietly waited while they worked.

Todd gave an excellent report; his instructor thanked him after the rest of the class had left the room.

EXAMPLE SHEET

Example Set I

1. Jane went to the pool.
2. Paul is a very nice guy.
3. Cakes lined the store window.
4. I love chocolate ice cream.
5. Bikes are very expensive.
6. Dad is strict.
7. Bananas taste good.
8. Kathy has a son named Jimmy.
9. Raccoons raid our garbage cans every night.
10. Flowers are in bloom everywhere.

Example Set II

1. The old gray mare limped down the lane.
2. The silver-winged plane soared.
3. Johnny's baby sister cried for hours.
4. The first three girls giggled.
5. Fourteen good pilots died in the war.
6. The chairman of the meeting left early.
7. The chrome-plated motorcycles glistened in the sun.
8. The pioneers in our family fled from England.
9. The dog's buried bones rotted in the ground.
10. Carol's best china plate broke into a hundred pieces.

Example Set III

1. The bus must have gone by now.
2. My best friend could not work tonight.
3. The light green grapes have been eaten.
4. The committee of environmentalists is working to solve the smog problem.
5. Steven's aunt is not following her new diet.
6. The old rickety wagon should not have been filled to the top.
7. The merry pied piper would have played a happy tune.
8. A stray sunbeam could have pierced the clouds.
9. The paint on the old gray house was peeling.
10. The peace treaty might have been signed today.

Example Set IV

1. Bill and Sue want to go to the movies.
2. Jason and his friends work together.
3. Are the car and truck parked outside?
4. The park and sidewalks are covered with snow.
5. Hiding and seeking are fun activities.
6. The old man and his black cat have lived long lives.
7. The station and its surrounding parking lot become dangerous after 9:00 P.M..
8. Arnie, Karen, and Ty went to buy a new van.
9. Peace and war are direct opposites.
10. Did Marty and Kathy travel 500 miles just to speak at the conference?

EXAMPLE SHEET (Cont.)

Example Set V

1. Sally swam and played all afternoon.

2. The dogs had barked all night and slept all day.

3. Michelle came home yesterday and did not work all day today.

4. The basketball team rode on a bus and flew in a plane to attend the game.

5. The park is dark and spooky at night and can be delightful on sunny days.

6. Did Jane call her father and tell him the news?

7. I miss my sister and want to see her again soon.

8. Children should not be allowed to watch T.V. and should be encouraged to play.

9. Will you sit by the sea and paint the ships?

10. The books were stacked on the floor and were ruined by the flood.

Example Set VI

1. The ponies and calves scampered and played in the field.

2. Kathy and her father do not like to play tennis and hate to jog.

3. The Army and the Navy had a football game and filled the stadium.

4. The two boys and their fathers were sick and did not attend the Father-Son Banquet.

5. Parties and dances are usually fun and can be thrilling.

6. Cards and dice were used at the party and had been scattered everywhere.

7. Radio towers and tall buildings must have lights and must be visible at night.

8. Candles and flowers can brighten the table and can make guests feel special.

9. Tape and string are needed to secure packages and can be used for other things.

10. The graduates and their parents posed for pictures and celebrated with a party.

Name: _____

SIMPLE SENTENCE
VERBAL PRACTICE CHECKLIST

Attempts

	1	2	3	4	5	6
Naming Strategy Steps						
Pick a formula	__	__	__	__	__	__
Explore words to fit the formula	__	__	__	__	__	__
Note the words	__	__	__	__	__	__
Search and check (MARK)	__	__	__	__	__	__
Giving Definitions						
Simple Sentence	__	__	__	__	__	__
Independent Clause	__	__	__	__	__	__
Subject	__	__	__	__	__	__
Verb	__	__	__	__	__	__
Compound Subject	__	__	__	__	__	__
Compound Verb	__	__	__	__	__	__

Naming Kinds of Simple Sentences

	1	2	3	4	5	6
S V	__	__	__	__	__	__
S S V	__	__	__	__	__	__
S V V	__	__	__	__	__	__
S S V V	__	__	__	__	__	__
Total	__	__	__	__	__	__
Percent Correct	__	__	__	__	__	__
Date	__	__	__	__	__	__

UNIVERSITY OF KANSAS CENTER FOR RESEARCH ON LEARNING

Name: _____

COMPOUND SENTENCE
VERBAL PRACTICE CHECKLIST

<u>Attempts</u>

	1	2	3	4	5	6
Giving Definitions						
Compound Sentence	___	___	___	___	___	___
Independent Clause	___	___	___	___	___	___
Coordinating Conjunction	___	___	___	___	___	___
Naming Kinds of Compound Sentences						
I , c I	___	___	___	___	___	___
I ; I	___	___	___	___	___	___
Naming Coordinating Conjunctions						
For	___	___	___	___	___	___
And	___	___	___	___	___	___
Nor	___	___	___	___	___	___
But	___	___	___	___	___	___
Or	___	___	___	___	___	___
Yet	___	___	___	___	___	___
So	___	___	___	___	___	___
Explaining Punctuation						
Use of a comma	___	___	___	___	___	___
Use of a semicolon	___	___	___	___	___	___
Total	___	___	___	___	___	___
Percent Correct	___	___	___	___	___	___
Date	___	___	___	___	___	___

Name:_____

COMPLEX SENTENCE
VERBAL PRACTICE CHECKLIST

<u>Attempts</u>

	1	2	3	4	5	6

Giving Definitions

Complex Sentence   —   —   —   —   —   —

Independent Clause   —   —   —   —   —   —

Dependent Clause   —   —   —   —   —   —

Subordinating Conjunction   —   —   —   —   —   —

Naming Kinds of Complex Sentences

D , I   —   —   —   —   —   —

I D   —   —   —   —   —   —

Explaining Punctuation

Between the I clause and the D clause:

when I is first   —   —   —   —   —   —

when I is last   —   —   —   —   —   —

Total   —   —   —   —   —   —

Percent Correct   —   —   —   —   —   —

Date   —   —   —   —   —   —

UNIVERSITY OF KANSAS CENTER FOR RESEARCH ON LEARNING

Name: _____

COMPOUND-COMPLEX SENTENCE
VERBAL PRACTICE CHECKLIST

<u>**Attempts**</u>

	1	2	3	4	5	6
Giving Definitions						
Compound-complex Sentence	__	__	__	__	__	__
Independent Clause	__	__	__	__	__	__
Dependent Clause	__	__	__	__	__	__
Coordinating Conjunction	__	__	__	__	__	__
Subordinating Conjunction	__	__	__	__	__	__

Naming Kinds of Compound-Complex Sentences

	1	2	3	4	5	6
D , I , c I	__	__	__	__	__	__
I D , c I	__	__	__	__	__	__
I , c I D	__	__	__	__	__	__
D , I ; I	__	__	__	__	__	__
I D ; I	__	__	__	__	__	__
I ; I D	__	__	__	__	__	__

Explaining Punctuation

	1	2	3	4	5	6
Between two I clauses:						
with coord. conjunction	__	__	__	__	__	__
without coord. conjunction	__	__	__	__	__	__
Between D clause and I clause when:						
D is first and I is second	__	__	__	__	__	__
D is second and I is third						
with coord. conjunction	__	__	__	__	__	__
without coord. conjunction	__	__	__	__	__	__
Total	__	__	__	__	__	__
Percentage Correct	__	__	__	__	__	__
Date	__	__	__	__	__	__

SENTENCE SCORE SHEET

Student Name: _____

Date: _____

Pretest/Posttest: _____

Practice: _____

Line Number

Sentence Type	1	2	3	4	5	6	7	8	9	10	11	12	13	14	15	Totals
Simple																
Compound																
Complex																
Compound-Complex																
Non-Sentence																

Total Sentence Attempts →

Calculating the Scores

Percentage of Complete Sentences

No. Simple + Comp. + Complex + Comp./Complex ⬚ / ⬚ X 100 = ____ %

Total No. Sentence Attempts   **Mastery = 100%**

Percentage of Complicated Sentences

No. Comp. + Complex + Comp./Complex ⬚ / ⬚ X 100 = ____ %

Total No. Sentence Attempts   **Mastery = 33%, 40%, or 50%**

(see criterion for each part)

Percentage of Complicated Sentences Punctuated correctly

No. Comp. + Complex + Comp./Complex Punc. Corr. ⬚ / ⬚ X 100 = ____ %

Total No. Complicated Sentences   **Mastery = at least 66%**

Student's Name: _____

SIMPLE SENTENCE PROGRESS CHART

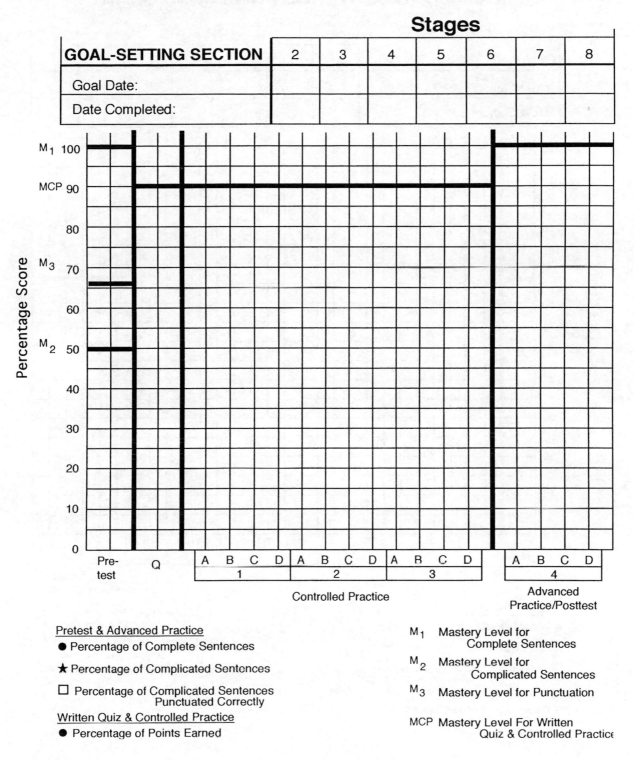

GOAL-SETTING SECTION	Stages							
	2	3	4	5	6	7	8
Goal Date:								
Date Completed:								

Percentage Score

M₁ 100
MCP 90
80
M₃ 70
60
M₂ 50
40
30
20
10
0

Pre-test   Q   A B C D   A B C D   A B C D   A B C D
                    1   2   3   4

Controlled Practice   Advanced Practice/Posttest

Pretest & Advanced Practice
● Percentage of Complete Sentences
★ Percentage of Complicated Sentences
□ Percentage of Complicated Sentences Punctuated Correctly
Written Quiz & Controlled Practice
● Percentage of Points Earned

M_1 Mastery Level for Complete Sentences
M_2 Mastery Level for Complicated Sentences
M_3 Mastery Level for Punctuation
MCP Mastery Level For Written Quiz & Controlled Practice

UNIVERSITY OF KANSAS CENTER FOR RESEARCH ON LEARNING

175

Student's Name: _____

COMPOUND SENTENCE PROGRESS CHART

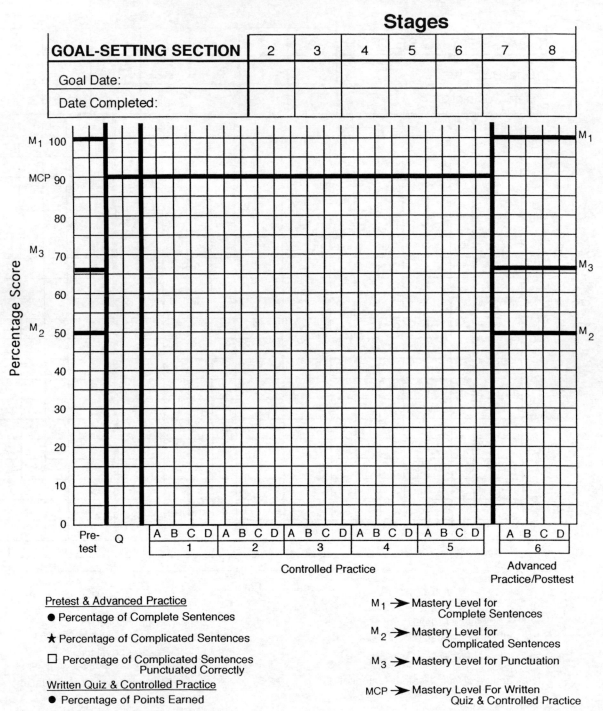

Stages

GOAL-SETTING SECTION	2	3	4	5	6	7	8
Goal Date:							
Date Completed:							

Percentage Score

M₁ 100
MCP 90
80
M₃ 70
60
M₂ 50
40
30
20
10
0

Pre-test Q A B C D | A B C D | A B C D | A B C D | A B C D ‖ A B C D
1   2   3   4   5   6

Controlled Practice

Advanced Practice/Posttest

Pretest & Advanced Practice
● Percentage of Complete Sentences
★ Percentage of Complicated Sentences
□ Percentage of Complicated Sentences Punctuated Correctly
Written Quiz & Controlled Practice
● Percentage of Points Earned

M₁ → Mastery Level for Complete Sentences
M₂ → Mastery Level for Complicated Sentences
M₃ → Mastery Level for Punctuation
MCP → Mastery Level For Written Quiz & Controlled Practice

176

Student's Name: _____

COMPLEX SENTENCE PROGRESS CHART

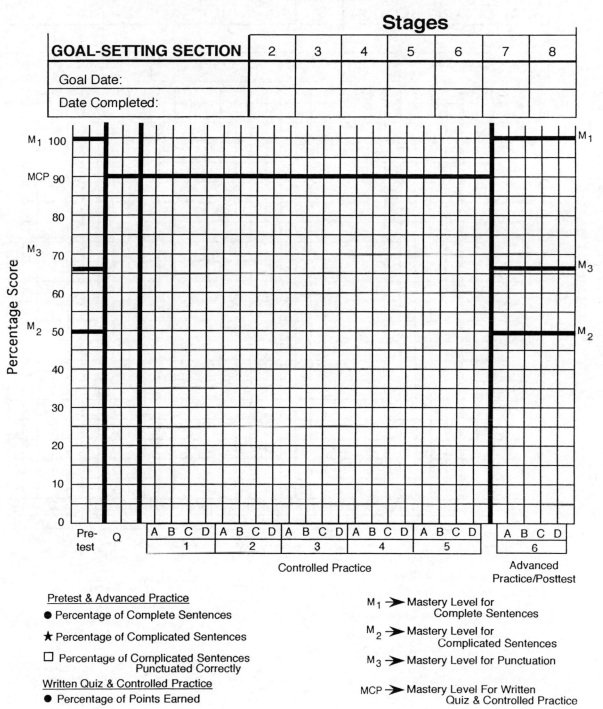

GOAL-SETTING SECTION	Stages						
	2	3	4	5	6	7	8
Goal Date:							
Date Completed:							

Percentage Score

M₁ 100
MCP 90
80
M₃ 70
60
M₂ 50
40
30
20
10
0

Pre-test   Q   A B C D 1   A B C D 2   A B C D 3   A B C D 4   A B C D 5   A B C D 6

Controlled Practice

Advanced Practice/Posttest

Pretest & Advanced Practice
● Percentage of Complete Sentences
★ Percentage of Complicated Sentences
□ Percentage of Complicated Sentences Punctuated Correctly

Written Quiz & Controlled Practice
● Percentage of Points Earned

M₁ ➤ Mastery Level for Complete Sentences
M₂ ➤ Mastery Level for Complicated Sentences
M₃ ➤ Mastery Level for Punctuation
MCP ➤ Mastery Level For Written Quiz & Controlled Practice

Student's Name: _____

COMPOUND-COMPLEX SENTENCE PROGRESS CHART

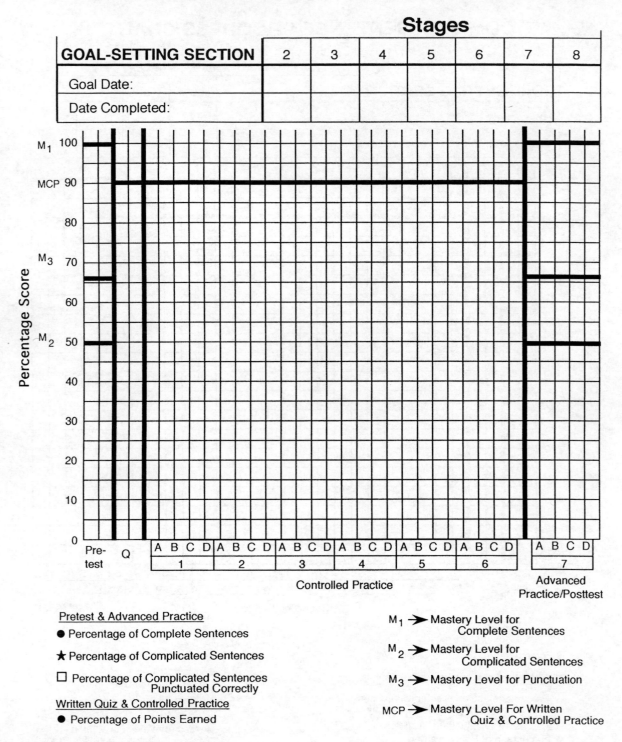

GOAL-SETTING SECTION	Stages						
	2	3	4	5	6	7	8
Goal Date:							
Date Completed:							

Pretest & Advanced Practice
- ● Percentage of Complete Sentences
- ★ Percentage of Complicated Sentences
- ☐ Percentage of Complicated Sentences Punctuated Correctly

Written Quiz & Controlled Practice
- ● Percentage of Points Earned

M_1 ➤ Mastery Level for Complete Sentences

M_2 ➤ Mastery Level for Complicated Sentences

M_3 ➤ Mastery Level for Punctuation

MCP ➤ Mastery Level For Written Quiz & Controlled Practice

UNIVERSITY OF KANSAS CENTER FOR RESEARCH ON LEARNING

Student's Name:_____

GENERALIZATION PROGRESS CHART
FOR —————————————————— SENTENCES

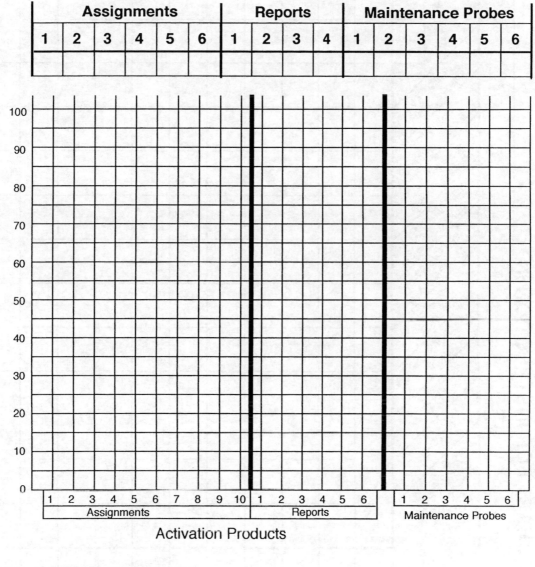

	Assignments						Reports				Maintenance Probes					
1	2	3	4	5	6	1	2	3	4	1	2	3	4	5	6

Percentage Score

100
90
80
70
60
50
40
30
20
10
0

Assignments: 1 2 3 4 5 6 7 8 9 10
Reports: 1 2 3 4 5 6
Maintenance Probes: 1 2 3 4 5 6

Activation Products

● Percentage of Complete Sentences

★ Percentage of Complicated Sentences

☐ Percentage of Complicated Sentences Punctuated Correctly

MANAGEMENT CHART FOR INSTRUCTION IN _____ SENTENCES

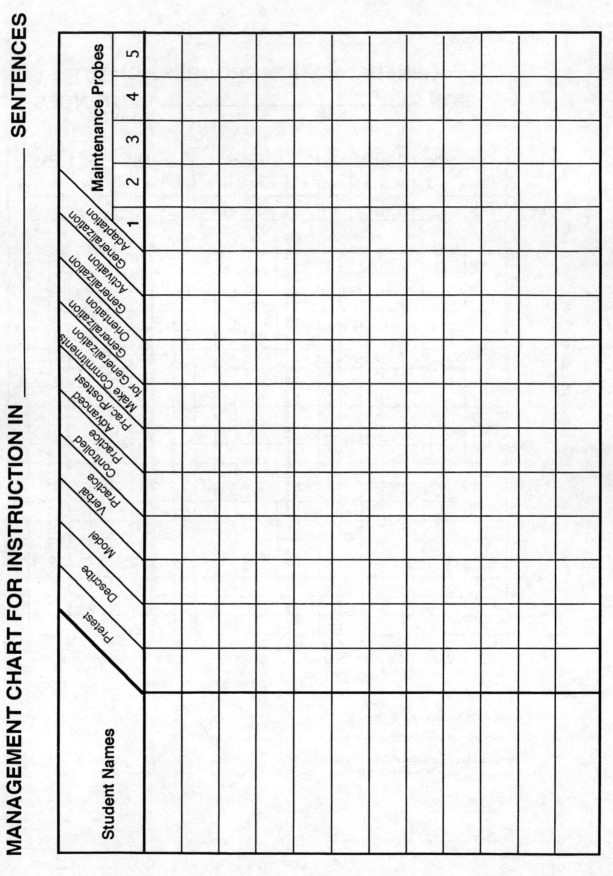

Student Names	Pretest	Describe	Model	Verbal Practice	Controlled Practice	Advanced Prac./Posttest	Make Commitments for Generalization	Generalization Orientation	Generalization Activation	Generalization Adaptation	Maintenance Probes 1	2	3	4	5

Name: _____

SIMPLE SENTENCE CHECKLIST

S V   _____

SS V   _____

S VV   _____

SS VV   _____

Name: _____

COMPOUND SENTENCE CHECKLIST

S V   _____

SS V   _____

S VV   _____

SS VV   _____

I , c I   _____

I ; I   _____

Name: _____

COMPLEX SENTENCE CHECKLIST

S V _____   D,I _____

SS V _____   ID _____

S VV _____

SS VV _____

I,cI   _____

I;I   _____

Name: _____

SENTENCE CHECKLIST

S V _____   D,I _____

SS V _____   ID _____

S VV _____

SS VV _____   D,I,cI _____

    ID,cI _____

I,cI _____   I,cID _____

I;I _____   D,I;I _____

    ID;I _____

    I;ID _____

Name: _____

Simple Sentence
Verbal Practice Checklist

	Attempts			
	1	2	3	4

Naming Strategy Steps

Pick a formula   ___ ___ ___ ___

Explore words to fit the formula   ___ ___ ___ ___

Note the words   ___ ___ ___ ___

Search and Check

     Mark out imposters *(infinitives &*
         prepositional phrases   ___ ___ ___ ___

     Ask is there a verb   ___ ___ ___ ___

     Root out the subject   ___ ___ ___ ___

     Key in on the beginning, ending, middle   ___ ___ ___ ___
       (capitalization, punctuation, & it makes sense)

Giving Definitions

Simple Sentence   ___ ___ ___ ___

Independent Clause   ___ ___ ___ ___

Subject   ___ ___ ___ ___

Verb   ___ ___ ___ ___

Compound Subject   ___ ___ ___ ___

Compound Verb   ___ ___ ___ ___

Question to ask in finding Subject(s)   ___ ___ ___ ___

Name the Linking Verbs   ___ ___ ___ ___
    (am, are, is, be, been, become, was, were, seem)

Naming Kinds of Simple Sentences

S   V   ___ ___ ___ ___

SS   V   ___ ___ ___ ___

S   VV   ___ ___ ___ ___

SS   VV   ___ ___ ___ ___

Total _____   **Percentage** _____

UNIVERSITY OF KANSAS CENTER FOR RESEARCH ON LEARNING

APPENDIX C: ENRICHMENT ACTIVITIES

The enrichment activities are to be used with students who progress quickly through the materials and who need to wait for other students to reach mastery before they are given the next part of the instruction.* They can also be used when a student makes inquiries about a certain sentence structure or when a student indicates he wants to learn more. They are not recommended for use with all students. For most low-achieving adolescents, it is most prudent to emphasize the basic instruction in the four kinds of sentences and to move on to instruction in the other writing strategies as quickly as possible.

AFTER SIMPLE SENTENCES

After a student has mastered the skills involved in writing simple sentences, you can provide supplementary instruction in the use of single words (e.g., adjectives and adverbs) and word groups (e.g., prepositional phrases, participle phrases, infinitive phrases, absolute phrases, gerund phrases) to expand the basic simple sentence. Analyze the student's writing carefully, and determine whether the student uses such sentence expanders as adjectives, adverbs, and prepositional phrases. If these expanders are missing in the student's sentences, provide brief (1- to 2-day) lessons on each missing expander. Follow these instructional steps for each sentence expander identified:

1. Describe

a. Define the expander (e.g., adjective) in one or two sentences.

b. Explain how the student will benefit from using the expander.

2. Model

a. Give a demonstration showing how to use the 'PENS' Steps with a question on expanders included in the final step (i.e., when you check the sentence to make sure that no words have been left out and it makes sense, you can also check to see if it needs an expander). Show how to insert the expander in some of the sentences the student has previously written.

3. Controlled Practice

a. Have the student take sentences she wrote for a previous lesson (e.g., *Simple Sentence Lesson 3A* or *3B*) and rewrite them inserting the expander. If this is inappropriate, given the sentences the student has written on previous lessons, give the student *Simple Sentence Lesson 3A* and have him write new sentences that include the expander.

b. Provide individual feedback.

c. Continue the practice until the student can appropriately add an expander to nine out of ten sentences.

4. Advanced Practice

a. Assign the task of writing 6 sentences on the same topic using the same requirements for *Simple Sentence Lessons* in the *#4 Series,* but also require the use of the expander in four of the sentences.

b. Provide individual feedback.

c. Continue the practice and feedback until the student can appropriately include the expander in four out of six sentences.

When the student masters the use of one expander, introduce another expander. Each time the student practices after learning two or more expanders, insist that the student use the previously learned expander(s) as well as the new one. For example, if the student is practicing using adverbs and has already mastered using

---

* Note: Alternatively, you can set up your instructional sequence to avoid such waiting. This is much preferred over deliberately slowing students' learning rates.

adjectives, require the student to have adjectives in two sentences and adverbs in four sentences for each advanced practice attempt.

AFTER COMPOUND SENTENCES

A student may wish to learn how to write compound sentences with more than two independent clauses. If so, follow these instructional steps:

1. Describe

a. Show the student these two formulas: I, I, cI and I;I;I. Explain that the formulas are similar regardless of how many "I"s are added. In the first formula, the initial "I"s are separated by commas, and the last two "I"s are separated by a comma and a coordinating conjunction. In the second formula, all the "I"s are separated by semicolons.

Explain that this type of sentence is typically used when three independent clauses are parallel or very similar in meaning and content. Have the student expand his Formula Card to include these new formulas.

2. Model

a. Show the student the following sentences:

The train went fast, the car went slower, but the bike was the slowest.

The farmer wore a straw hat; the cook wore a chef's hat; the construction worker wore a helmet.

b. Ask the student to identify the formula for each sentence and to explain how the independent clauses in each sentence are parallel (very similar in structure and content).

3. Controlled Practice

a. Ask the student to write three sentences for each formula in the same format as that of the *Simple Sentence Lesson Series #3*.

b. Provide individual feedback.

c. Continue the practice and feedback until the student masters the skill.

4. Advanced Practice

a. Ask the student to write six sentences about a topic. Require the inclusion of one compound sentence with two clauses and one compound sentence with three clauses.

b. Provide individual feedback.

c. Continue the practice and feedback until the student masters the skill.

AFTER COMPLEX SENTENCES

Complex Sentences with Two Adverb Clauses

If a student wishes to learn how to write complex sentences with more than one dependent clause, follow these steps:

1. Describe

a. Show the student these three formulas: DD,I D, ID IDD. Explain that the comma rule still applies in each case. A comma is required between the D and the I when the D comes first. It is not required when the I is before the D.

b. Have the student add these formulas to her Formula Card.

2. Model

a. Show the student these sentences:

Until I get my new bike, I won't be able to come because I don't have any transportation.

We will stay at Bob's house until the fog lifts as long as we are welcome.

Although the team was tired because they fought hard, they won.

b. Ask the student to identify the independent clause and the dependent clauses in each sentence and the correct formula for each sentence.

3. Controlled Practice

    a. Ask the student to write two sentences for each formula in a format similar to the format of the *Complex Sentence Lesson Series #3.*

    b. Provide individual feedback.

    c. Continue practice and feedback until the student masters the skills.

4. Advanced Practice

    a. Ask the student to write six sentences about a topic. Require the inclusion of one compound sentence, one complex sentence with two clauses, and one complex sentence with three clauses.

    b. Provide individual feedback.

    c. Continue practice and feedback until the student masters the skill.

Complex Sentences with Adjective Clauses

Some students (especially students at the college level) will inquire about sentences that include adjective clauses. Follow these steps in providing instruction on complex sentences with adjective clauses:

1. Describe

    a. Review adverb clauses. "We have been learning about complex sentences with *adverb clauses.* The dependent clauses we've been writing provide additional information about the verb in the sentence. They tell us, for example, when, how or why an action takes place."

    b. Define adjective clauses. "A second kind of complex sentence contains a dependent clause called an *adjective clause*."

[Write "Adjective Clause" on the board.]

"An adjective clause modifies a noun in the independent clause. It either simply tells us more information about that noun or it identifies a particular person, place, or thing."

[Write the definition on the board and have the students make their own Cue Cards.]

"The words that are used most often to connect or relate this kind of dependent clause to the independent clause are called *relative pronouns*. The most common ones are: who, whom, whose, whoever, whomever, which, what, whatever, and that."

[Write "Relative Pronouns" and the list of words on the board and have the students make their own Cue Cards.]

"Let's look at an example. In the sentence, 'I called Todd, whose father works at the University.', what's the dependent clause?"

[Write the sentence on the board, and elicit the answer, "Whose father works at the University."]

"Right. What word in the independent clause does the dependent clause tell us more about?"

[Solicit the answer, "Todd."]

"Good. 'Todd' is a noun, and this dependent clause tells us more about Todd."

    c. Explain how to sequence independent clauses and adjective clauses. "When you write a sentence with an adjective clause in it, you usually put the adjective clause right after the word it modifies. There are two ways of sequencing independent clauses and adjective clauses."

        (1.) Explain how to put the adjective clause after the independent clause. "The example we discussed is a complex sentence in which the adjective clause modifies the last word in the sentence. Thus, the adjective clause comes after the independent clause. This is the first way of sequencing independent clauses and adjective clauses."

        [Point to the clauses in the example, and specify the sequence.]

        (2.) Explain how the adjective clause can be imbedded within the independent clause. "We've seen how the dependent clause can come after the independent clause.

A second way of making a complex sentence with an adjective clause is to have the dependent clause inside the independent clause."

"Let's look at an example of a complex sentence where the dependent clause is inside the independent clause."

[Write, "My house, which I bought 5 years ago, needs a new coat of paint." on the board.]

"In this sentence, the dependent clause is inside the independent clause. What is the dependent clause?"

[Solicit the answer, "which I bought 5 years ago," and underline this clause with one line.]

"What is the independent clause?"

[Solicit the answer, "My house needs a new coat of paint." Underline the independent clause with two lines.]

"That's right. You'll notice that the independent clause is divided into two parts with the dependent clause in between the two parts. That's why we say it's 'inside' the independent clause."

(3.) **Explain how complex sentences with adjective clauses are punctuated.** "You may have noticed when I wrote this sentence on the board that it has two commas separating the dependent clause from the independent clause. There are times when a comma or commas are necessary and times when they are not necessary."

"Commas are necessary when the adjective clause is simply providing additional information about a noun. In this example, . . ."

[Point to the sentence, "My house, which I bought 5 years ago, needs a new coat of paint."]

". . . what two words does the clause, 'which I bought 5 years ago,' modify or tell more about?"

[Solicit the answer, "My house."]

"That's right.'My house' has been clearly identified already. I only have one house. Thus, the adjective clause just tells more about my house. In a sentence like this . . ."

[Write, 'Houses which people built 100 years ago need a lot of care.', on the board.]

". . . what is the dependent clause?"

[Solicit the answer, "which people built 100 years ago."]

"Right. What word does the dependent clause modify?"

[Solicit the answer, "Houses."]

"Correct. In this sentence, particular houses are being identified. If we were to take out the adjective clause . . . "

[Cross out the adjective clause or cover it up.]

". . . we wouldn't know what houses were being talked about. When the adjective clause is needed to *identify* a particular person, place, or thing, then no commas are needed in the sentence. It's an important part of the sentence."

"Thus, we have two punctuation rules to remember. Whenever the adjective clause is an important part of the sentence and identifies the particular persons, places, or things talked about, no comma or commas are needed."

"Whenever the adjective clause is just adding information and the person, place, or thing is already clearly identified, we do need a comma or commas."

"How can we remember these rules?"

[Discuss with the students a way of remembering the rules.]

"Let's look at two more examples."

[Write, "The shoes which the store sold yesterday made a lot of customers happy." and "Sally's new blue shoes which she bought yesterday made her happy." on the board.]

"In which sentence do we need commas to separate the dependent clause from the independent clause? Remember, we do not need commas when the dependent clause identifies *particular* persons, places or things. If they're identified and clear, commas are needed."

[Solicit the answer, "The second sentence." Ask where to put the commas and add them to the second sentence. Ask the students to identify the independent clause, the dependent clause, the words being modified by the dependent clause, and the relative pronoun in each sentence.]

"Here are two more sentences."

[Write, "Paul is proud of the desk which he varnished yesterday." and "Paul is proud of Jesse who is his son." on the board or on a blank transparency.]

"In these sentences, the adjective clause comes after the independent clause so only one comma may be needed to separate the dependent clause from the independent clause. In which of these sentences is a comma needed?"

[Solicit the answer, "The second sentence."]

"That's right. In the second sentence, Jesse is already clearly identified and the dependent clause only adds information to the sentence. Whenever you have a name of a person that is being modified, you always use a comma."

(4.) **Give examples of the sequences.** **"Let's think of some other examples of sentences where the dependent clause is an adjective clause."**

[Put the following relative pronouns on the board and ask the students to contribute two examples for each: who and that. One example for each conjunction should illustrate the adjective clause at the end of the sentence, and one example should illustrate its placement within the sentence. Write the sentence on the board, ask if a comma or commas are needed, add a comma or commas if necessary, and provide feedback as appropriate.]

d. Introduce the formulas for complex sentences with adjective clauses. **"We've talked about four kinds of complex sentences with adjective clauses: sentences where the adjective clause comes after the independent clause and a comma is needed; sentences where the adjective clause comes after the independent clause and a comma is not needed; sentences where the adjective clause is inside the independent clause and two commas are needed; and sentences where the adjective clause is inside the independent clause and commas are not needed."**

"Let's use an 'I' to represent an independent clause and a 'D$_2$' to represent an adjective clause. What should the formula for a sentence with an adjective clause that comes *after* the independent clause and that needs a comma look like?"

[Solicit the answer, "I,D$_2$", and write it on the board.]

"Good. Now what would the formula be for the same kind of sentence that does not need a comma?"

[Solicit the answer, "ID$_2$", and write it on the board.]

"Fine. What should the formula look like if the dependent clause is inside the independent clause and commas are needed."

[Solicit ideas. If no one comes up with an acceptable idea, write the formula I ,D$_2$, on the board.]

"What should the formula look like for the same kind of sentence where commas are not needed?"

[Solicit the answer, I D$_2$, and write it on the board.]

e. Expand the Formula Cards. [Ask the students to add the four formulas for complex sentences with adjective clauses to their Formula Cards under the heading, "Complex Sentences." Have them add a "1" as a subscript to the Ds in the formulas for complex sentences with adverb clauses. Show them your own card as a model. Check each student's card to ensure it is correct.]

f. Make *Example Sheets*. [Have the students make an *Example Sheet* for complex sentences with adjective clauses. Ask them to add the correct formula next to each example on their *Example Sheets*. Check each student's *Example Sheet* to ensure it is correct.]

2. Model

a. Provide a model of how to use the 'PENS' steps to write complex sentences with adjective clauses following the instructions on pp. 84-85, but substitute a complex sentence with an adjective clause for the model.

3. Verbal Practice

a. Ask the students to verbally rehearse the definitions for complex sentence, independent clause, dependent clause, adverb clause, and adjective clause; the words that are used to connect adjective clauses to independent clauses; the four types of complex sentences with adjective clauses; and the punctuation rules for adjective clauses. Require the students to reach mastery (100% correct) in an individual oral quiz.

4. Controlled Practice

a. Make up a lesson similar to those used in the *Complex Sentence Lesson Series #3*. Choose a formula and a relative pronoun for each sentence (e.g., who, whom, whose, which, that), and write them to the left of the sentence number. Require the students to write ten sentences (two for each of the four formulas and two of their choice) for each lesson.

b. Provide individual feedback.

c. Continue practice and feedback until the student masters the skill.

5. Advanced Practice

a. Ask the student to write six sentences about a topic. Require the inclusion of one compound sentence, one complex sentence with an adverb clause, and one complex sentence with an adjective clause.

b. Provide individual feedback.

c. Continue practice and feedback until the student masters the skill.

6. Trouble-Shooting

Often students write dependent clauses of the following nature:

My father, who has lots of patience, lost his temper.

In this sentence, the word, "who," serves as both the subordinating conjunction *and* the subject of the dependent clause. In the following sentence,

My father, whom I love very much, is visiting me.

the word "whom" serves as the subordinating conjunction and the word "I" is the subject of the dependent clause. Both types of sentences are appropriate and should receive full credit. The relative pronouns that can serve as subjects for dependent clauses include: who, which, and that. Whenever a student writes a sentence in which the relative pronoun serves as the subject of the dependent clause, explain to the student what she has done and why it is acceptable. Contrast this kind of a dependent clause to a group of words that do not form a dependent clause. In the following sentence, "While running fast, Jane tripped," the introductory clause cannot be accepted as a dependent clause because it has no subject and no helping verb. The word "while" cannot serve as a subject of a dependent clause.

Complex Sentences with Adverb and Adjective Clauses

Students who have learned to write complex sentences with adjective clauses may want to combine adverb and adjective clauses in the same sentence. Follow these steps to provide instruction:

1. Describe

a. Explain to the students that the formulas for complex sentences with adverb clauses and with adjective clauses can be combined, and the punctuation rules are still the same. Have the students suggest ways of combining the formulas. Some possibilities are:

D_1, I	$I D_1$	D_1, I	$I D_1$
$\boxed{,D_2,}$	$\boxed{,D_2,}$	$\boxed{D_2}$	$\boxed{D_2}$
D_1, ID_2	ID_2, D_1	D_1, I, D_2	I, D_2, D_1

2. Model

Show the students the following sentences:

> After the war was over, many people who had been employed lost their jobs.

> My mother, who came from Scotland, lived in Philadelphia before she was married.

> Many people who had been employed lost their jobs after the war was over.

> Before I was born, my mother, who came from Scotland, lived in Philadelphia.

Have the students identify the independent and dependent clauses in each sentence and match a formula to each sentence.

3. Controlled Practice

a. Ask the students to write 2 sentences for each formula in a format similar to the format of the Complex *Sentence Lesson Series #3*.

b. Provide individual feedback.

c. Continue practice and feedback until the student masters the skill.

4. Advanced Practice

a. Ask the student to write six sentences about a topic. Require the inclusion of one compound sentence, one complex sentence with two clauses, and one complex sentence with three clauses.

b. Provide individualized feedback.

c. Continue the practice and feedback until the student masters the skill.

Complex Sentences with Noun Clauses

Another type of complex sentence that has not been covered in the manual is the complex sentence containing a noun clause. A noun clause is a dependent clause that is used as a noun or a pronoun in a sentence. A noun clause can be used as the subject, direct object, predicate nominative, appositive, indirect object, or as an object of a preposition (see pp. 140-141 for examples). If a student writes this kind of sentence spontaneously, give such sentences full credit, and explain to the student what he has done. Teachers of students with adequate background in the parts of speech may want to present this kind of complex sentence after the students have mastered the types presented here. Refer to an English textbook for the content of your presentation. Use the same instructional steps as those suggested for complex sentences with adjective clauses: define a noun clause, provide example sentences, design formulas, provide a model, conduct controlled and advanced practice, provide feedback, and require mastery.

AFTER COMPOUND-COMPLEX SENTENCES

Students who have learned to write complex sentences with adverb and adjective clauses may wish to learn to write compound-complex sentences with adjective clauses or with both adverb and adjective clauses. Follow these instructional steps.

1. Describe

a. Discuss with the students ways of combining the formulas for compound sentences and complex sentences with adjective and adverb clauses. Write the formulas on the board. Some possibilities are:

Compound-complex sentences with adjective clauses

I; I $\boxed{,D_2,}$	I , cI $\boxed{,D_2,}$	I, D_2; I	I,D_2,cI
I; I $\boxed{,D_2,}$	I, c I $\boxed{,D_2,}$	I; I,D_2	I,cI,D_2
I; I $\boxed{D_2}$	I,c I $\boxed{D_2}$	ID_2; I	ID_2,cI
I: I $\boxed{D_2}$	I,cI $\boxed{D_2}$	I;ID_2	I, cID_2

Compound-complex sentences with adverb clauses and adjective clauses*

ID_2;ID_1	ID_2,cID_1
D_1,I;ID_2	D_1,I,cID_2
I ;ID_1 $\boxed{D_2}$	I,cID_1 D_2
D_1,I;I $\boxed{D_2}$	D_1,I,cI $\boxed{D_2}$

Stress with the students that the possibilities are many and that they just need to be careful that the sentence makes sense. Although sentences with more than four clauses can be written, encourage students to master sentences with three or four clauses and to limit themselves to these kinds of sentences. Students who are just learning to write sentences often have trouble coordinating the content of more than three clauses. Additionally, sentences with more than four clauses are often difficult to read.

2. Model

a. As a group, pick one or two of the formulas you have designed and work through the 'PENS' Steps. Write the sentence for each formula on the board and provide feedback as needed.

3. Controlled Practice

a. Have the student practice writing different kinds of compound-complex sentences. Choose six formulas, and write them on a piece of paper. Ask the student to write a sentence for each formula.

b. Provide individual feedback.

c. Continue practice and feedback until the student masters the skill.

4. Advanced Practice

a. Ask the student to write six sentences about a topic. Require the inclusion of one compound sentence, one compound-complex sentence with an adjective clause, and one compound-complex sentence with an adjective clause and an adverb clause.

b. Provide individual feedback.

c. Continue practice and feedback until the student masters the skill.

---

* These are only a few of the possibilities.